AN AUTOBIOGRAPHY
TOM LANDRY

TOM LANDRY
with Gregg Lewis

HarperPaperbacks
A Division of HarperCollinsPublishers

HarperPaperbacks *A Division of* HarperCollins*Publishers*
10 East 53rd Street, New York, N.Y. 10022

A hardcover edition of this book was copublished in 1990 by Zondervan Publishing House and HarperCollins*Publishers*, New York.

The publishers gratefully acknowledge the help of NFL Properties (6701 Center Drive West, Suite 1111, Los Angeles, California 90045) and Bob Kelly and Kevin Terrell, in the composition of the photo section. In addition, the publishers acknowledge David Woo/*The Dallas Morning News*, David J. Sams, and New York News Inc. for their contributions to the same.

All Scripture quotations, unless otherwise noted, are taken from the *Holy Bible: New International Version* (North American Edition). Copyright © 1973, 1978 , 1984 by the International Bible Society. Used by permission of Zondervan Bible Publishers.

First HarperPaperbacks printing: October 1991

Printed in the United States of America

HarperPaperbacks and colophon are trademarks of HarperCollins*Publishers*

10 9 8 7 6 5 4 3 2 1

*To Alicia for a lifetime of love,
devotion, and strength—
and to our children and grandchildren.*

Contents

Chronology of Events

1924 Born September 11 in Mission, Texas
1938 Began junior varsity football career
1940 Starting quarterback of Mission High School Eagles
1941 Undefeated Mission Eagles win regional championship
1942 Enrolled in University of Texas on football scholarship
1943 Inducted into the Army Air Corps and began flight training
1944 Stationed in England as B-17 bomber pilot
1945 Discharged from Army Air Corps as First Lieutenant after thirty bombing missions over Europe
1946 Reenrolled at the University of Texas
   Played for Texas Longhorn team that went to the Cotton Bowl after the season
   Drafted by the New York Giants of the National Football League and the New York Yankees of the All-American Football Conference
1947 Starting fullback for the Texas Longhorn team that won the Sugar Bowl at season's end
   Named second-team All-Southwest Conference fullback
   Met Alicia Wiggs
1948 Captain of Texas Longhorn football team

1949   Finished college football career on New Year's
            Day by running for 117 yards in Texas's Or-
            ange Bowl victory
        Signed professional football contract with the
            New York Yankees of the All-American Foot-
            ball Conference
        Married Alicia Wiggs on January 28
        Graduated from University of Texas
        Played for Yankees as backup fullback, defensive
            back, and punter
        Son Thomas Wade Landry, Jr., born October 31
1950   Began career as defensive back for the New York
            Giants after NFL and AAFC merger
1952   Daughter Kitty born in August
1954   Named as assistant coach of the New York
            Giants defense
        As player/coach won All-Pro honors as defensive
            back
1955   Last active season as football player
1956   Assistant coach of defense for the World Cham-
            pion Giants
1958   Daughter Lisa born in March
        New York lost the NFL championship in over-
            time to Johnny Unitas and the Baltimore Colts
            in the game that marked the marriage of tele-
            vision and pro football
1959   Made personal commitment of life to Christ
        Last season as assistant coach of New York
            Giants
        Named as head coach of the new NFL franchise
            in Dallas
1960   First year as coach of the Dallas Cowboys who
            went 0–11–1
1961   The Cowboys' first run
1964   Signed unprecedented ten-year contract to coach
            the Cowboys despite losing record
1965   Cowboys finally broke even with a 7–7 record
1966   Won first Eastern Division title but lost to Green
            Bay in the championship game
        Named coach of the year for the first time

1967 Won Eastern Division title again before losing in the infamous Ice Bowl to Green Bay

1968 Won division title again before losing in playoffs to Cleveland

1969 Lost once more to Cleveland in playoffs

1970 Won last five regular season games and two playoff games before losing Super Bowl V to Baltimore in final seconds

1971 Won the NFL championship and Super Bowl VI in New Orleans

1975 Young Cowboy team with "Dirty Dozen" rookies won the NFC Championship and lost Super Bowl X to the Pittsburgh Steelers

Coach of the Year Honors

1977 The 12–2 Cowboys won the NFC Championship again and then defeated the Denver Broncos in Super Bowl XII

1978 After a fine 12–4 season the Cowboys lost to Terry Brandshaw and the Pittsburgh Steelers in Super Bowl XIII

1981 Won 200th regular season game as head coach

1984 Clint Murchison sold the Cowboys to Bum Bright

1985 Final Eastern Division Championship

1986 Cowboys end their pro football record of twenty consecutive winning seasons

1987 Signed final three-year contract

1988 The Cowboys went 3–13 in final season as coach

1989 On February 25 fired as coach when Cowboys were sold to Jerry Jones

Dallas celebrates Tom Landry Day on April 22

1990 Elected to the Pro Football Hall of Fame

Acknowledgments

You never realize how much is involved in writing a book until you do it. A project like this takes so many people doing so many different things.

The folks at Zondervan Publishing House have been great to work with—particularly my publisher Scott Bolinder who helped persuade me to do this book and my editor John Sloan who helped set and maintain our course. I couldn't have written this book without the sensitive professional skills of Gregg Lewis who has coached me through the whole process—prodding my memories, understanding my feelings, and recounting an entire lifetime of experience in the following pages.

I'd also like to thank all those writers who covered the Cowboys over the years for the many articles, columns, and books that refreshed my memory, filled in forgotten facts, and provided background for the writing of this autobiography.

I want to express my gratitude to my friends, my colleagues, and my family for their shared memories. Special thanks go to Alicia who not only lived so much of my life with me but helped me remember and relive so much of this book. I'm also deeply grateful to my son Tom, Jr., for carrying so much of the load of my personal business this past year, including serving as my agent on this book.

Appreciation is due photographer David Woo and the extremely helpful archives staff at NFL Properties for their assistance in pulling together the photos in this book.

But in addition to thanking those people who helped make this book possible, I'd like to acknowledge two unique organizations that helped make my career in football possible.

For ten years I had the great privilege of playing and coaching for the New York Giants and the Mara family. Then for my first 24 years in Dallas the Murchison family owned the Cowboys. In Wellington Mara and Clint Murchison, Jr., I worked for two of the finest owners in the history of professional sports whose management styles gave their businesses a family feel and a lasting sense of security that accounted for their franchises' long-term successes. Wellington and Clint weren't just bosses but encouraging and supportive friends. Not only my career, but so much of my life is owed to the opportunities, responsibilities, and trust granted me by these men and the organizations they owned.

Finally I'd like to acknowledge a group of men without whom I could never have lasted as an NFL coach for 29 years—my assistant coaches. Many fine football men worked with me during my career, but I'd like to extend special recognition to those with me the longest: Jerry Tubbs, 29 years; Jim Myers, 25 years; Ernie Stautner, 24 years; Ermal Allen, 23 years; Danny Reeves, 16 years; Gene Stallings and Bob Ward, 14 years; Mike Ditka, 13 years; Dick Nolan, 12 years.

These men and their long-term commitment to the Dallas Cowboys and to me played a major role in the Cowboys' success. For that they have my everlasting gratitude and respect.

Introduction

Every autumn Sunday afternoon for twenty-nine years Tom Landry stood like a rock along the Dallas Cowboy sidelines. On television screens across America the stone-faced visage that peered from beneath the brim of his trademark hat became as instantly recognizable as the face of Walter Cronkite.

There was something about the man Tom Landry that commanded respect from his players, his NFL colleagues, and football fans everywhere who watched him work at a game he, as much as any other single person, helped transform from a second-rate sport into a cultural icon. When new management took over the Cowboys and fired him in February 1989, the public outpouring of indignation in newspapers throughout America and the thousands of encouraging, supporting personal calls and letters—from presidents and schoolchildren alike—proved the Cowboy coach was not just admired, he was loved.

Despite a successful career that made him a very public figure for decades, Tom Landry always remained a very private person. While his face is recognized around the world, few people really know the man. Millions of people admire him, but most of them really don't know why.

As a lifelong sports fan, I began this project knowing full well the popular public image of Tom Landry as the coolly-controlled, quiet, cerebral, intensely serious, perhaps even emotionless, Cowboy coach.

His longtime friend and former teammate on the New York Giants, Frank Gifford, once observed that Tom Landry is difficult for others to understand only because he is exactly what he seems to be. But after months of working closely with him, sitting for hours at a time, day after day, poring over old scrapbooks and digging together through boxes of personal memorabilia, eating Mexican food at Rosie's, flying with him in his Cessna across the plains of Texas, and watching the NFL playoffs on TV with him in his sitting room, I think I have a much clearer picture of the man than people outside his family have ever had.

In some ways Gifford was right. Much of that public image is true.

He *is* always a Christian gentleman. Not just when the cameras are on or when he is with "important" people. He's just as gracious and cordial when a restaurant dinner is interrupted by autograph seekers or when strangers stop him on a New York sidewalk just to shake his hand. He is quiet; perhaps that's because despite a lifetime of experience with the media, he remains a basically shy man. He is indeed extremely intelligent and can be very intense at times. But I found him neither cool nor emotionless. He smiles easily and has an easy-going, somewhat dry sense of humor.

Tom Landry isn't perfect. He knows his own weaknesses. And despite a colossal collection of honors and awards acquired during a lifetime in the limelight, he remains humbly uncomfortable with praise and personal recognition.

You have to get beneath the public image to answer the real questions of what he's like:

How can a man known for his unflappable self-control be the longtime mentor of a human hydrogen bomb like Chicago Bear coach Mike Ditka? How can a man with his serious, businesslike commitment to the task put up with the irreverent zaniness of fun-loving characters like a Dandy

Don Meredith? What enables a soft-spoken, humble man to endure a fast-talking big-mouth like a Hollywood Henderson? Why would a straight-shooting disciplinarian try to work with recalcitrant troublemakers like a Duane Thomas? How could it be that a man with an image as a no-nonsense, conservative coach was also one of the greatest innovators in the history of the sport?

This is Tom Landry's story as it has never been told before—in his own words. It's a uniquely personal perspective from a man who competed against every great quarterback from Otto Graham to Joe Montana. A man whose career in football began when professional players wore leather helmets and bought their own cleats with meager, part-time paychecks and lasted to see the days of plexiglass face shields and multi-million dollar sportswear contracts.

Tom Landry's story provides an inside look at the growth and history of professional football from a man whose countless strategic innovations helped revolutionize and popularize the game. It offers an inside look at the Dallas Cowboys—America's Team—through the eyes of the man who reigned on the Dallas sidelines from 1960 through 1988. But first and foremost, the story that follows will give readers, for the first time, an inside look at Tom Landry. The man under the hat.

Gregg Lewis

part one

TROUBLE AT VALLEY RANCH

chapter one
THE BREWING STORM

THURSDAY. February 23, 1989.

Some new rumors floated around the office, but I didn't pay any attention. There had been many rounds of speculation since Bum Bright, the owner of the Dallas Cowboys, had gone public with his desire to sell the team almost a year before. Reliable reports had it Bright needed a quick supply of cash to shore up his crumbling real estate and banking empire. Yet none of the rumored buyers had panned out so I had no reason to believe anything would develop soon.

Two months had passed since the end of the Cowboys' worst season (three wins, thirteen losses) in twenty-eight years—the poorest record since my winless first season coaching the original Cowboys' expansion team in 1960. We were ready to begin gearing up for a better '89 season. I'd hired two new coaches who were moving to town. We had been working through the scouting reports in anticipation of the annual college draft; because we had the very first pick in the entire draft we knew we could select the very best college football player in America, someone who could make a strong and immediate contribution to our team. My assistants and I had just started putting together a revised playbook for 1989. And every coach in the Cowboys' organization was preparing for the first team meeting of the year scheduled for the following Monday, when the entire squad would assemble at the Cowboys' Valley Ranch headquarters to begin our official off-season conditioning program.

It was that time of year when I always try to put the past season, good or bad, behind me and begin thinking about the coming fall. After three losing seasons in a row, I'd gained some new critics who felt it was time I retired— the inference being I was too old to coach and that the game had finally passed me by. One columnist speculated that senility had already set in.

While no one likes to be criticized, I've taken enough criticism in the press over the years that I no longer lose any sleep over it. I weigh the opinions of knowledgeable writers I respect and shrug off the rest. In this case, while I knew there was much to be done in order to bring the Dallas Cowboys back into the top echelon of the National Football League, I also felt confident I knew how to do it. I had worked out plans to correct some of the mistakes I'd made in recent years. And I was ready to begin implementing those plans for the future.

It wasn't until Thursday night that I had any real indication I might not have a future with the Cowboys.

I spent the evening at home with Alicia, the charming, beautiful, and patient woman with whom I had celebrated my fortieth wedding anniversary less than a month before. After a quiet dinner we sat together on the couch in our den. We'd turned on the television, but were as oblivious to it as we were to the constant silent stream of headlights out on Northwest Highway just visible through the winter-bare limbs of the trees across the creek. Alicia, propped comfortably on pillows, was reading a magazine. I'd been totally engrossed in my preparation for the next day when I heard Alicia say, "Tommy!"

"Hmm?"

"Listen!"

"Mmm . . . hmm."

"Did you hear that?"

"Hear what?"

"On TV!"

Alicia wasn't sure of all the details. She had just caught the end of a local newsbrief. Something about the Cowboys being sold and a new Cowboys' coach. More details were promised on the 10 o'clock news.

The clock on the VCR said 9:30.

The phone rang. Alicia answered.

After a few seconds I heard her say, "We don't know anything about it." She listened another minute or so before saying we'd just seen the report and it was the first we'd heard anything. After she said good-bye and hung up she told me the caller had been Dale Hansen, a Dallas TV sportscaster, who said he'd just heard the story and was calling to try to confirm it. When Alicia told him we didn't know anything about a sale of the team, he had said he just called Tex Schramm, the general manager and president of the Dallas Cowboys. Tex had said he knew nothing either.

So we watched the news. KXAS-TV, Channel 5, in Fort Worth reported that oilman Jerry Jones, president of Arkoma Exploration of Little Rock, Arkansas, had reached an agreement with Bum Bright to buy the Dallas Cowboys. The report also said he planned to bring in his good friend and former University of Arkansas teammate and roommate, Jimmy Johnson, current head football coach at the University of Miami, to coach the Cowboys.

Alicia reacted first with shock. And then, with a loyalty characteristic of our life together, she became indignant at the idea anyone could believe the story. "It can't be true," she insisted.

I didn't know what to think. On a hopeful note, the report included no statement from any of the principals. Neither Jones nor Bright had confirmed the story. And the clearest indication I had that this was just another rumor was Tex Schramm's reaction. When we had talked earlier in the afternoon he had said he'd heard nothing from Bright.

I knew Tex well enough to know he was telling the truth. And since it was inconceivable to me that Tex, the Cowboys' president and CEO for twenty-nine years and two different owners, wouldn't know if a deal was about to be made, the whole thing sounded farfetched to me.

For another reason, the name Jerry Jones had surfaced out of nowhere several months before. And then only briefly. In the past year there had been several prospective buyers with bigger names and bigger portfolios. As early as June 1988 Denver oil billionaire Marvin Davis had approached Bright and looked over the Cowboys' books before backing off. Hotelier Robert Tisch, president of Loews Corporation, briefly considered buying the Cowboys before deciding Bright's $180 million asking price was too high. There had been other offers: from Donald Carter, owner of the Dallas Mavericks; from a group led by one of the Cowboys' minority owners; and most recently from Los Angeles Lakers' owner Jerry Buss. But all proposed deals had been rejected or fallen through.

As startling as this report was, and as definite as the reporter made it seem, I wasn't at all ready to believe it. I've seen enough "scoops" about the Cowboys over the years on TV and in newspapers when I'd been in a position to know they weren't true, that I figured this one would probably blow over in the light of a new day.

So I just assured Alicia, "We don't know anything for sure. If Tex doesn't know about it, there may be nothing to this. There's certainly nothing we can do tonight anyway. Let's just get some sleep and see what we find out tomorrow."

Come morning we found out the story wasn't about to go away. It made front-page news in Friday's papers. The *Times Herald* headline read, "Arkansas Man Likely to Buy Cowboys." The article cited the KXAS report, which had said the deal was done, but the newspaper lead only went so far as to say, "Arkansas oilman Jerry Jones has emerged as the leading candidate to buy the Dallas Cowboys. . . ." Again nothing final. But the same article did mention "persistent rumors" circulating in South Florida that Jimmy Johnson would become head coach of the Cowboys under Jones.

The paper pictured both men. I didn't know Jimmy Johnson well. We'd met on occasion at one public function or another over the years. He and some of his college coaching staff had once been the Cowboys' guests for a visit to our preseason training camp out in California. The last time I'd seen him was just the month before when he'd been the guest of Cowboys' vice president Gil Brandt in the Cowboys' box at Super Bowl XXIII.

By the time I got to my office out at Valley Ranch, the sprawling Cowboys' headquarters on the northwest outskirts of Dallas, the switchboard had lit up with calls, a flock of reporters had landed, and the halls buzzed with questions and speculation. I talked to Tex briefly; he told me he still didn't know a thing. But I sensed obvious distress.

Through three decades of partnership Tex and I learned to read each other pretty well, although I suspect that took a lot more effort on his part than on mine. He's much more of an open book than I am; no one would ever mistake him for a stoic or accuse him of being a "plastic man." Where I've usually kept my own emotions buried out of public view, Tex's volatile feelings often bubble, or even burst, through the surface.

A lost football game sometimes hit him like the death of a friend. Big wins could prompt a volcanic eruption of exuberant cheer. He could often be a warm, gregarious, and compassionate gentleman. At other times he seemed to revel in red-faced shouting matches with anyone—friends as well as foes—who disagreed with him. Where my personality often forced people to try to guess my feelings or doubt I had any, Tex's feelings were usually obvious— sometimes even through closed office doors.

Yet as different as we were in personality and lifestyle, we always understood and respected one another. And after a lifetime of experience together, I doubt anyone, but maybe our wives, knew us better than we knew each other.

I thought I had seen the gamut of Tex's emotions. But this Friday morning was different.

For twenty-nine years Tex had always been the man in charge. Because of our division of labor, and because I preferred to concentrate on the football field, I seldom concerned myself with front office business or issues related to the ownership of the football club. That was Tex's territory. If I ever had any questions about it, I could go to him. If he didn't have an immediate answer to any question regarding the Cowboys' organization, he always knew right where to go to get it.

But not this time. Tex was totally shut out. He was angry and obviously hurt. Beneath his obvious agitation I sensed a frustrated helplessness I'd never known in Tex Schramm before.

Bum Bright had left Tex hanging on this one. And I was hanging with him. It was an awful, exposed, and vulnerable feeling neither of us had ever known. Or ever imagined possible.

If the story was just a rumor, it was a whopping big one. I still wanted to believe that's all it was.

The moment I walked into the conference room for my scheduled morning meeting with all my assistant coaches, they hit me with a barrage of questions. I could only say, "I haven't heard anything and neither has Tex. We'll just have to wait and see what happens." We proceeded with the planning and preparation for the Monday meeting with the team.

Tex finally reached Bum Bright by phone sometime during the morning to ask what statements should be made. But all Bright would tell him was that a statement clarifying the situation would be made over the weekend. So about lunchtime Tex read his own prepared statement to the press saying only: "The status of the sale of the Cowboys will be clarified within the next forty-eight hours. Until that time, I have no comment."

After that, when I encountered reporters in the hall outside my office I simply told them, "I'll let Tex's statement stand for today."

While Bum Bright still wouldn't give Tex any information, Tex did get a call from his good friend, Don Shula, coach of the Miami Dolphins. Don phoned to tell him Jimmy Johnson had already contacted his son David Shula about becoming an assistant coach with the Cowboys. Maybe it was all true.

Slowly the hours passed. We still had the team meeting on Monday to prepare for, and I tried to go about my business as usual. But it was impossible to ignore the constant ringing of the phones in the outer offices and the tension and uncertainty building up throughout the day.

The Cowboys' coaches' office area is off-limits to the press unless a reporter is invited in for an interview. So it was pretty easy for me to avoid the crowd of reporters gathered in the press room and the public hallways of the Cowboy Center. But every time I passed in view of reporters they called out questions: "Are you fired? . . . Do you have any plans for the future, Tom? . . . What are you going to do now?"

Finally, replying to the last question, I told them, "I'm going to keep on working and go home when I finish." Pressed with a direct question about the story I was to be replaced by Jimmy Johnson I responded, "I know nothing at all about a coaching change. No one has said anything at all to me." Then I added, "It very well could be true. Stranger things have been known to happen, but I can't worry about things I can't control. We'll just have to wait and see."

Despite limited success at continuing my planned routine, Friday was not a routine day at the office. Before I left at five that afternoon I checked with Tex again. He'd heard nothing new.

I told him I was flying down to Austin the next morning to spend the weekend at our vacation home in the Hills of Lakeway. I intended to play some golf and enjoy an early birthday celebration for my youngest daughter, Lisa, who lives there in Lakeway. "If you need me or hear anything, give me a call."

Tex assured me he would. And as I drove away from the tension-filled halls of the Cowboys' headquarters, the idea of escaping Dallas and the press for the weekend sounded like a wonderful idea.

I tried to reassure Alicia when I reached home. But in telling her the details of the day, I had to admit, at least to myself, that things didn't look good.

The story dominated the early evening newscasts on every station in the Dallas metroplex. But all anyone seemed to have was more speculation. Camera crews lurked outside Bright's office all day, but Bright had confirmed nothing. We did catch a statement by one of Bum's assistants who told reporters he could confirm nothing but assuring them and the public that whatever happened would be "good for the Cowboys and good for Dallas." Obviously something was going on behind the closed doors down at Bum Bright's bank headquarters.

After dinner we received a curious phone call from an unidentified man who told Alicia, "Don't worry. Some of your friends are putting together a bid and we're gonna buy the team out from under him." While I couldn't put much faith in an anonymous caller, it gave us reason to think the story might not be over yet. At the very least it was one more crazy puzzle piece in what had become, in little more than twenty-four hours, a very bizarre business.

Whatever was happening between Bum Bright and Jerry Jones, there seemed nothing for me to do but wait. And to go on with our weekend plans. So a short time before we went to bed for the night, I called the local flight service number for a weather report to make sure I'd be able to fly my single-engine Cessna 210 down to Lakeway the next morning for our getaway weekend.

Yet by that time, I realized there would be no getting away from whatever was about to happen.

chapter two
FIRING DAY

SATURDAY dawned with the promised good flying weather. But the storm clouds over the Cowboys continued to build. The front-page stories of the two Dallas dailies dwarfed the tragic reports of a jumbo jet being ripped open in midair over Hawaii with bigger, more prominent headlines that read: "Cowboys Sale Near; Landry Likely Out" (*Dallas Morning News*) and "Cowboys Deal Near; Landry Likely to Go" (*Dallas Times Herald*).

The *Morning News* coverage, which I read while eating a large bowl of oatmeal for breakfast, featured a front-page, color photo of Jerry Jones and Jimmy Johnson dining together Friday night at Mia's Mexican Restaurant, one of Alicia's and my favorite eating spots, not far from our north Dallas neighborhood. From the picture, I instantly recognized not only the restaurant, but the table where Jones and Johnson were sitting beneath Cowboys' photos, clippings, and assorted sports memorabilia hanging on the walls above and behind them.

Tex phoned minutes before we left for the airport. He wanted to tell me he was on his way to a meeting at the Bright Banc offices downtown—presumably to finally learn something official. He also wanted to know: "If I need to reach you later today, where are you going to be?"

I told him we were about to take off for Lakeway as planned. We would be at our house there for a short while later in the morning. Then we'd drive out to Hidden Hills, a newly developed club nearby, for an afternoon round of golf. Tex promised to reach me when he knew anything definite and we said good-bye.

My son, Tom, Jr., who was going to Austin with us for the weekend, arrived. Together we took the five-minute ride from our home to Love Field where we keep our plane at the Daljet facility. Tom asked if I'd seen the *Morning News*. I admitted I had, but that I didn't know any more than I had the night before. And I told him about the call from Tex.

At the airport we quickly loaded our golf clubs and what little luggage we needed for the weekend into the cargo area in the back of the cabin. And I carefully went over the complete preflight checklist I keep on a laminated card. Donning my headphones, I received clearance from the tower and taxied out to the end of the runway to wait permission for takeoff.

As we lifted off, banked toward the south, and began climbing as we headed out over downtown Dallas, I tried not to think about the Cowboys, Tex, or the meetings taking place a few thousand feet below. I focused instead on the instrument panel gauges in front of me and the instructions of the air traffic controller's voice in my headset.

Alicia and Tom, Jr., may have exchanged a few words during the flight. But with my earphones on I certainly couldn't hear them over the cockpit noise. I was very much alone with my thoughts for the next hour—until the flat Texas plain stretching out below suddenly met the edge of the hill country outside Austin. Descending over Lake Travis and circling the tiny Lakeway airstrip on our final approach, we could see our house. After we touched down safely and turned to taxi back from the end of the runway, we spotted Lisa, waiting for us near the gate.

*   *   *

It was afternoon by the time Alicia, Tom, Jr., Lisa, her husband, Gary Childress, and I all teed off at Hidden Hills, a fairly new golf course designed by Arnold Palmer in the rugged rolling hills rising above the shores of Lake Travis, several miles from our vacation home west of Austin. We just completed the first hole when the club pro came trotting out on the course.

"Coach Landry!" he called. "You have a phone call."

I hurried back to the clubhouse by myself. It was Tex.

"What's happening?" I asked.

"It isn't good," he replied.

"All right," I said. I knew what that meant.

"Jerry Jones and I are flying down to Austin to see you right away."

I felt like saying, *Tell him to save his gas*. Instead I gave Tex directions for the hour-plus drive to Hidden Hills from the Austin airport where Jones's pilot intended to land his private jet.

Then I rejoined my family waiting for me at the second tee. I told them what they already knew, that the call had been from Tex. And I relayed what he'd said, that he and Jones were flying right out to talk with me. I didn't say what I knew that meant. I didn't have to.

Alicia gave me a warm reassuring hug. Maybe it's because she's been married to me for so long, but she's not big on public displays of emotion. Yet the feeling was there in that brief embrace. I knew she too felt the pain, perhaps more than I did at that moment.

I told her I thought it would be best if she went back to the house at Lakeway. Lisa volunteered to drive her. And I promised to call as soon as I talked with Tex and Jones.

After Alicia and Lisa went home, there wasn't much left to say. And nothing to do but wait. So with too nice an afternoon to waste, Tom, Gary, and I played out our eighteen holes. I can't say I remember much about the round. I do recall it was tougher than usual to concentrate on the weak points of my game.

* * *

Tom, Jr., and I saw the rental car drive up from where we had been practicing on the putting green. When Tex and Jerry Jones climbed out in front of the clubhouse, we walked over to meet them.

The two of them looked uncomfortable. And it wasn't just the dark business suits and ties. Jones reached out to shake hands as Tex introduced him.

"We can talk over here." I motioned toward the sales office for the Hidden Hills development, which was across the practice green from the clubhouse. It was closed late Saturday afternoons and Gary, who worked for the Hidden Hills development, had arranged for us to use it after we had finished our round of golf.

No one said anything else until we were inside the office, a cottage renovated into a sales office with a tastefully appointed arrangement of contemporary-style living room furniture. Tex and I settled into two mauve and gray easy chairs facing a matching couch where Jones sat. Tom, Jr., stood a little off to the side, toward the kitchen area, behind Jones. A sense of awkwardness filled the room.

Jones began quickly by saying Tex had suggested he come down personally and let me know face to face what was happening. I don't recall his exact words, but he went on to say he'd bought the Cowboys and he was bringing in Jimmy Johnson to be his head coach.

I don't remember much of anything he said after that. A jumble of feelings crowded my mind. Anger. Sadness. Frustration. Disappointment. Resignation.

I sensed how upset Tex was by the body language I caught out of the corner of my eye. But I fixed my eyes on Jones, who was still talking. The longer he went on, the more uncomfortable he looked.

When he finally stopped, I was thinking about the rebuilding plans I'd had for the Cowboys. So I said what was on my mind at the moment. "It's unfortunate we're not gonna be finishing what we've started. But," I sighed, "that's not going to happen now."

Jones said something about wishing there was some

way he could make this easier for me. And I guess that's the only time I let my frustration and anger about the uncertainty and secretive events of the past week come through, because I told him I didn't think the situation had been handled the way it should have been.

He apologetically tried to explain why things had developed the way they had over the preceding few days. But we all knew there wasn't much to say at that point.

I did ask about my assistants. I felt particularly concerned about the two new men I'd just hired, who had just uprooted their families and moved to Dallas. Jones didn't say anything specific, just that he would have to wait and see. He assured me he'd do the right thing by all the assistant coaches.

I also asked what we should do about the team meeting scheduled for Monday. He didn't know anything about that. So I decided the team should come in as scheduled to begin the off-season training program.

And that's all there was to the meeting.

We stood up. Jones shook my hand, went around the couch to shake hands with Tom, Jr., and headed for the door.

I don't have any idea how long the meeting took. Just a few minutes and a lot of that was a blur.

Tex stopped to shake my hand. He looked like a disaster survivor—wounded and in shock. Tears filled his eyes; he could barely choke out the words, "I'm sorry."

My own eyes misted over and I mumbled something in response. I have no idea what I said. There weren't any adequate words for that moment. Just raw emotion. And understanding—soul-deep understanding forged by nearly three decades of friendship and trust.

For twenty-nine years we'd been partners. During those long losing years at the beginning, then through all those heartbreaking seasons when we "couldn't win the big one" Tex had stood with me. Side by side on draft days and in joyous Super Bowl locker rooms. We had lived a lifetime of shared memories.

We had built a professional football team like no other. But we'd *been* a team as well.

In that instant, with that final handshake, it was all over. At least for me. And some of the pain we each felt was because we both realized Tex's days with the Dallas Cowboys were over, too.

As the office door closed behind Tex, Tom, Jr., walked over beside me and said, "I'm sorry, Dad."

I tried to smile. I could tell he felt awkward and had no idea what to say. How many men ever have to be in a meeting and watch their own father get fired? I knew he felt terrible and out of place. But it made me feel better just having him there with me; I appreciated and needed that support.

Everyone who had been in that room was emotionally spent—Jones, too. My son-in-law, Gary, told me later he'd been waiting outside the door with the message that Jones's pilot had landed on the Lakeway airstrip so they wouldn't have to drive all the way back in to Austin. But when a visibly pale Jones walked out of the sales office he had been too flustered to follow Gary's verbal instructions on how to find Lakeway.

"Can you just draw me a map?" he had asked. After Gary did so, he walked quickly to a car where he tried unsuccessfully for a couple minutes to get the key in the door before realizing it wasn't the car he'd been driving.

Tom, Jr., and I left the sales office together and walked to the clubhouse dressing room to change. No one else was there. And no one came in while we were there. For a few days I guess I'd been bracing myself for what had just happened. Now all the energy I had used to keep going drained right out of me. I felt empty and exhausted. And older than I'd ever felt in my life.

Tom and I changed in silence as the reality of the afternoon slowly began to sink in through the numbness.

With it came the question I had refused to think about for the last forty-eight hours. The question I had been putting off since I'd begun my life in professional football forty years before. "What do I do now?"

The first order of business was to call Alicia and confirm what she already knew. She didn't react emotionally at all. Perhaps she was as numb as I was by that time. But I knew the feelings had to be there, churning beneath the surface. As she'd done at so many of my low points over the years, she was supporting me with a heartening show of strength and resolve.

When Alicia told me she was already dressed for dinner, we agreed to go ahead with our evening plans. (Though we never for a moment considered doing anything else.) She and Lisa drove back to join Gary, Tom, and me for dinner at the Hidden Hills Club.

I'm afraid Lisa's birthday celebration wasn't a wildly happy occasion. But it wasn't completely somber either. I guess everyone tried to buck up for my sake. My family made small talk and even laughed a little. I tried to enter in, but I admit I was a bit preoccupied.

As it turned out, the Hidden Hills Country Club may have been the only place in the state of Texas where we could have eaten a quiet meal that evening. As a new club in a new development, only a handful of members and guests showed for dinner. And the security gate effectively kept the gathering press off the grounds.

By the time Alicia and Lisa had gotten back to Lakeway that afternoon, a number of TV crews and reporters had already congregated outside The Hills of Lakeway security gate, but hadn't recognized Lisa's car before the guard let them through. During the afternoon one TV crew had attempted to land a helicopter at the The Hills clubhouse, just a stone's throw from our house. But the manager had refused them permission to land and ordered them to take off immediately.

One reason we'd come to Austin for the weekend was to escape the press. And I didn't feel up to facing them yet. So we left Hidden Hills by a back way and made it home to Lakeway without having to face a single microphone or camera.

*   *   *

Getting ready for bed that night I asked Alicia if she'd mind if we made our return flight to Dallas early the next morning instead of waiting until afternoon. She said that would be fine with her.

My thought was to get back so I could clean out my office on Sunday when there wouldn't be many people around Valley Ranch. I hoped to avoid a public scene. And I wanted to get at least one emotionally difficult task behind me before I faced my players for the last time on Monday.

Sleep didn't come easily that night. My mind kept racing.

I'd experienced a lot of low times during my career. I'd suffered numerous gut-wrenching losses in big games. This was the biggest. Worse than any playoff loss marking the sudden end of a season. After this, there were no more seasons.

I couldn't help thinking about the past forty years in professional football. Even a quick mental review of the important people and events in my life made me feel very thankful. My Giants' teammates in the fifties. The World Championship in New York. My friendship and rivalry with Vince Lombardi. The Super Bowls. All those Cowboys' comebacks. The twenty straight winning seasons. And so many great players . . .

But I couldn't think only about the past. I immediately had to face the hard adjustments of an as-yet-unimaginable future. For that I knew I would need and could ask God's guidance and help—as I'd learned to do so many times before.

I fully expected the next couple days to be two of the most emotionally trying days of my life. And that they would prove to be. But as I fell asleep that Saturday night, I could never have imagined—at sixty-four years of age, standing at the sad, sudden, involuntary end of a long and fulfilling career—that the weeks and months to come would hold the most satisfying, most rewarding, and the most incredible days of my life.

part two

FROM A
TEXAS TOWN
TO THE BIG APPLE

chapter three
SMALL-TOWN TEXAN

LIKE ANY true Texan who will jump at the chance to tell you how everything is bigger-'n'-better in the Lone Star State, I could be tempted to exaggerate in describing my hometown. Except there was hardly enough to it to exaggerate about.

Mission lies deep in the Rio Grande Valley just miles from the Mexican border. It has never been and never will be a glamour spot. But there wasn't a prettier-smelling place on earth when the winds would waft the sweet fragrance of flowering lemon, orange, and grapefruit in from the great citrus groves stretching up and down the valley.

The town of Mission wasn't big enough to boast a traditional Texas town square—just a few side streets branching off Conway, the main drag running from one end of town to the other. And yet, for the first seventeen years of my life, that tiny town made up my world.

Unlike many of my friends, my own family's roots didn't stretch far back in that part of Texas. My Canadian great-grandfather, Stanislas Landrie, was one of six children born to French immigrants. Somewhere along the line the spelling of the family name got changed to Landry.

French remained my family's primary language until Stani's son, my own grandfather, Alfred, married my grandmother, Lillian Celena Anderson, in 1893. She taught him English and bore him six children, two of which died during difficult Illinois winters.

My own father, Ray, born November 17, 1898, suffered from muscular rheumatism. So when the family doctor suggested they leave Bradley, Illinois, and move to a warmer climate, the Landrys packed up and headed south. My dad's rheumatism problem disappeared in the warmth of southern Texas and he developed into a natural athlete who made his mark locally as a pitcher and a football player.

During high school Dad noticed a new girl in town, Ruth Coffman, a beautiful young woman with long auburn tresses and striking blue eyes. Her farmer father had moved his family from Virginia to Tennessee to Oklahoma, before arriving in Mission in 1915.

Mom was a quieter, more serious student than Dad. She loved to sing, joined the school glee club, and went on to become valedictorian of her high school class. As an attractive new girl in town she had more than her share of admirers. But once she began dating Dad, neither of them dated anyone else again.

In 1918 Dad graduated from Mission High School and went off to Texas A&M. After Mom graduated the following year, the Coffmans moved again—this time to Los Angeles. Dad dropped out of A&M and followed her to California where he got a job and took training to become a mechanic. On May 8, 1920, they married and moved back to their old hometown of Mission. By the time I was born on September 11, 1924, my big brother Robert was almost four and my sister Ruth was a year and half old.

What made for a small town, made for a big extended family. And that's the role Mission played in my life and the lives of my peers. Anyone you'd meet on the street knew who you were, where you lived, and often where you were heading. And while that meant privacy was at a premium and kids had a hard time getting into serious mischief, it proved to be good preparation for the kind of public life I've lived for more than forty years. I learned a sense of accountability early in life, accepting the fact that people were always watching—even when I wished they weren't.

One such occasion occurred when I was five or six and just learning to ride a bike—a true challenge on hard-baked dirt streets full of bumps and ruts like the road that ran along the irrigation canal at the far edge of town. Its high roadbanks served the dual purpose of keeping wobbling riders on course while at the same time providing a safe place for short-legged youngsters to dismount from the lofty heights of a big brother's bicycle seat. But one day I either pedaled too fast, hit a particularly bad rut, or simply panicked—maybe all three. Whatever the cause, I crashed into the roadbank so hard I flew head over handlebars and landed on my bottom, smack in the middle of a large cluster of cactus.

I jumped up and lit out for home screaming for Mama. But the pain in my posterior was nothing compared to the agony of embarrassment I suffered over her quick-thinking solution to my prickly predicament. Somehow she sent out an alarm, probably by way of my brother and sister, and the next thing I knew I was lying face down and bare-bottom up on a table surrounded by neighbor ladies armed with tweezers.

I have no idea how long it took, but it seemed like hours as my mother and her friends pulled scores of needles from my backside. Looking back I suspect there may have been only two or three women there, but it seemed like a capacity crowd. I felt like a public spectacle and I can still vividly recall horrible embarrassment that lasted far longer than my sore bottom.

For years I had a childhood speech impediment that probably contributed to my already quiet and shy personality. I never said much because I was too self-conscious to speak up. Yet, despite my shyness, I felt a strong sense of belonging growing up in a town like Mission and a solid feeling of security—especially in my family. They were always there to love and accept and protect me—not just my immediate family but also my grandparents, aunts, uncles, and cousins.

One of my earliest memories is fishing with my Grandpa Landry and my dad's brother, Uncle Arthur. We'd spent a lazy afternoon fishing on the Rio Grande where the old pump station diverted river water into the canal that supplied Mission and the local citrus groves. We'd caught three catfish before Uncle Arthur announced, "It's time to go back home, Tommy. You can bring the fish."

I hauled the stringer of fish out of the water and headed across the catwalk stretching across the canal. But my bare feet slipped on that wet, wooden walkway and I plunged into the water churning out from under the pumphouse. No sooner did that dark brown water close over my head than I felt a big adult hand grab my hair and drag me back up into the light. One moment of terrifying darkness was all I experienced before Uncle Arthur was there. And when he pulled me safely out of that rushing water, he and Grandpa exclaimed in amazement, "Would you look at that! Tommy never let go of the fish!" There they were! I had the stringer of catfish still clenched tightly in my hand.

In my childish innocence I assumed their obvious relief and happiness was because I'd held tight to the fish, not because my uncle had miraculously snatched me from the swirling waters of the canal before I was swept under and drowned. And for years afterward, whenever the incident was recounted by my family and friends, my overwhelming memory was one of pride that I hadn't lost those catfish.

But it was impossible for any family, no matter how attentive, to protect an active little boy from potential disaster. One warm autumn day at my grandparents' house I was playing on the front porch, watching and waiting for my dad and my uncle to return any moment from a deer hunting trip. Finally, I spotted them! Before my uncle's Model T coasted to a stop across the street, I flew off the front steps and bolted for the car. I never saw the other car coming from the opposite direction.

The next thing I knew I was lying on a table in the doctor's office upstairs over the drugstore. My screams drifted out of the open windows above downtown Mission as my father and his sister, Aunt Viola, tried to pull my leg taut enough for the doctor to set it without benefit of any anesthesia. When I opened my eyes again, I realized my father was gone. I screamed even louder and he came rushing back to my side. I didn't know till my aunt told me years later, that Dad, an experienced volunteer fireman who'd never been squeamish about treating the worst accident victims, had left the room because he was about to pass out at the sight of my suffering. Yet when he came back, he stayed until the doctor finished applying the cast. Then he gently carried me home in his arms.

Like most little boys, I thought my dad could do anything. It certainly wasn't hard to respect him, because everyone else did. He knew most everybody in town by name and they knew him—if not as the mechanic they depended on to fix their car, then certainly as chief of the town's volunteer fire department, a post he held for forty years before he retired. For twenty-seven years he served as Sunday school superintendent at the little Methodist church a block from our house. Whenever an emergency arose in town, a civic project required manpower, the Lions' Club needed a volunteer, or a big barbecue demanded a great cook, the people of Mission knew they could call on Ray Landry. At one time or another it seemed most of them did.

I can't count the number of times we had to delay our own family celebrations on Christmas Day because Dad had been called to a fire. But the fire department duties that so often disrupted his personal plans provided his sons with a source of great excitement. Whenever the alarm sounded, Dad would run to his shop in the garage across the alley where he kept the fire chief's official red Chevrolet. As he roared off to the scene of a fire, I'd take off after him on my bike, feeling proud of my brave father, the fire chief.

Our self-important role as sons of the fire chief gave Robert and me the opportunity to spend many thrilling days playing at the firehouse, sliding down the fireman's pole, and climbing on the town's first fire truck—which Dad had built in his shop across the alley from our house. Occasionally we even spent the night on one of the cots upstairs in the fire station, a building that was home for a number of young single guys through the hardest years of the Depression. I remember that's where my dad took me to stay on the night my little brother Jack was born in 1931.

Where Dad's personality made him a true public servant, Mother was much more of a private person. I think I inherited my studious, perfectionistic, and quiet nature from her. For some time during the Depression she fed and clothed a family of six on less than $1.50 a day; yet we always had enough left over to provide a hot meal to any transient who ever showed up at our back door.

We never had a lot of anything, including privacy. All four of us kids shared a single attic bedroom that ran the full width of the small frame house. And the attic stairs descended into my parents' bedroom. Yet our cramped house served as the neighborhood gathering ground, and it was to our home that our extended family often came for reunions and holiday get-togethers because my folks always made people feel welcome.

Both my parents were more doers than talkers. Their examples taught me much about values such as community service, dedication, dependability, hard work, and integrity. They seldom vocalized their Christian faith, but church was clearly important to them. Whenever the church's doors opened—Sunday morning, Sunday night, and Wednesday evening as well—our entire family showed up. The church congregation, like the fire department and the town itself, provided another sort of "family" to which I belonged. And while neither of my parents were ever overtly affectionate, with each other or with their children, I never doubted their love.

I probably spent more time with my sister Ruthie than with either of my brothers because she was my closest sibling in age. A tomboy with excellent athletic skills, Ruthie often played baseball and football with me and my friends—keeping me humble with a sprinter's speed I couldn't match until we reached our teens. I do remember always looking up to my older brother Robert as the student, the athlete, the person whose shoes I most longed to fill.

Frequently when Dad kept customers' cars overnight, he'd let Robert and me sleep on cots in the shop to keep an eye on things. What Dad didn't know was that long before Robert was old enough to get a license, he had begun honing his driving skills in that garage—late at night, when we figured everyone was asleep. I'd ride shotgun and provide moral support as he turned on the ignition, slipped the car into gear, and eased it across the garage floor and then back into its original position after an exciting round trip of twenty-five or thirty feet.

One fateful night Robert moved Dad's official red fire chief's car out into the middle of the garage, but when he went to pull it back into its stall, he mistakenly shifted into reverse. Then, instead of hitting the brake, he stepped on the gas and sent that Chevrolet hurtling backward into the alley, through the sliding wooden garage doors, which crashed down around us. The commotion brought Dad running. I don't ever remember seeing him any angrier than he was that night. And it was the last time Robert and I ever took one of those late-night test drives in Dad's car.

Because conscientious, hard work was an obvious family value, I found jobs to earn money from a very early age. I sold newspapers on the street before I finally graduated to a route of my own. And from the time we stood as tall as a golf bag, my best friend Wade Spillman and I would caddy at our local golf course, toting bags as big as we were, for a twenty-five cent tip. Of that, we had to kick back a nickel to the caddy-master for lining us up with the golfers.

But neither work nor school ever really interfered with the most important business of being a kid and enjoying the freedom to play games, explore the world, and have fun. There wasn't much in the way of organized activities in Mission, but then we didn't need any. My friends and I played football and basketball in season—sometimes down at the park, but more often in our yard or in the vacant lot next to our house. We lived outdoors and went barefoot pretty much year-round; I don't remember regularly wearing shoes until junior high. I learned to swim in the irrigation canals outside town and soon became a proficient swimmer and diver with daily practice during the summers at the Crystal Waters Pool. We would hike down to the Rio Grande to fish whenever we wanted, and come hunting season, we'd take to the fields outside town to hunt deer and shoot the white-wing doves that flew in flocks so big they sometimes darkened the sky.

We found plenty to keep us busy. And whenever the days did drag and small-town life began to feel a bit dull, all we had to do was wait till Saturday. Because Saturdays were never boring.

For a nickel apiece, my friends and I could get into the local theater to watch the Saturday morning serials with the Lone Ranger, Hopalong Cassidy, Tom Mix, and sometimes Tarzan. And along about five o'clock every Saturday afternoon, Dad would drive the family Buick down the block and around the corner and park it as close to the drugstore on Conway Street as he could. You had to go early to get a prime parking spot. When night came, the entire family would walk downtown and find a familiar fender to lean on as we talked with neighbors and watched the crowds gathered for the usual Saturday night excitement.

Saturday night in Mission was a weekly melting pot when Methodists mingled with Baptists, rich mixed with poor. Children played tag up and down the sidewalks. Their parents greeted each other like long-lost friends instead of as neighbors they had chatted with last Saturday and would probably see again in church the next morning. It was all part of the familiar small-town ritual that helped give meaning to life in Mission—the only world I knew.

When we had an extra nickel, my friends and I would take in a Saturday night feature or two at the local theater. I guess the silver screen provided the only real fodder for young boys' fantasies in those days. Unlike kids today who often idolize big-name athletes, I knew little or nothing about organized, professional sports. Once in a while I'd sit with the old black gentleman who shined shoes at the barber shop and listen to a radio broadcast of a New York Yankees' game. Even in Mission we knew about the Yankees. But I couldn't have named a half-dozen big-league baseball teams. And I never knew there was such a thing as professional football.

So I didn't find my boyhood heroes on the playing field. I watched them in western movies, riding across fields on horseback. Whenever I imagined a glamorous and exciting future life beyond the borders of Mission, Texas, I always dreamed of becoming a cowboy.

chapter four
A HIGH SCHOOL COACH'S INFLUENCE

MY FAMILY, my church, and the small-town environment of Mission served as filters for the basic values I learned as a boy. But it was sports that shaped and reinforced those values.

We had no Little League or Pop Warner programs in my day, so we learned to organize and mediate our own contests. Long before I ever played a down of organized football, I practiced leadership skills by drafting a team of friends and calling the plays in thousands of sandlot football games. That lack of parental involvement in our recreational activities wasn't as much a disadvantage as it was an opportunity to develop independence and initiative. It also meant the season never had to end.

Some days, all day, we would wear out the dirt and what little grass remained in the empty lot next to our house on Dougherty Street. Supper served merely as a long time out, with the action continuing by porch light in our front yard until our mothers announced bedtime and we had exhausted their patience with multiple appeals for "just one more play!"

In the course of those endless games I first tapped the

flow of my own competitive juices—savoring the sweetness of hard-won success and learning to swallow the bitterness of disappointment and defeat. The cuts and bruises inflicted in equal measure by hard-nosed opponents and hard-baked earth caused plenty of painful tears. But eventually they also instilled a gritty toughness in anyone who played day after day, year after year.

From the time my big brother Robert began tossing me passes and occasionally letting me center the ball in pickup games with his older pals, I saw football as a chance to prove myself. To measure myself against my peers. And eventually to feel good about who I was and what I could do. Competition helped create and crystallize my self-identity.

Organized sports, when I finally got a chance at them in high school, played an even bigger role in shaping me as a person. And my very first coach very quickly became the single most influential person in my young life.

Bob Martin couldn't have stood over 5'10" or weighed more than 170. But to a scrawny, 112-pound freshman boy like me, he seemed an imposing figure. He must have been about twenty-two years old, fresh from college, and facing his first job at Mission High as a teacher and junior varsity football coach. But to me Bob Martin was an experienced man of the world. After all, he had lettered in football at South Texas State Teacher's College in San Marcos. And he was my coach.

About two dozen boys turned out the first day of junior varsity practice. When Coach Martin held up a football and said, "I need a smart, tough kid who will take this ball and initiate every play for our team," I immediately volunteered. I believed I was tough, but I'm not sure how smart I was because that's how I became the 112-pound center of the Mission High School junior varsity football team. I'd rather have been a back and carried the ball, but my JV experience as a center helped teach me the importance of teamwork and an appreciation of every player's role on a football squad.

Bob Martin himself taught me much more. He convinced me success always requires effort. That self-respect demands your maximum effort at all times. And that your best effort always made you a winner because it meant you'd never lose your pride. He lectured us about the value of teamwork and how the whole can be stronger than the sum of its parts. He taught me the importance of knowing and taking care of my body. He modeled self-discipline in his own life and demanded no less from his athletes. And I listened because I knew what Bob Martin said, he also lived.

For the next four years I was to spend more time with Coach Martin than any other person—including my family. His word would become my law, his approval my inspiration. And football would become my life.

As much as I respected Coach Martin at the time, I didn't fully appreciate what he taught me or what he achieved in Mission, until years later. While Martin is an Anglo name, Bob's Mexican mother's ancestry was evident in his features and his dark complexion. And the railroad that ran the length of the valley in those days clearly divided the Hispanic population from the Anglo-Americans in every Texas town along the Rio Grande. Mission was no exception. The town's school system was segregated up through the lower grades; even in our combined high school, an obvious division remained with each group sticking pretty much to itself. While we mixed without incident on the Mission athletic teams, and I counted a number of Hispanic kids among my good friends, prejudice ran deep in South Texas. So that Bob Martin's hiring to teach and coach at Mission High and the fact he lived on the Anglo side of the tracks (just two doors away from my house) undoubtedly caused a lot of talk around town and meant Bob Martin had far more to prove than most young coaches.

By the summer before my junior year, however, Bob had shown enough to the school board that he got appointed head varsity football coach. Those of us who had played for him two years already on the JV team welcomed the announcement and anticipated a great varsity career. We already believed in our coach and he'd taught us to believe in ourselves.

I had put on a few pounds and weighed about 145 by that summer of 1940. Dad had hung a tire from a tree beside our house, and I'd practiced throwing a football through it for months. Evidently the coach had been watching from his garage apartment two doors down, because he moved me from JV center to varsity quarterback/tailback that year.

As a single A school, we went 6–4 my junior season playing against A and larger AA schools. We won the district championship by going undefeated during the regular season against teams in our district. That gave us the right to host the high school team from Alice for the single A championship of the bi-district. However we lost the game by a tough score of 7–6.

I finished the season with a total of 46 points scored, several other touchdown passes, plus All-South Texas honors. But I wasn't satisfied with that level of success. And neither was Coach Martin. We were already looking to the next year when the heart of our district championship team would all be back again.

I have to admit football dominates my high school memories. In part that's because several other aspects of my teenage years proved more easily forgettable.

Perhaps the biggest advantage of a small school like Mission with just over two hundred students was that I got involved in everything. Unfortunately, that didn't mean I was good at everything.

One year I took band. Since I couldn't play any other instruments, the director put me on drums. But it was no use; I had no rhythm.

I showed even less talent in singing. The boys' glee club needed bodies and Clayburn Norris, the assistant football coach, directed the choir. So when he told me I *would* join, I did what Coach Norris ordered. In practice I even tried to sing. But when it came time for a performance or for competition with choirs from other schools, I just mouthed the words. The one time I lost my concentration and actually sang out loud during a performance, the guy in front of me winced, turned, and gave me such a withering look I never again forgot my understood role as a silent singer. The next year the assistant coach didn't even try to draft me for glee club, and I had to put any hope for a singing career on hold for over fifty years before I finally got my big break in country music. But that story comes later.

Perhaps my most embarrassing high school experience came when I won the male lead for our senior play. I felt honored and figured it could be interesting. I hadn't bothered to read the entire play until we began practicing and suddenly realized the script called for me to kiss the female lead (one of the prettiest girls in town) during the last scene.

It was one thing to kiss a girl on a date when you were alone. I'd had little enough experience in that area. But to stand on a stage and kiss a girl in front of friends, family, and the entire school? I'd sooner have been gang-tackled in my own end zone.

However, I saw no way to duck or fake my way out of this one. So I determined to stand in there and take it. I tried to hide my embarrassment, but even in rehearsals it was obvious. The closer we would get to that scene, the more of my lines I'd mess up.

I would like to be able to say that the actual performance of the play wasn't as bad as I'd anticipated. It was though. Maybe worse. The moment my lips touched the girl's, my teammates and friends hooted and whistled and cheered me on. If a person could ever die of embarrassment, I would have done it.

My feelings about my romantic stage role fairly accurately reflected my experience with the high school social scene. I found it took far more courage to ask a pretty girl for a date than it did to try to run through the biggest, meanest, and ugliest opposing lineman in South Texas. I wasn't any smoother as a talker than I was as a kisser. And as a dancer in the day of the fast-stepping jitterbug, I was nothing more than an accomplished shuffler.

My teenage social life revolved more around my own gang of friends and teammates than around girls. Our idea of a good time was sitting at the drugstore soda counter on Saturday mornings rehashing the big plays of the game the night before, letting the welcome attention of other customers soothe the usual postgame soreness and any bruises to our bodies or egos.

Another blow to my manly image came with the "honor" of my election as "Cutest Boy" at Mission High. I would have felt honored to be named "Most Likely to Succeed." "Smartest" or "Friendliest" would have been all right. As a tough athlete I might have aspired to those. But never to "Cutest."

Fortunately I wasn't too macho to take my academics seriously. In fact, what I'd learned on the field about effort and doing my best, I applied in the classroom. It never seemed easy to me like it did to my sister Ruthie or my friend Wade. English and literature particularly proved challenging; any natural aptitude seemed to lie more in math and the sciences. But with a lot of hard study and the encouragement of my enthusiastic young math teacher, Miss Frances Dusek, I actually made the National Honor Society before I graduated. That achievement gave me great satisfaction and enough confidence to think just maybe I had what it took to make it in the world beyond the valley.

In a school the size of Mission, anyone with any athletic ability at all got the chance to compete in any sport. I loved baseball and played a few summers for the Mission 30–30 Rifles, a local semipro team made up mostly of Hispanic men in their late teens and twenties. But Mission High never fielded a baseball team, so I had to make do with other spring sports. Though I never had great speed, I did letter in track by running in relays and doing my best in field events like the high jump and the broad jump. I played a little tennis, too; but I didn't ever measure up to Wade

Spillman, who made it all the way to the state tennis championship his senior year.

Other than football, basketball was my most competitive high school sport. In Mission during those days both were outdoor sports. A number of the other schools around had gymnasiums, but we played our basketball games on a clay court beside the school. That meant before every game the surface had to be rolled smooth and lined—much like clay tennis courts are maintained. It also meant that a home basketball game sometimes had to be called on account of rain. But the arid winter weather of South Texas provided a suitable climate for outdoor basketball. And our lack of a gym gave us a great home court advantage against opponents who weren't used to shooting free throws with the sun in their eyes.

At the end of our very successful junior season Bob Martin began to challenge us to prepare and commit ourselves to aim even higher the next year. He gave us a motto: "Eleven brothers are hard to beat." And then that Christmas of 1940 he sent each member of the football team a card with a motivational poem challenging us to a higher goal as individuals and as a team.

By the time our senior football season rolled around, we could hardly wait. And I had learned an important lesson in motivation: For a team to be motivated enough to win, each individual member must be motivated. And we were.

The coach clamped down harder than ever with training restrictions. He announced that he didn't even want us drinking cokes during the season. And that, as a matter of team pride and with the added intent of keeping us focused on football, he told us he didn't want to see one girlfriend wearing a football letter sweater. Those sweaters were to be a special badge of honor for players only.

No one complained about the rules.

In the opening game of our '41 season, I threw for two touchdown passes in a 12–0 win over Edinburg. The following week we downed San Benito by a score of 25–0 and I had touchdown runs of 66 and 20 yards. I tossed a couple more touchdown passes in a decisive 28–0 victory over Raymondville.

By the time we'd ripped Mercedes 40–0 and captured an even more lopsided 47–0 victory against Weslaco, newspapers up and down the valley had taken note of Mission's powerhouse football team. And I got more than my share of attention from sportswriters who called me "Terrific Tommy Landry, a six-foot, 170-pound back who can run, pass, and punt with the best of them." I tried not to let all the attention go to my head; I understood even in those days you can't believe everything you read in the papers. In spite of the hype, I knew I weighed only 157 pounds.

At the same time, I can't say I didn't bask in the glory that shone on me, on our football team, our school, and our entire town that fall of 1941. While the tension-filled winds of war gathered around the world, and history-changing forces began to build in Europe and the Far East, one little town in South Texas remained oblivious to it all.

Each week the tension began building on Monday as everyone in school and around town began talking about Friday's opponent. The signs and banners in the school halls and in storefronts multiplied as the week went on. You could taste the excitement that grew and encompassed you as game day approached. By game time Friday night, the mounting pressure of all that anticipation and expectation, including your own, focused you completely on the task at hand. And with each victory the intensity increased.

The growing fanaticism of our fans won them the label of "Missionaries." By the sixth week of the season, Mission had more fans in the stands at our game in Donna than the home team did. They all witnessed a game marked by a controversy still debated in South Texas five decades later.

We led 12–0 when Donna drove the ball deep into our territory. On a third down play the Donna quarterback lofted a pass toward the end zone. Playing defensive safety,

I read the play and headed for the intended receiver. The football and I arrived at roughly the same time; both ball and opponent hit the ground before the official threw his flag for interference and signaled a touchdown for Donna on the penalty.

An incredulous Bob Martin surprised me and everyone else by racing onto the field. The official saw him coming and shouted, "Get out of here!"

"You can't call a touchdown on a penalty!" Bob shouted. "They should get the ball on the one-yard line."

But the official wouldn't listen and ran Bob off with the threat of another penalty. "All right," Bob said, "but you're going to have to apologize to me later."

We held on to win by a score of 12-7. And sure enough, when the area officials held their weekly meeting on Monday, Bob got a phone call from the man who had called the penalty. "You were right, Coach, and I apologize. It shouldn't have been a touchdown." But the damage had been done. The Mission Eagle defense had given up its first points of the season and I was the culprit.

I made amends the following week with three touchdown runs and a long pass to set up another in an impressive 46-0 win over AA rival McAllen. The toughest game of the year so far promised to be the following week against Harlingen, another Class AA school. Sometime during the first quarter I took a big hit just below the right eye. But I stayed in the game to boot a 46-yard punt, which went out of bounds on Harlingen's 4-yard line. We threw them for a loss in the end zone for a 2-0 lead and then took the ensuing kick after the safety and drove for another score.

But by the end of the first quarter, the entire right side of my face had swollen so much I had to come off the field. I never made it back in the game, but we held on to win 9-0.

My cheekbone was broken and I wasn't sure whether I'd be able to play the next week against LaFeria. Wearing old leather headgear without facemasks left my sore face exposed to a lot of pain and vulnerable to additional injury.

But Bob Martin rigged my helmet with a couple facemasks, one upside down, to give me a little added protection. I played only the first quarter against LaFeria and we had scored both of our touchdowns in the 14–0 victory before I came out of the game. I didn't play much the following week either as we downed Pharr 34–0 and clinched the district title in the final game of the regular season.

Excitement soared to an all-time high the next week before the bi-district championship scheduled in Aransas Pass. The local Lions' Club held a special banquet in the team's honor. My teammates voted me the team's "Most Valuable Player" and "Best Sport." And I was named, along with halfback A. B. Ward, end Darroll Martin, guard Donald Albrecht, and center Jimmy Mehis, to the all-district team. But what was even more amazing, the townspeople of Mission, Texas, presented Bob Martin with a brand new $906 Chevrolet.

Friday's December fifth edition of the *Mission Times* pictured the Aransas Pass team on page one next to the lead story headlined: "Special Train Will Leave This Morning Bearing Team, Fans to Aransas Pass Game Tonight."

The story itself recounted the excitement and events of that week:

Approximately 400 local football fans, members of the Mission High School Band and Mission Eagle squadmen are expected to be aboard the "Eagle Special" when it rolls from the Missouri Pacific station this morning at 10:30, bound for Aransas Pass, where the Mission Eagles will meet the Aransas Pass Panthers tonight at 8:00 at Roosevelt Field to determine the bi-district championship. . . .

Spontaneous enthusiasm over the possibility of securing the first special train trip in the history of Mission High School football overflowed the school campus and came surging down Mission's main street Wednesday morning. The school band, holding aloft the well-known Aransas Pass road sign, "They Bite Every Day," staged a parade and pep rally in the downtown business section. Later in the day a number of students circulated a petition asking merchants to close their stores Friday so that their employees could ride the special train to the game tonight.

Meeting hurriedly Thursday morning, the retail trade committee of the Chamber of Commerce decided to underwrite the special train and allow their employees to attend the game. . . .

The town of Mission had never seen anything like it. The sheer glory of it all was heady stuff for a bunch of high school boys intent on establishing a permanent place in valley history.

After the incredible buildup, the game itself seemed almost anticlimactic. But not quite. I scored three times on runs of 4, 38, and 76 yards as we shut out Aransas Pass by a score of 19–0. We rode a joyous victory train home, knowing we had won the right to host the regional championship for all of South Texas below San Antonio. This game, against Hondo, would be the last high school game our team would play, because single A schools didn't have a state championship in those days.

Two days later, on Sunday morning, December 7, 1941, the Japanese attacked Pearl Harbor. Suddenly high school football took on a very different perspective. But it wasn't until sometime later that the full impact of a war starting half a world away finally reached Mission, where talk of football mixed with talk of war for at least another week.

Over three thousand Mission fans packed the stands of Burnett Field to watch the regional championship game. Not even a muddy field slowed us down that night. I passed for one TD and ran for two more, including a 65 yard run—for my final high school touchdown—in a game we won handily, 33–0.

En route to our 12–0 championship season we had amassed 3,866 yards and 174 first downs while limiting our opponents to just 600 yards and 60 first downs. We'd scored 322 points and given up only those 7 awarded on my interference penalty. In fact, years later when I had made All-Pro as a defensive back, my high school teammates used to laugh and remind me that I'd been the weakest link in the 1941 Mission Eagle defense.

That autumn of glory, shared with my boyhood friends and teammates, remains perhaps my most meaningful season in my fifty years in football. The game was never more fun, the victories never sweeter, the achievement never more satisfying.

The entire globe stood on the brink of a war that would change life for all of us. But for one wonderful moment in history, a handful of small-town boys in Mission, Texas, knew what it felt like to have conquered the world.

chapter five

INTO THE WORLD
AND WAR

GROWING UP in Mission, I never gave a lot of thought to my future. Because I focused so closely on the immediate goal before me—whether it was the next game or the next test—I never looked very far ahead. But also as a young man who had never really been out of the Rio Grande Valley, I had such a narrow worldview I couldn't imagine very many options to consider.

Success on the football field my senior year changed all that. It flung open the door between South Texas and the rest of the world, immediately bringing me face-to-face with a future full of more questions than I had answers.

First came the question of where I'd go to college. Sometime early during that senior football season, I remember getting a call from Doc Newhouse, an oilman headquartered in Mission. He invited me to come to the bank he owned in downtown Mission—said he wanted to talk about my plans after graduation. I remember walking into his office for my appointment wondering just what a rich, successful oilman wanted from the likes of me.

As it turned out, Doc was a University of Texas grad, an avid Longhorns' supporter, and a big donor to the school's athletic program. He wanted to encourage me to give some very serious thought to enrolling at UT next year. "Best school in the world," he told me. "And you're just the kind of football player the Longhorns need."

I felt flattered he thought so, but I wasn't so sure. The team had been pictured on the cover of *Life* magazine earlier that fall as the preseason favorite to win the national collegiate title. Coach D. X. Bible fielded a team so loaded with talent I wasn't sure they needed anyone, let alone a kid like me from a podunk school they had never heard of.

I thanked Doc Newhouse for his interest and told him I hadn't given much thought at all yet to choosing a college. He said that was fine but that when I did, he sure hoped I'd consider the University of Texas. I assured him I would, and that's the way we left it for the time being.

One Saturday in November a friend drove me all the way to Houston to see Rice University. I met Coach Jess Neely, talked with some of his assistants about their football program, and met a few of the players. They arranged for tickets to that afternoon's game.

I couldn't believe the size of Rice's stadium. The entire population of Mission wouldn't have filled the end zone seats!

Sitting in the stands that day, listening to the deafening noise of that awesome crowd, and watching the surprisingly fast and hard-hitting action down on the field, I realized, *This is the big time*! But with the excitement of that realization also came the doubts. *Do I really have what it takes to play Southwest Conference football?*

Only a few Mission High players had ever gone on to play football in college. One of them, John Tripson, who had played high school ball with my older brother Robert, went on to play at Mississippi State. And after our undefeated season in 1941 he tried to convince me I should consider that Southeastern Conference school. I can't imagine they'd ever have heard of me, if it hadn't been for John braggin' about his hometown high school team. I suspect it was merely as a courtesy to him that they invited me to visit the campus. I didn't want to make a big trip like that by myself, so they sent me two bus tickets and told me to invite a friend.

Jimmy Mehis, who played with me at ˙ssion, agreed to go along. The two of us had quite an adv nture, hitting every bus stop in half the towns in Texas and Louisiana before we even reached the mighty, muddy Mississippi River we had read about in Mark Twain stories our English teacher had assigned. The Starkville campus appeared nice enough and the people acted friendly, but the homeward half of our trip seemed a lot less exciting than the first half. And much, much longer. The twenty-four-hour-plus bus-ride gave me plenty of time to conclude: *Starkville, Mississippi, is just too far from home.* I decided the state of Texas was where I wanted to stay.

As a good, churchgoing Methodist, I briefly considered Southern Methodist University up in Dallas. But Doc Newhouse kept talking to me about the University of Texas. And he had begun talking to the coaches at UT about me.

One of D. X. Bible's assistant coaches, a burly, big-talking, bear of a man aptly named Bully Gilstrap, came to Mission early that winter. I met him down at Doc Newhouse's bank and he took me out to dinner at the Manhattan Cafe on Conway Street. He knew just how to impress a hungry football prospect; he bought me the biggest steak on the menu. While I cleaned my plate, he talked.

"Tommy," he told me, "just look around here in Mission, here in the valley, anywhere in the state of Texas. Look at all the really important people and you'll find most of them went to the University of Texas. Whether you look at church leaders, the oil business, the citrus business, farmers, lawyers, your big politicians . . . most all of them come out of the university."

With the long bus trip to Mississippi still fresh in my mind, his next argument hit home. He said, "If you go to another school, even SMU in Dallas, it'll be awfully far for your parents to go see you play. Austin's a lot closer to home. Your family and friends can easily make that trip."

I wasn't ready to make my final decision that night on a full stomach in the Manhattan Cafe. But I was close. Not only was Texas the closest Southwest Conference school, but I would know people there.

My friend Wade Spillman, who'd skipped a grade and graduated a year ahead of me, was already in school up at Austin. And another good friend and high school teammate of mine, Don Bentsen, Senator Lloyd Bentsen's younger brother, was going to UT. (Just as an aside, the Bentsen and Landry families go way back. When Lloyd Bentsen, Sr., first came to Mission from up north, my dad befriended him, introduced him to one of the prettiest girls in town, and advised Lloyd if he wanted to win her over he'd better be sure and go with her to church. Lloyd took Dad's advice, eventually married the girl, and thus began one of the most prominent families in the valley.)

After talking over my decision with my family and Coach Martin, I accepted the full scholarship offer from UT. That answered one big question. And I knew in time it would also answer the personal question I'd been asking myself: *Could I play Southwest Conference football?*

The summer between high school and college, Doc Newhouse used his clout to land me a job as a roughneck for a driller in the oil fields out near Rio Grande City. The rig operated twenty-four hours a day, which meant three towers or shifts. With no seniority, I worked the graveyard tower, from midnight till 8:00 in the morning. From Mission it took between one and two hours of rough-road driving through a wasteland of mesquite and cactus to reach the rig, so I had little time for anything but work and sleep. I wouldn't have had the energy anyway.

Even for a seventeen-year-old athlete in his physical prime, working the floor of a drilling rig can be backbreaking labor. Eight hours of wrestling and fitting together heavy and awkward thirty-foot sections of pipe, with the drill's diesel engines pounding beside you, while the driller screamed orders, warnings, and threats, left you sweat-soaked, mud-coated, and absolutely drained of everything but the desire to lie down and sleep. But I wasn't about to complain because the big money I made—over four dollars an hour—would last me all school year in Austin.

Halfway through the summer I got transferred to a second rig even farther out of Mission, which meant I stayed in a motel room all week—my first taste of life on the road. Stuck by myself, in a two-bit town where I didn't know a soul, with nothing to do but work and sleep and eat, I lived a very lonely life. It certainly convinced me a college education could provide a very nice advantage in life.

I worked the day shift on my second rig. The staggering heat and the merciless sun soon had me longing for the slightly cooler temperatures of the midnight shift. And I began counting the days until August when I would leave the oil field for the playing field and the relative ease of two-a-day preseason drills.

Just the week before I planned to head off to Abilene for the state high school all-star game, my crew had to change the drilling bit on our rig—which meant we must pull up and disconnect every section of pipe we had put down so far. Mud from the pipe caked both floor and crew by the time the driller told me to go down in the hole under the rig and shut off the valve. I took off on the run, slipped on the muddy top step, and sailed into the hole—a ten-foot drop. I landed on a pile of spare pipe, a metal spigot sticking into the bone of my shin.

The injury brought an end to my career as a roughneck. And it didn't do much to further my football ambitions either, limiting me to the role of sideline spectator for most of the all-star game. I still limped a little when I headed off to Austin—excited and scared by the prospect of college.

It's a good thing I hadn't chosen a school in a city like Dallas or Houston. In those days, the capital had little more than the state government and the university. Yet coming from Mission, Austin seemed a teeming metropolis. The enrollment at UT outnumbered the population of my hometown.

Wandering among the imposing buildings of the sprawling campus, I often felt lost.

My first look at the freshman football team was just as overwhelming. Coach D. X. Bible built his program by being a master recruiter. During his tenure, Texas was a lot like Notre Dame is today; any high school player D. X. wanted, especially in the state of Texas, he got. Most of the AA all-state players from the year before played on our freshman squad—three of the four first-team backs. This meant I was a third-string back on the freshman team and raised serious doubts in my mind about ever getting a chance to test myself as a Southwest Conference football player.

However, I did begin to look like a football player. Eating the great training table food served to the team, my weight quickly climbed to a solid 190. But life in Hill Hall, the college athletic dorm, had its down side. Hazing of freshman players was a favorite pastime of upper-class players who kept the frosh humble by making them run errands and giving them countless demeaning orders.

All freshmen lived on the first floor of Hill Hall. And often, during study time after supper, the dreaded call would come down and one or more freshmen would have to report to one of the upperclassmen's floor where you might be ordered to bend over and take a hard, painful lick from a big wooden paddle wielded by a big senior lineman. Or you might be ordered to sing your high school fight song.

The older players heaped the most abuse on the freshmen who acted cocky or tough. If they took a disliking to someone, they could make his life pretty miserable. I didn't have to endure much of the hazing. I'd like to think that was because I was smart enough to keep a low profile and nice enough to be well liked. But I suspect it may have had more to do with my attempts to sing "Mission High forever, Firm forever stand" to the approximate tune of "On Wisconsin." I don't recall anyone ever asking me for an encore.

Coaches encouraged players not to sign up for too many heavy courses; they wanted us to stay academically eligible. But while my summer experience may have convinced me I didn't want to try to make it in the oil business by working from the bottom up, I wasn't at all averse to finding some other role in Texas's biggest industry. So I signed up that fall for a full load of prerequisite courses on an engineering track and soon found the competition in the classroom as tough as that on the field.

I felt I made a good enough showing in practice and in the few games we played during the abbreviated freshman schedule to begin moving up on the depth chart. But I knew I still had a long way to go.

However, any disappointment I felt about the progress in my football career became suddenly insignificant when the tragedy of war struck home. One day that fall I got a phone call from my family with the terrible news that my brother Robert was missing in action. Like so many thousands of others, he had enlisted soon after Pearl Harbor, been assigned to the Army Air Corps, and gone almost immediately into pilots' training. While ferrying a B-17 over to England, his plane disappeared over the North Atlantic near Iceland.

Naturally my parents weren't ready to concede Robert's death. We all hoped and prayed that by some miracle he would be found alive. But the sudden, sickening emptiness I felt after that phone call grew greater with each day and week that passed without additional word. I suppose the way we learned about Robert should have made the official acknowledgment of his death at least a little less shocking when it came some weeks later. I don't know that it did.

I still couldn't believe it. *Robert dead? It couldn't be.* How can any eighteen-year-old kid cope with the undeniable reality of a loved one's death? I tried to shut it out by focusing on my classes and football. It didn't work because they no longer mattered. Robert was dead. The big brother I had looked up to all my life was gone forever from the face of the earth—without my ever having told him how much he meant to me.

I knew nothing I did could bring Robert back. But that November, just a couple months after my eighteenth birthday, I enlisted in the army reserves and applied for pilots' training in the Army Air Corps. Most of the football team enlisted in some branch of the service.

As a reservist, I stayed in school until February when I got called up and had to leave Austin. After basic training at Shepherd's Field in Wichita Falls, and preflight training at Kelly Field near San Antonio, I got assigned for several months to a college training detachment up at Eastern Oklahoma State College. There I continued my studies and got my first taste of flying in a single-engine, two-seater trainer.

I'll never forget my first training flight. Having never been in a plane before, I could hardly wait to take off as my pilot taxied to the end of the grass runway of that little field in Ada, Oklahoma. My first step toward becoming a bomber pilot.

We began to roll down that strip, the engine whining, the plane gathering speed. The ground dropped away. Ten, twenty-five, fifty, a hundred feet. We climbed, nose up, into the big blue sky. What a feeling to fly!

At two hundred feet, everything went deathly silent. Something was wrong! And in the split second it took me to realize the engine had died, my heart began hammering in my chest. But my icy-cool instructor never so much as flinched as he worked the flaps and the tail rudder and slipped that plane sideways to land pretty-as-you-please in the middle of a cow pasture. My heart and I both were glad they didn't make us go up again that day.

After that introduction to flying, the remainder of my pilots' instruction seemed like a breeze. I went on to do my primary flight training in Missouri where I soloed for the first time in a single-engine, open-cockpit trainer. From there I went to Kansas for more basic and on to advanced training where I earned my wings in twin-engine aircraft at Lubbock. After that I transferred to Sioux City, Iowa, where at the age of nineteen, I trained for war as a copilot at the controls of a giant B-17. My pilot, Kenneth Saenz, was a much more mature man of twenty-two.

When our combat orders finally came in the fall of 1944, our crew sailed for England with thousands of other servicemen aboard the *Queen Mary*. Despite the nightly entertainment, including a show-stopping, comedy-music-and-dance routine by none other than Mickey Rooney, my trip on that luxury liner never felt like a pleasure cruise. Even in the officers' quarters they packed us into bunks stacked four or five high. And I could never forget that I was on my way to a war across the very ocean in which my brother Robert had died.

After landing in Liverpool, we crossed England by train to our assigned base with the Eighth Air Force, 493rd Squadron in Ipswich, not far from London. By the time we arrived in England in the fall of 1944, the Allies had already destroyed most of the German Luftwaffe. So when we made our first combat flight as part of a two thousand plane bombing mission into Germany to destroy the Mersburg oil fields, we didn't have to worry as much about fighters as we did about the ground guns.

I can still picture the angry black cloud of exploding flak filling the sky as we approached our target that day. And I remember the helpless, sinking fear I felt as we followed our squadron leader into the heart of that cloud. Nothing they had ever told us about during training prepared me for that experience. I could see the flak exploding all around us. And even though I couldn't really hear it over the roar of the giant B-17 engines, I could sometimes feel the shock vibrations through the plane.

The sky was so dark that day we had no idea how close our bombs came to the target. When the lead bombardier in our squadron dropped his load, we dropped ours and suddenly banked for England. In our hurry we lost our squadron, eventually hooked onto a pattern with another squadron, and followed it home.

All our bomber bases had to be camouflaged from the Germans; but that same camouflage also made them almost impossible for our own planes to find in the fog. At the time we didn't have the radar guidance systems available today; when we went into fog we were literally flying blind. And with hundreds of planes returning to England from a bombing run at the same time, you couldn't afford to wander off course looking for your field. On several occasions we had to drop below the fog and skim the surface of the channel along the English coast until we spotted a familiar tributary and could turn inland, cut our engines, and land at Ipswich.

Many missions carried us so far over Europe we had to use every bit of our fuel capacity to make it home. Sometimes the margin of error was so slim the slightest change in course or an unexpected increase in headwinds might force us to ditch our plane.

On one long mission we leaned out the fuel mixture as far as possible and still keep the engines running. We'd been flying that way for hours without risking any changes in the controls. Suddenly, over the Netherlands, all four engines quit at once. Ken and I quickly ran through our checklist and tried repeatedly to restart the engines as the plane fell through the sky. "We're going to have to bail out!" Ken said. He gave the order to the crew even as we tried to steady the plane.

The thought of bailing out over enemy-occupied territory was a terrible prospect. We would undoubtedly be captured and made prisoners of war—if we survived. We had a pilot at Ipswich whose crew had bailed out over friendly territory. In his ten-man crew, his was the only chute that opened. He lived, but he broke emotionally and never flew another mission.

We had no choice but to jump. I unbuckled and stood up to head back for the bomb bay doors to bail out. But as I straightened up between my seat and the pilot's something stopped me. I turned and looked back at the controls and shoved the knob on the fuel mixture control all the way forward. I nearly fell down when the engines roared back to life and the plane surged ahead. Ken and I jumped back into our seats, pulled that plane out of its dive, and headed for home so close to the ground we had to zigzag to avoid the gunfire from the Germans in Amsterdam.

A little later in the war we flew another particularly long mission to hit a target in Czechoslovakia. By that time the Allies occupied much of France, which meant we had an alternate base on the mainland where we could land if we couldn't make it back to Ipswich. So when our fuel gauges dropped toward empty on the return, we decided not to risk ditching in the Channel. However, by that time fog had set in over France and we had to circle a few times, wasting the last of our precious gas in a fruitless search for the signal beacon at the alternate base.

We finally dropped below the ceiling, nearly brushing the tree tops, our engines coughing and spitting on the fumes. We could see nothing but forests ahead. When a clearing suddenly opened up beneath us we dropped the plane and plowed a furrow through some farmer's land, hurtling toward a windbreak of trees at the far end of the field. We had no control and no steering as we slid between two trees that clipped off both wings. Slowed considerably, we jerked to a crashing halt against another tree.

After all the violent crashing, the world suddenly fell silent. Then the crew began to yell. We quickly leaped from the plane and ran some distance away to avoid any explosion. But we had no gas left to explode.

Incredibly, every member of our crew walked out of that crash without a scratch. Together we hiked out to the nearest road, hitched a ride from some Allied soldiers to the nearby base, and flew back to Ipswich where we were assigned another B-17.

I flew thirty combat missions in all before the war ended and I headed back across the Atlantic to home. While at the time I don't guess I stopped to seriously ponder my experience, looking back now, I marvel at all that happened to me. During the course of three short years, I went from a scared college freshman lost on his university campus to a grizzled war veteran of twenty-one. I knew what it meant to look my own fear in the face and go on to do my duty because the lives of my crew and the destiny of my country depended on it. I had seen a big chunk of America during my training, sailed across an ocean, walked the blacked-out streets of war-torn London, and crisscrossed the airways over most of Europe in a B-17.

War had tested me, but I had survived. And that experience had given me not only a broader perspective on life, but a confidence in myself I had never known before.

I'd seen the world. And it was far bigger than anything I expected to face back in Austin at the University of Texas.

chapter six

LONGHORN IN LOVE

I A R R I V E D back in Austin for the 1946 spring semester to discover UT's enrollment had exploded. The same thing happened all over the country as millions of veterans on GI bills transformed the atmosphere on college campuses everywhere. The somber pain of the war years gave way to a new sense of hope and optimism about the future. College was no longer just a place where kids went to grow up and find direction in life; the older students brought with them a seriousness, a maturity, and a sense of purpose that made for a unique era in college education and in college athletics as well.

Returning veterans also created an age spread among college athletes that had never occurred before. At Texas we had men almost thirty years old competing on the same team with kids fresh out of high school. While I didn't think much about it at the time, this age spread had to demand some changes in the way college coaches dealt with their players.

I injured a leg and finished spring drills in '46 on a pair of crutches. Then in preseason practice, I sustained another injury and saw only limited action as a backup fullback that fall of my delayed sophomore season. But our star junior quarterback, Bobby Layne, led us to the Southwest Conference Championship and a berth in the Cotton Bowl on January 1, 1947.

Prospects looked promising for the next year, but the retirement of Coach D. X. Bible raised a giant question mark prior to the '47 season. When assistant coach Blair Cherry took over and announced his intentions to switch from a single wing to a T-formation, pro-style offense, that raised another. But over that summer of '47, Cherry took Bobby Layne with him to visit the Chicago Bears' training camp to learn how Bears' coach George Halas and his star quarterback Sid Luckman ran their offense. So by the time the season started, the Longhorns looked like they might stampede right through the schedule.

My assignment that fall was to learn to direct the new system as a backup for Bobby Layne. While substituting for an All-American is a tough way to get playing time, Cherry in effect made me a defensive starter by always sending me in for Bobby when we gave up the ball.

I know Bobby Layne became legendary as much for his off-the-field exploits as for his football skills. But, since I wasn't the first person Bobby thought of when he needed a drinking partner or party company, the stories I know of his wild side are all hearsay. I do know that just weeks after I got out of the service following the war, I went to Dallas to watch Texas play in the Cotton Bowl. A friend of mine told me he had seen Bobby the evening before the game at Dallas's Touchdown Club, drinking and carousing nearly the whole night through. Yet by the next afternoon he had an astounding day passing the football and running up 40 points in an impressive victory over Missouri.

Bobby never trained. Not in high school, college, or after he became a star pro quarterback. And I've often wondered how much greater he might have been if he had. Not only did he possess remarkable athletic skills—he never lost a game as a starting pitcher on the Longhorns' baseball team—but he commanded respect as a natural-born leader.

When he called the signals in the huddle, everyone believed the play would work because Bobby wouldn't let it fail.

Most doubts about Texas's coaching change and our new offensive system quickly faded after we launched the season with convincing wins over Texas Tech (33–0) and Oregon (38–13). Unfortunately I didn't fare as well as the team did. During the Oregon game I broke my right thumb right at its socket when I hooked it in an opponent's hip pad trying to make a tackle. Because of the injury to my throwing hand, the coach moved me out of the backup quarterback role, shifting me to fullback. With the thumb splinted and heavily bandaged, I started at fullback and played my usual role as defensive back the very next week when we achieved national attention by annihilating North Carolina, one of the top teams in the country, 34–0.

We held the Tarheels' All-American ChooChoo Charlie Justice to only 18 yards while I ran for 91 yards, a touchdown, and one black eye on twelve carries. Yet I never should have played again so soon. The thumb didn't heal right; the joint froze up, and I could never again grip a football well enough to throw a proper pass. Even if I had realized my quarterbacking days were over, it might not have mattered. Because our team kept rolling and I began to rack up yardage and touchdowns at fullback.

We remained undefeated going into our contest with conference favorite SMU, a team led by eventual Heisman Trophy winner, best friend, and former teammate of Bobby Layne at Highland Park High School in Dallas—Doak Walker. The Mustangs fooled us with a big reverse on the opening kickoff and scored soon after that on another sneaky reverse.

We drove right back down the field and I scored on a short run. But a little later, running out of a spread formation, Gil Johnson, the SMU quarterback, hit Doak Walker on a short pass over the middle. Doak broke by me and ran all the way to the 2-yard line to set up their second score. Bobby Layne threw a touchdown pass for us and we missed the extra point. So the score stood at 14–13 late in the game as we drove into SMU territory. We needed only a few more yards to set up the winning field goal when Bobby called my number on third and 1.

The instant the center snapped the ball I accelerated out of my stance, but I'd set up in the wettest spot on the field, and my feet went right out from under me. I can still see the look of shocked dismay on Bobby Layne's face when he pivoted to make his handoff and saw me on my knees in the mud. He turned and tried to run himself but was thrown for a loss. SMU held, we gave up the ball, and the 14–13 score stood.

That slip of mine against SMU was the one play that prevented us from going undefeated all season. We won the remainder of our games handily and capped off an outstanding year by downing Southeastern Conference powerhouse Alabama in the Sugar Bowl by the score of 27–7. Our second-string fullback caught the flu, which meant I played that entire game—offense and defense. So while most of the team went out that night and celebrated in New Orleans' French Quarter, I went back to my hotel room and fell dead asleep.

That 1947 team probably ranks as one of the greatest football teams in University of Texas history. Bobby Layne and tackle Dick Harris made All-American, the two of them and end Max Bumgardner won first team All-Conference honors, and I was named second team all-SWC fullback. And yet for me, the greatest highlight of 1947 didn't involve gridiron glory.

I met a girl.

That was no small feat at UT in those days. While enrollment soared to seventeen thousand in 1947, we only had about five thousand coeds.

With those kind of odds against me, I knew I needed help. So I asked Gloria Neuhaus, the girlfriend of teammate Lew Holder, if she could get me a date with one of the girls in her sorority. Gloria talked to a beautiful blonde freshman named Alicia Wiggs, suggesting she make a blind date with me, and the two of us could double-date with Gloria and Lew.

Alicia didn't like the idea, but Gloria kept after her and finally pulled rank as an older sorority sister—insisting that as a pledge, Alicia had to go. So we went on our first date— a picnic in the woods at Bull Creek—the day after the North Carolina game. I must have made a great impression when I showed up with my bandaged thumb, a scraped-up face, and a black eye. I guess she took pity on me because we seemed to hit it off.

Not only was she good looking, but I found her easy to talk to and fun to be with. So I asked her out again the next week. And the next and the next. For a time, Alicia dated some other guys during the week, but she saved the weekends for me. With football practice on top of studies, I didn't have much time for a social life. We would usually go out on Saturday nights after the game and then I'd take her to church on Sunday.

On most dates we went to a movie at one of the two Austin theaters that gave UT football players free passes. Then I'd take her to dinner at the nearby El Matador Restaurant. Alicia loved Mexican food and thought it was great we shared so much in common. I didn't tell her the main reason we went there: It was the cheapest place to eat in town.

I introduced Alicia to my parents one Saturday that fall. Mom and Dad drove up to see every one of my home games. They would leave Mission before dawn on Saturday, arrive in Austin shortly before kickoff, visit with me a few minutes after the game, then head back and get home well after midnight.

I met Alicia's parents the first time they drove over from Houston to visit her for a weekend. The three of them waited outside the stadium as I hurriedly showered and dressed. Alicia introduced us and we stood there talking just a few minutes before she informed her parents, "Tommy and I have to be going. I'll see you later." And we headed off on our usual date. It wasn't until years later I learned that as we walked away, Alicia's mom had turned to her dad and said, "There she goes, Dear! We've lost our little girl!"

I wasn't that sure of myself when it came to girls. I hadn't ever had a steady girlfriend. Yet everything seemed so natural with Alicia. We had very different upbringings. She'd grown up in big cities, living in Dallas all her life until her family moved to Houston just before her senior year in high school. Her dad was chairman of the board of his own insurance company.

To me Alicia seemed much more sophisticated than eighteen. To her, I seemed a mature, experienced man of twenty-three. And I let her think that as long as I could because I was crazy about her from the start.

She finally knew I cared when she opened the Christmas gift I bought her that year. All fall, every time we went to the movies, we would stop and look in the window of the jewelry store next door to the theater. And Alicia always exclaimed over the same item—a gold lapel-pin watch in the shape of a little man in a pointed hat. She called it "little man" and seemed to think it was just about the cutest thing she'd ever seen.

It wasn't cheap, but I splurged and bought it for her just before Christmas. Now she says she was overwhelmed by my thoughtfulness in selecting that particular pin, and she knew then I had to love her to be so sensitive to her feelings. I'm not sure how much credit I can take though: How sensitive does a guy have to be after six or eight stops at a jewelry store window? But if that "little man" helped make me a big man in Alicia's eyes, it was worth every penny.

At Thanksgiving I took Alicia with me to Mission to meet all my friends and relatives. Everyone approved. And we dated regularly the rest of the school year.

That summer between my junior and senior year I worked as a boys' counselor at a combination kids' camp and dude ranch out in Kerrville called Silver Spur Ranch. Alicia and her family came for a week at the ranch that summer, which gave me a chance to spend some off-campus time with her and get to know her parents a little better. Fortunately I hit it off so well with her folks that her mother told Alicia's dad, "If she doesn't marry Tommy I'm just going to adopt him."

But while I knew by this time I was seriously in love, I wasn't ready to start talking about marriage. I just couldn't see a way to swing it financially any time soon. I still had a year of school left—I'd switched my major to Business Administration after the war—and had no solid prospects for a job after I graduated. Any ideas about marriage had to be put on hold.

For a time, even my football season was on hold when I came down with impacted wisdom teeth, and missed the start of my final college season. I didn't play much or regain my full strength until the last few games of what was, for me, a very disappointing football year.

On an encouraging note, after I'd turned in some solid games at the end of the regular season, a couple professional football teams expressed some initial interest in me. I knew the New York Giants had already selected me during the National Football League's annual draft of senior college football players. They'd picked me back in 1946, the year my original college class had been scheduled to graduate. Steve Owen, the Giants' coach, had come to one of our practices, seen me practicing punting, and had decided to chance a seventh-round pick on me as a "future," even though I wouldn't graduate for another three years.

But now, at the end of the '48 season, I learned I'd also been drafted by the New York Yankees' Football Club in the All-American Football Conference, a rival league of the NFL. The football Yankees were owned by Dan Topping, the same man who owned the great New York Yankees' baseball team.

I'd never seriously considered the prospect of playing professional football. I knew virtually nothing about it at the time; it wasn't a sport that received any coverage in Texas. But I still loved the game, and if someone would actually pay me to play it, well . . . I didn't have anything else lined up after graduation. Maybe I could even make enough money to get married.

But first I had one more college football game to play. Despite a 6–3–1 record during the '48 regular season, the Longhorns received an invitation to play the mighty Georgia Bulldogs in the Orange Bowl. Many sportswriters and other critics complained that the Orange Bowl had scraped the bottom of the barrel and settled on a third-rate opponent for Coach Wally Butts's Georgia team.

That 1949 bowl game was my third different New Year's Day bowl game in three years. Even back then, the Orange Bowl had a reputation for pageantry. That was the only game I've ever seen in my life where the players had to warm up outside the stadium because we couldn't get onto the field due to a pregame procession. We found a little patch of grass out by the parking lot for our pregame exercises and drills.

Once again my backup got injured and I had to play an entire bowl game on offense and defense. But I turned in the best personal performance of my Longhorns' career as the game's leading rusher—117 yards on seventeen carries.

The timing couldn't have been better. As I walked off the field after the game Jack White, an assistant coach with the football Yankees, stopped me, pulled a contract out of his pocket, and handed it to me. I signed that night for a $6000 salary—big money in those days. But what excited me far more was the $500 signing bonus. With that I could afford to get married!

Back in Austin, I took Alicia to dinner. Even after hours of mental rehearsal, I felt so nervous I couldn't think of a way to get the words out. Finally, I said to her, "If you'd find us a place to live, we could move in at midterm break."

She looked puzzled. "You want me to find you and Tom Hamilton an apartment?" (Tom was my roommate.)

"No," I told her. "You and me. We could get married."

I know it wasn't the most romantic proposal. But she accepted. And a few days later on her birthday, January 12, I presented Alicia with the engagement ring I'd purchased on sale a few months before.

Alicia's mom was not thrilled when we told her we wanted to get married on January 28. She didn't think sixteen days was enough time to plan a wedding. But she managed beautifully and I think she eventually forgave me. Once I'd made up my mind, I was ready.

After taking my final semester exam on the morning of January 28, Alicia and I drove to Houston, where we were married that evening in a small chapel ceremony. With my big $500 bonus, we managed a honeymoon in Mexico City, paid the first month's rent on a furnished apartment not far from campus, and had enough left over to cover expenses for some time afterward.

Looking back, it all seems so naive. We knew so little about each other, about marriage, about anything. We had no idea in the world what the future was to hold for us. We just knew we were in love. And we would face whatever came together.

That's just what we've done.

chapter seven

NEW YORK LIVING

MARRIAGE experts say the first year is often the toughest. Unfortunately ours overlapped my first year in professional football, which is also the toughest year for players. Somehow Alicia and I survived both rookie seasons. Probably due to our we-can-manage-anything-because-we're-in-love attitude.

The $500 bonus was all the money I had received from the Yankees, and all I was going to receive, until the regular season began in September. And there would be more then only if I made the team.

So when I headed off to my rookie training camp in August, Alicia, about six months pregnant at the time, moved in with her parents in Houston to save on expenses. We had already come to the difficult decision she would stay in Houston to have the baby even if I made the team. As much as we both hated the thought of being separated for the duration of an entire football season, the idea of moving and having to find a new doctor in the big city of New York, where we didn't know anyone, just seemed too overwhelming. Besides, we both wanted our children born in Texas.

That way if any of them wanted to run for governor when they grew up, they could claim to be born-'n'-bred Texans.

Actually, my own identity as a Texan prompted my original decision to sign with the Yankees instead of the Giants. Their roster had so many players with Texas roots— including Gil Johnson from SMU, Pete Leyden from UT, Baylor's Jack Russell, Bruce Alford of TCV, and Martin Ruby out of Texas A&M. I figured I would feel a lot more at home with the Yankees than with the Giants where I didn't know anyone. I'd heard enough about the name players in the league to believe the competition in the All-American Football Conference, conceived and founded by *Chicago Tribune* sports columnist Arch Ward after the war in 1946, had already reached a par with the older NFL. I never gave a thought to the possibility the '49 season might be the last for the fledgling AAFC.

Even at the age of twenty-five, my first pro football training camp brought back many of those same feelings and doubts I had as a goggle-eyed freshman back in Austin. Shared roots or not, veterans didn't do much to make a rookie feel welcome. Football was their job and rookies presented a threat to their livelihood. Hazing seemed as much a training camp tradition as it had been in Hill Hall. Rookies toted buckets of ice, performed other menial chores for veterans, and always had to wait for the veterans to get taped and treated in the training room before we took our turn. While I wasn't expected to endure the humiliation and pain of paddling, the older guys did require me to stand and sing UT's anthem, "The Eyes of Texas are Upon You." (It seemed at every level of football—high school, college, and now as a professional—people wanted me to sing. But only until they heard me.)

Looking around the dressing room the first day in camp I noted all those thirty- to thirty-five-year-old bodies and thought, *These guys are football players*? In those days, no one trained during the off-season. Most of the veterans appeared drastically out of shape—overweight and, to someone fresh from college, ancient.

I soon learned the rigors of training camp were designed to get anyone into shape. I had come into camp at my college playing weight of 190 and quickly lost 20 pounds to the two-a-day workouts in the muggy heat of a late Connecticut summer. I also learned once they began to shed their excess winter weight, those "old guys" could play football. And I faced a big challenge just to prove I could compete with them.

Most rookies could never be sure of a spot on the roster until the final cut. But I got a break when the Yankees' regular punter went out with an injury during our preseason game against the Cleveland Browns, the runaway champions of the AAFC in all three of its previous seasons. I had such an impressive day punting that our coach, Red Schrader, sought me out in the Cleveland railway station as we stood waiting for our train after the game. "Well kid," he said, "you made the team today." I couldn't get to a phone fast enough to call Alicia and tell her I had a job playing football.

Experiencing New York City itself for the first time seemed almost as exciting as making the team. I'll never forget the thrill of walking into the dressing room in Yankee Stadium and seeing those long-familiar names above the lockers— DiMaggio, Henrich, Rizzuto, Ruffing, and all the rest. The very first major-league baseball game I ever saw was during the final weekend of the '49 season. The Yankees came from behind to take two straight games and steal the American League Championship from Ted Williams and the Boston Red Sox.

I watched that day as Yankee Stadium and all of New York went berserk. What an introduction to the fantasy of professional sports in America. And I was now a part of that fantasy!

But I certainly wasn't a very big part that first season. I punted, played a little defense, and occasionally backed up Buddy Young at halfback. I ran so much slower than Buddy, a world-class sprinter, that whenever I relieved him, I'm sure I relieved the opposing defense as well.

Despite the shortage of playing time, the season offered a memorable initiation into professional football life. Every trip became another personal first—an opportunity for a country boy to see yet another big, interesting American city. I particularly remember my first time in California. We played the Los Angeles Dons in the Coliseum on a hot day with smog so thick I would choke and have to run to the sidelines sick with dry heaves between plays.

We played in many of America's great stadiums, but we didn't exactly fill them. I remember a game against the Chicago Hornets when so few people showed up in Soldiers Field I don't think they even bothered to turn on all the lights. Compared to the size of the baseball crowds at Yankee Stadium, or the size of football crowds I'd played for in college, professional football crowds in those days—even for NFL teams—often felt more like high school than the big time.

I lived during the season with a bunch of other single players in Manhattan at the old Henry Hudson Hotel on West Fifty-seventh. I would catch the subway up to Yankee Stadium for practice and in the evenings I'd go out to a movie or over to Madison Square Garden to watch a fight. While I enjoyed exploring the big city, I very quickly developed a terrible case of loneliness. I missed Alicia so much I wrote her every day and could hardly wait until our game was over to make my weekly phone call home. The closer time came to the baby's due date, the more I wished I could just pack up and head home.

My most memorable game that year came against the great Cleveland Browns. Using his contacts from coaching days at Ohio State and from his days coaching the best athletes in the service at Great Lakes Naval Station during the war, Paul Brown had created an instant dynasty in Cleveland when the AAFC began in 1946. The Browns' roster read like a Hall of Fame program. All-time tackle Lou Groza and great guard Bill Willis anchored the lines. Otto

Graham, one of the best quarterbacks ever to play the game, threw to All-Star receivers Dante Lavelli and Mac Speedie. Plus the Browns ran perhaps the best-all-around fullback ever to play the game. As one of the country's finest black athletes coming out of the service during the war years, Marion Motley not only helped break the color barrier in professional football, he broke a few opponents' helmets with his punishing runs and devastating blocks.

My first professional start came against these most formidable foes because of an injury to one of our starting defensive backs. And Paul Brown and Otto Graham knew a raw rookie when they saw one. They threw at me all day. Mac Speedie turned me inside out and hung me out to dry. He set the official AAFC single-game record for receiving that day—well over 200 yards.

That game was the most embarrassing athletic performance of my entire life. But it also proved to be one of the most important. Because the primary lesson learned that day, and reinforced over the next few years, served as the very foundation of my philosophical approach to playing and coaching pro football. I realized my own limitations. I conceded that it was impossible to succeed solely on skill, on emotion, or even on determination. Any success I ever attained would require the utmost in preparation and knowledge. I couldn't wait and react to my opponent, I had to know what he was going to do before he did it. With my 10.4 speed in the hundred, I could never cover a 9.6 receiver by running with him; but if I knew where he was going, I could be there when he arrived.

That day in Cleveland was the starting point, the beginning of the challenge to really learn the game of football.

If that Cleveland debacle was the low point of my season, the high point came on October 31 when I got a message to call Houston. The instant I heard Alicia's voice on the phone I wanted to know: "What'd we get?"

"A boy!" Alicia insisted on calling him Thomas Wade Landry, Jr.

I poured out my new happiness that evening in a letter addressed to "My Darling Wife":

> When I heard your voice tonight . . . I couldn't believe we had a son. I must have sounded all jumbled up, because I wanted to tell you how grand it was and how much I missed not being there, but all I seemed able to do was mumble. . . .
>
> I can't get over the size of Tom, Jr. We might have to make a tackle out of him instead of a quarterback. Though I'm liable to make a golfer out of him anyway. It will save a lot of bumps and bruises. . . .
>
> Have I told you how much I love you? I would like to tell you a million times more that I do. I guess today I miss you more than ever. To think that today we two have become three is really something. I could almost get sentimental, but you would never believe it. . . . Let's make this next month fly by. I love you lots, Tommy, *Sr.*

My loneliness multiplied the last four weeks of the season. The moment the final gun sounded in our last game of the season on Thanksgiving Day in San Francisco, I raced for the airport to catch the first flight home to my new family. After ten months of marriage and four months apart from Alicia, it felt like a honeymoon all over again. Only better. Because I was a daddy.

When the financially shaky AAFC folded after the '49 season and only three teams—the Browns, the San Francisco '49ers, and the Baltimore Colts—merged into the NFL, I learned my first lesson about the uncertainty of professional sports. I felt somewhat encouraged when the New York Giants exercised their territorial rights and selected me along with several of my Yankees' teammates from the AAFL talent pool. But I also knew I had to prepare for life after football. So during the off-season I began taking night school classes toward an industrial engineering degree at the University of Houston while working for Cameron Iron Works during the day.

Alicia and I decided we would never again spend a

season apart like we'd done in 1949. We had to be separated a few weeks during the Giants' training camp. But then she and Tom, Jr., would join me in New York. It might be a hassle establishing a second home for our family, but we'd get our own apartment in a hotel with the families of other Giants' players. I would show her life in the big city and it would be fun. We'd treat whatever time we had in New York, as well as the unpredictable life of the NFL, as a family adventure. But we never imagined how long that adventure would last.

To start with, the '50 season with the Giants felt like a second rookie year. My former Yankees' teammates and I had to prove to the Giants' veterans that we belonged in the NFL. But the Cleveland Browns made that easier for all of us—proving the caliber of AAFC football the very first week of the season by trouncing the reigning NFL champion Philadelphia Eagles 35–10. Then, unfortunately, we had to face the Browns the following Sunday.

Giants' coach Steve Owen told us early in the week, "We're going to use a 6–1–4 defense against the Browns Sunday. It'll confuse 'em. And that's what will beat 'em." Steve, a pudgy, balding, and bespectacled man from the Knute Rockne school of motivation, had directed the Giants for twenty years. An excellent overall strategist, he didn't worry much about the details. Since he never explained how we were to execute this new defensive alignment, our defensive squad tried to coordinate the individual assignments in practice during the week.

When we had our defensive meeting in a Cleveland hotel room before the game, Steve stepped to the chalkboard and sketched in a 6–1–4 alignment. "This is the defense we're going to play," he said. Then he turned around, looked over the room, and focused on me, "Landry, come up here and explain how it's going to work." So I stepped to the board and reviewed everything the other players and I had figured out during the week. "If the ends rush, the backs will do this. If they drop off the line, then we'll do . . ." It is the first coaching experience I remember.

Steve's strategy worked. The Browns never figured out what we were doing on defense. Graham's passing attack went nowhere, and we completely frustrated the seemingly invincible Browns by a score of 6–0. The next day's papers dubbed Owen's new alignment the Umbrella defense because they said, from high in the press box, the single linebacker down on the field looked like a bumbershoot with our defensive backs in an umbrella-looking semicircle flexing up and down, forward and backward, depending on the play.

Before we played the Browns in New York a few weeks later, Steve announced a variation on the umbrella—a 5–1–5 alignment. Again he left it to the players to work out the details of a new defense that sufficiently confused Cleveland for us to win 17–13. Unfortunately, Cleveland's potent offense ran up big winning scores against everyone else in the league. We lost to two other teams and ended up tied with Cleveland at 10–2 for the American (Eastern) Conference crown. That meant we had to play them yet again in Cleveland for the right to go to the NFL Championship.

In the brutal cold and ice on the windy shore of Lake Erie, we battled the Browns to a 3–3 tie, until Lou Groza kicked a field goal late in the fourth quarter. We eventually lost 8–3. Though we had held the Browns' high-scoring offense to just one touchdown while defeating them two out of three games, Cleveland went on to win the World Championship over Norm Van Brocklin and the Los Angeles Rams.

The next year the Giants lost only two games, but both losses came in low-scoring losses to the Browns who once again won the conference title. New York had built a solid defensive football team; we just needed a better offense to go with it. In '52 we signed a promising young halfback out of USC by the name of Frank Gifford, and Kyle Rote played his first full season as a pro; but we lost a disappointing five games and again finished second in the conference to Cleveland.

Perhaps the most memorable loss that year occurred in Pittsburgh. The Steelers' offense ran up touchdown after touchdown in the first half while their defense knocked our starting quarterback Charlie Conerly out of the game and then kayoed his backup, rookie Fred Benners from SMU. Since I was the only other Giant who had ever played quarterback, Steve Owen ordered me into the game. I'd never taken a snap as a pro and didn't know any Giants' offensive plays. But fortunately there never was much grass in old Forbes Field, so in the huddle I'd kneel down in the dirt and scratch out the pass routes I wanted for the next play. I'm proud to report that even though the Steelers had us down 38–0 when I went in at quarterback in the second quarter, I helped engineer a Giants' offensive attack that brought us all the way back to a final score of 63–7 at the final gun—the worst shellacking in Giants' history. I had to play quarterback again the next week in another losing effort against the Washington Redskins—allowing me to retire forever with a perfect 0–2 record in games played as a professional quarterback.

If the Giants' '52 season was disappointing, you would have to term '53 a complete disaster. Even with the addition of several promising new faces including eventual great Rosey Grier, and the switch of Gifford to the offense (he'd played mostly alongside me in the defensive backfield his rookie season), we managed only three wins all season. And our humiliating 62–10 defeat at the hands of the repeating champion Cleveland Browns in our next-to-last game, forced the retirement of Coach Steve Owen after the season. The end of an era had arrived for the New York Giants. And another was about to begin.

When I began playing in the fifties, NFL football had much the same flavor it had when it started in the twenties with great players like Jim Thorpe and Red Grange and legendary coaches such as Curly Lambeau in Green Bay and George Halas in Chicago. (In fact, both of them still coached.) Several teams still ran variations of the old single-wing offense. Pro football remained a violent, sometimes brutal game where the ability to take, or better yet, *dish out* physical punishment was often the mark of a man. And a reputation for toughness was a high honor, hard sought.

The most brutal player of that era may have been Hardy (The Hatchet) Brown, a linebacker for the Colts and the '49ers. His trademark tackling technique brought an early end to more than one football career and struck terror in the hearts of every running back in the league. Instead of going for an opponent's legs, Brown would crouch low and launch his body like a ballistic missile at the head of a running back in an attempt to deliver what amounted to a flying shoulder block to the unprotected face of the ball carrier.

Hardy Brown may have been a major factor in the sudden, universal acceptance of the facemask on football helmets. I heard tell of one time in San Francisco when he hit a runner's jaw with such force the man's eyeball popped out of the socket and dangled on his cheek by a tendon. I saw the hit he put on Joe Scott, one of our Giants' backs, one Sunday in Baltimore. The blow shattered Joe's nose, splitting it open from the nostril to the bridge. Blood went everywhere. After the game we had to carry Joe out of the stadium and lay him out full length on the floor in the aisle of the train for the ride back to New York.

But Hardy Brown certainly wasn't alone at the top of the NFL's most violent list. Most teams had at least a player or two with well-earned reputations for toughness. Bucko Kilroy in Philadelphia was one; Ed Sprinkle in Chicago, and Ernie Stautner in Pittsburgh were two others. In that game I quarterbacked against the Steelers, after they had already knocked out our two quarterbacks and established an insurmountable lead. Ernie came crashing through the line and busted me with a forearm to the nose after I'd released yet another incomplete pass. It made me so mad and hurt so badly I leaped to my feet and began screaming at Stautner, who quickly backed off and even apologized. He'd meant nothing personal; that was just the way he played the game.

While you expected to take a share of physical punishment, there always seemed to be an understood line of violence beyond which you dared not go without risking retaliation. One of the funniest things I ever saw in pro football took place during a preseason game we played against Detroit in Norman, Oklahoma. The Lions' Jack Christiansen did something that provoked our quarterback Charlie Conerly. So Charlie decided to take revenge; he called the Bootsie play. Most teams had some variation on this where the center snaps the ball to his quarterback and then everyone else goes for the culprit on the opposing side. The first vigilante to get to him tackles him and the rest of the team piles on with the intent of delivering as much pain and punishment as possible before the officials can untangle them.

Conerly brought the team out of the huddle and lined up just like a normal play. But the moment the ball was snapped, Christiansen recognized the Bootsie. He turned and hightailed it down the field, through the end zone, and completely out of the stadium with the entire Giants' offensive team in angry pursuit as those of us on the sideline howled at the sight.

Things were just as tough off the field in those days. Sports medicine was not the refined science it is today. In New York, the official team physician, Doc Sweeney, got the job primarily because he was Steve Owen's brother-in-law.

I split my lip wide open during one game, covering my uniform with blood. No one considered taking me out of the game. But when Doc Sweeney examined me in the locker room after the game he decided I would need a few stitches. He made me lie down right there on the training table, opened his medical kit, and proceeded to sew up my face without even bothering with so much as a local anesthetic. I felt the burning pain as Doc Sweeney worked the point of that needle into my lip at one point and then part way out

another when he stopped abruptly and began to laugh.
He'd suddenly realized he had forgotten to string any
surgical thread onto the needle. He and everyone else
around me had a hearty laugh at my expense while he
rummaged around in his bag to find the thread. And the
entire time I sat there with a surgical needle sticking through
my lip.

That was sports medicine in the early fifties. Playing
hurt was expected. Injuries were to be ignored or simply
laughed off. Football was a tough man's game.

The business side could be just as hard-nosed as the
play on the field. The top stars made somewhere around
$25,000. Most of the rest of us settled for far less. You pretty
much took what the owners offered you, or you were apt to
find yourself cut, traded, or made an example of. I remember the year one of our linemen, Tex Couter, held out for
more money and missed most of training camp. Steve Owen
was so mad about it that just a few days after Tex reported,
Steve started him in an exhibition game in Dallas and left
him on the field for the entire game, on offense and defense,
in 98-degree heat. Tex lost 25 pounds that day and the rest
of the team gained a new understanding of the price you
pay to fight management.

Football life could be hard on families as well. We
always had to plan our year around moving twice and
learning to live in two different cities. Though we earned a
good-sized paycheck for a six-month job, most players had
to find a second job in the off-season to make ends meet.

I'm sure the life was hardest on football wives. Looking
back I'm afraid I expected far too much of Alicia during
those years. Every summer I would head off to training
camp, leaving her with the job of packing and closing up our
place in Texas, and moving everything the family would
need for a four-month stay in New York. Our daughter Kitty
was born in 1952 when I was again away, this time at
training camp. And after that, Alicia had two small children
to care for while she pulled off the yearly cross-country
move by herself.

*   *   *

Yet the hardships of those years, both on and off the field, were more than offset by the positives. For two transplants fresh from the open spaces of Texas, the opportunity to live part of the year in the world's biggest city really did seem like an adventure. Some years our family lived with several other Giants' families out in Long Beach, Long Island. We'd go in together and rent an entire shorefront hotel—which was closed for the off-season—where we could walk right across the street with our children and take family strolls along the oceanfront boardwalk. Other years a number of families rented apartments together in some New York hotel. One year it was the Excelsior off Central Park West, right across the street from the Museum of Natural History. Tom, Jr., loved that. And there was nearby Central Park, a great place for family outings in those days.

When the kids got a little older, they attended a private school right in Manhattan. One of the player's wives would walk all the children to school in the morning, and in the afternoon someone from the school would drop them back at the hotel. One year when we stayed at the Concourse Hotel up close to the stadium, Frank Gifford played the regular role of after-school baby-sitter, taking a whole gang of youngsters every afternoon to play in the little park across the street. Until the day some official in the city office building next door ordered a policeman to "tell that man with all those kids they can't play there anymore. It's killing the grass."

But as a rule, New York City in those days was as hospitable as it was glamorous. More like a huge friendly hometown than a dangerous big city. Alicia thought nothing of carting the children anywhere in the city by subway. And the two of us took in all the great Broadway shows of the day: *South Pacific, My Fair Lady, Sound of Music, Peter Pan*. City life was fun. And we shared it all as a family.

We made so many lifelong friendships during those years. Unlike today's players, who earn enough money to buy homes anywhere and everywhere and see most of their teammates only on the field and in the locker room, many of my Giants' teammates, their wives and their kids, became like an extended family.

And then there was the game itself. The older, more experienced, and slower I became as a player, the more I had to anticipate my opponents' moves. My analytical engineering training, which I finished in 1952 at the University of Houston, helped change my perspective of football, enabling me to visualize the entire offensive and defensive schemes and quickly break the whole down to its component parts. I watched game films by the hour every week, studying, learning—so I would understand what I had to do to succeed on Sunday.

What I learned fascinated me and added a whole new level of challenge to the game for me. That challenge has lasted a lifetime and became a driving motivation all through my coaching career—a career I never aspired to, and had never even considered. Until 1954.

chapter eight

COACHING
WITH LOMBARDI

BEFORE the '54 season, the Mara family—Tim, who had brought the Giants into the NFL for $500 in 1925, and his two sons, Jack and Wellington—offered the head coaching job to former, part-time assistant coach Jim Lee Howell. A long-legged, soft-spoken, teddy bear of a man (at 6'6" and upwards of 250 pounds), Jim Lee was perfectly content in his part-time roles coaching the Giants' ends and coaching Wagner College out on Staten Island. But he agreed to take over head coaching duties if the Giants would hire him two assistants—one to take charge of the offense and one the defense. The Maras accepted the plan and suggested he might want to head over to West Point and talk to a young, untried assistant coach under Earl Blaik at Army. Jim Lee liked what he saw and hired Vince Lombardi to coach the Giants' offense.

He offered me the defense—as a player-coach. I had no plans for a coaching career; I intended to go into business when my playing days ended. And I didn't know how it would work to be player-coach; some of my teammates were older and more experienced than I was. But Jim Lee expressed his confidence; and since I had already taken a lot

of leadership in working out the defensive details of Steve
Owen's overall strategies, I told Jim Lee I'd give the plan a
try. At the age of twenty-nine, I became the youngest
assistant coach in the league.

If I ever thought the change would be a lucrative one, I
quickly learned the truth when Wellington Mara offered me
a contract for the '54 season at little more than I had been
making as a player in '53—right around $10,000 as I recall.
When I reminded him of my increased duties, he indicated
he would try to make it up to me with a bonus at the end of
the season if we had a good year.

I can't say I patterned my coaching style or philosophy after
any one coach I played for—or competed against. But it is
easy for me to point to the one man whose coaching played
the biggest role in shaping both my football strategy and the
kind of coach I became. That man was Paul Brown.

From 1946–55, Paul Brown and his Cleveland Browns
epitomized success in professional football. In each of those
ten years (four in the AAFC, six in the NFL) the Browns
played for their league's title—winning eight of ten championship games. The accomplishment was tantamount to
playing in ten straight Super Bowls and winning eight.

Because the Cleveland Browns clearly had no equal,
they became the measuring stick for the entire NFL. From
the time Mac Speedie humiliated me in my first encounter
with the Browns, playing Cleveland always presented my
greatest challenge as a football player. It allowed me to test
myself against the best. As an assistant coach I felt the same
challenge. What Sir Edmund Hillary must have felt in 1953
looking up at Mount Everest, I felt in 1954 looking at the
seemingly insurmountable Cleveland Browns.

It wasn't merely that Paul Brown's teams achieved a
string of championships that will probably never be equaled;
it was the way they did it. The pro game had only slowly
evolved from the gritty, grind-it-out style of single-wing
football played by Red Grange and Jim Thorpe in the
twenties to the more open, airy approach of the T-formation

that the Chicago Bears' George Halas, Clark Shaughnessy, and Ralph Jones popularized in the forties. Even then pro football remained very much a brutal game demanding more guts than guile, more strength than strategy.

Paul Brown and his Cleveland teams changed football overnight; they transformed it from a game to a science. They took offensive football from the rough-draft stage and created the final blueprint for the foundation of the game as we know it today.

For the first time, football became a game of finesse. Not that the Brown teams weren't strong or tough; they were. But they never beat you with brute strength; they used precision.

When you played against the Pittsburgh Steelers, guys would stuff extra padding under their hip pads and anywhere else they could get it. Everyone wanted all the protection they could get. Though you expected to win the game against a Pittsburgh club that didn't post a lot of wins in that era, you knew the Steelers would punish you physically. Even with extra padding Pittsburgh's opponents would be bruised and hurting for the next week. In contrast, teams would go into Cleveland, lose by three or four touchdowns, and wake up Monday morning feeling as if they had taken Sunday afternoon off.

And yet because everyone knew they were the best, it was never hard to get a team up for a game against Cleveland. My competitive juices would kick in and I'd shift into a higher emotional gear whenever I played against the Browns. And while this may be hard for a lot of people to believe, I was an intensely emotional football player.

On the field, as a defensive back, I had an acute hatred for receivers. If a guy caught a ball against me, I'd try to hit him so hard he wished he hadn't. And nothing made me madder than to have someone catch a touchdown pass on me. I remember one day against the Los Angeles Rams, their great halfback and former Army star, Glenn Davis, got past me. I was more than 5 yards behind him when he gathered in a perfect Van Brocklin pass and raced down the field. No way I could ever catch Glenn Davis, but I was mad. Though he crossed the goal line 10 yards ahead of me, I never stopped. When he slowed to a touchdown trot, I slammed into him from behind. He leaped back to his feet, snarled, "You want the ball so bad. . . . Here!" and slung it at my head. I chased him all the way to his bench where, realizing I was greatly outnumbered, I turned and beat a hasty retreat to my own side of the field.

I usually managed to control my emotions better than I did that day. But they were always there.

I realized from my own experience that emotional play wasn't the key to beating the Browns. And they regularly beat stronger, tougher, more physically talented teams. You couldn't play traditional defense, simply reacting to the offensive movement of the ball. The Browns' offense was so precisely designed, and Otto Graham executed it so well, that opposing defenses couldn't react quickly enough to keep Cleveland from moving the ball down the field. Any hope at all of consistent success against Paul Brown meant you had to somehow counter his game of precision football.

At this time in the evolution of pro football, defenses were pretty basic. Defensive players were simply taught to react to the ball. However, I'd learned as a defensive back that it wasn't enough for me to react to the movement of the ball; by the time I saw where the ball was being thrown and tried to get there it would be too late to stop the play.

My own survival as a defensive player had forced me to learn to "read" an offense, to anticipate what plays my opponents ran. Some of my ability was probably instinctive and enhanced by my analytical engineering education; but a lot of it came only after thousands of hours watching and dissecting game film. Eventually I learned that by watching or "keying" on players, on their movements, and the overall formation or positioning of the offensive players, I could consistently tell where the ball would be going. I no longer had to react, I could anticipate the offense—sometimes breaking up even the most well-executed plays. That mind game—recognizing what the other team was wanting to do and stopping them from doing it—was the intriguing challenge of defensive football.

It was on this basic premise that I created the coordinated defense I began to teach my Giants' teammates. Fortunately, the offenses of that day, even Cleveland's, weren't terribly complex. Teams had only a couple basic offensive formations; we called them red or brown. If a team set up in the red formation and the halfback went one way, you could expect one or two possible plays. If the fullback went the other direction you could expect one or two other plays. The offensive alignments and movement were limited enough that most defensive players had to learn only a few simple keys to watch for in order to determine what play was coming.

But even before I could teach my defensive teammates the new principle of reading keys, I had to convince them not to do what they had always been taught to do, which was to simply wait and react to ball movement.

Some players seemed skeptical at first. One of our new young players, Dick Nolan, always had questions. I'd say, "If the Redskins line up in this formation and this man goes here, then the ball's going to go there." And Nolan would raise his hand and ask, "But what if it doesn't go there, but goes over here? What if . . ."

I'd say, "It won't."

And Dick would say, "But what if . . ."

I finally got to the point I just said, "There are no what ifs!" And I said it so often someone finally put a sign up on the wall declaring, "There are no whatifs!"

Truth be known, my confidence was sometimes a bluff. But if I didn't believe in my system, how could I ever get the other players to believe in it? It was the uncertainty that provided the challenge for me, that forced me back to the films of the opposition again and again, until it was no longer a matter of guessing where a play was going, but knowing. At least most of the time. The more often I was right, the more confidence the players gained in the new system. And the more they believed in the defense, the more demanding I became.

I understood Paul Brown started his offensive lectures in training camp each year by holding up a ball and saying, "Gentlemen, this is a football!" From there he'd go on to cover every step of every offensive play and expect every player, the oldest veteran as well as the rookies, to take detailed notes, in pencil, on notebook paper, of his own exact assignments on every single play. I was just as demanding because I knew to beat the Browns' disciplined offense, our defense had to be just as disciplined.

I remember one game early in his career when Frank Gifford still played defensive halfback alongside me in the Giants' backfield. He intercepted a pass and headed downfield in a spectacular run for a touchdown. I followed him all the way to the end zone where, as he turned to accept the congratulations of his happy teammates, I said, "Frank, you were out of position on that play." Then I turned and ran to the bench.

Sure I was glad he scored a touchdown. But to me that wasn't nearly as important as his learning to play his position. To work perfectly the defense needed to be executed perfectly. And perfection was always the goal.

The Giants were far from perfect in 1954, but the defense began to solidify. It was never as tough, however, as it felt one day to Deacon Dan Towler of the Rams in what was one of my funniest football memories. Thirty years before Mike Ditka unleashed William "The Refrigerator" Perry as a 300-pound short-yardage running back, the Los Angeles Rams used the same principle in a goal-line offense featuring a full-house backfield consisting of three massive men—two to block and one to carry the ball on a power run. It was almost impossible to stop.

When the Rams drove the ball to our 1-yard line, we knew what was coming. Jack Horner, Tank Younger, and big Deacon Dan Towler raced onto the field. I figured they would run the play off-tackle to Nolan's side since he was a rookie and smaller than I was. I warned him to be ready.

Sure enough, at the snap of the ball the Los Angeles line surged forward, opening a huge hole in front of Nolan. The quarterback faked the handoff to Younger, who plowed through the opening looking for someone to crush. Deacon Dan took the ball, lowered his head, and charged into the gaping hole behind Tank. If he'd have looked up he could have waltzed into the end zone untouched. He would also have seen the goalpost, which in those days stood right on the goal line.

But Deacon Dan drove with his head down, straight toward the goal line, at full speed, head first . . . right into that goalpost. I watched that solid wooden beam give under the momentum of the blow, bending farther and farther until it stopped and sprang back with a force that sent Deacon Dan Towler catapulting right back through the line. He landed in a semiconscious heap somewhere about the 5-yard line, the ball bounced free, and we recovered the fumble.

Deacon Dan finally staggered to his feet, shaking his head as if to say, "What happened?" And there stood Dick Nolan, whom he outweighed by a good 75 pounds, scowling at him. "If you run at me again, Towler," Dick told him, "I'll really hit you." Then, as a bewildered look of respect filled Deacon Dan's eyes, Nolan turned to jog off the field, and the entire Giants' defensive unit nearly died laughing.

We bounced back that year to a respectable 7–5 record to finish third in the division. Personally I had my best year ever as a pro, tying future Hall of Famer Emlen Tunnell for the team lead in interceptions at eight, finishing fourth in the NFL in punting with a 42.5 average, and being named to the All-Pro team at the end of the season.

I figured that kind of showing on the field, plus the progress the defensive team had made during my first year of coaching, had earned me my bonus. So before I went home to Texas I stopped in the front office to ask about it. It seemed I'd misunderstood; Wellington had meant that if the Giants' *organization* had a good enough year, he would consider giving me a bonus. And while the box office take had admittedly improved over 1953, he told me the Giants couldn't afford to pay me any more than my contract called for. I walked out of his office disappointed and a little irritated. But not too irritated to eventually agree to another contract calling on me to perform my player-coach duties again in 1955 for the grand salary of $11,000.

Prospects looked pretty good when the Giants opened training camp in the summer of '55 at St. Michael's College in Winooski, Vermont. Not only did we draft defensive tackle Rosey Grier, fullback Mel Triplett, and defensive back Jim Patton, but we picked up experienced linebacker Harland Svare in a trade with the Rams. And on top of that, the Maras raided the Canadian Football League to sign the Montreal Alouettes' powerful halfback, Alex Webster—the CFL's leading rusher and Most Valuable Player in 1954. While I wasn't sure at first how much Webster was worth since he was one of the worst practice players I ever saw, he showed amazing running power and a real nose for the end zone, once he got in a game.

We began the '55 season losing three straight on the road and were a sorry 1–4 after five weeks. Then Vince's offense began to click, the defense jelled, and we finished strong to end up with a 6–5–1 record, serving notice that the Giants would be a team to contend with the following year.

The '55 season marked my last as a player. In 1956 I would serve solely as the assistant coach in charge of the Giants' defense. But I quickly learned that my change in status didn't make training camp any more pleasant. Less than two weeks into camp I wrote Alicia from Vermont:

. . . Don't think you're the only one who is lonesome. Don't ever think these football players can take your place. I miss you so much. We've stood it before, so I guess we can

this time. But let's hope this is it. Maybe I'll get a break next
year and have a job that will support us. . . .

I wasn't the only person disillusioned by training camp
that year. Two of our rookies, a baby-faced, third-round
draft pick out of West Virginia by the name of Robert E. Lee
"Sam" Huff and a would-be punter named Don Chandler
became so discouraged they snuck out of camp one night
and headed for the nearest airport. Somehow Vince Lombardi learned of their desertion and caught up with them in
the Burlington, Vermont, airport terminal where he chewed
them out, told them in no uncertain terms that they weren't
quitting, and drove them back to camp. Don Chandler went
on to become the premier punter in football for the next
decade and Sam Huff went on to become, well, Sam Huff.

In college Sam had played tackle. But at 6'1" and 230,
he wasn't really big enough to play in the Giants' line—
which was the reason for his frustration in training camp.
But the more I saw the kid play, the more I liked his fiercely
competitive, hard-hitting style. He seemed bright and eager
to learn, so I decided to teach him the position of middle
linebacker in a defensive alignment I'd been experimenting
with for a couple years—the 4–3. Sort of a combined
variation on the old Eagle defense developed by Greasy
Neale in the late forties and my old coach Steve Owen's
Umbrella.

For years the standard defense in football had been the
5–3–3 with five down linemen, three linebackers, and just
three backs to defend against the pass. But the Bears' T-
formation with two tight ends and a man in motion meant
there were too many receivers for three backs to cover.
Greasy Neale had countered that offense with a 5–2–4
defense that allowed for four defensive backs to cover the
receivers deep. When offenses began beating the Eagle
defense with short passes over the middle, the 4–3 seemed
like the obvious evolution. It had four down linemen to
contain the run, three linebackers including a middle

linebacker to fill the gaps and defense the short pass, and the four defensive backs to defend the long pass.

We started strong that season with two wins in our first three games on the road, including one in Cleveland that marked the end of the modern age of the electronic quarterback almost before it got started. I don't know whose idea it was, but the NFL had just legalized the use of a radio receiver in quarterbacks' helmets so coaches could talk directly to their quarterbacks on the field. Jim Lee Howell didn't feel we needed that kind of contact with our veteran quarterback Charlie Conerly, but Paul Brown used a radio to send instructions in to George Ratterman, his replacement for the just-retired Otto Graham.

As soon as the game began, our rookie end Bob Topp donned the earphones and tuned our radio to the Cleveland frequency to hear Paul Brown's instructions to Ratterman. Bob would call out the play. One of our running backs, Gene Filipski, who had spent some time on the Browns and knew their play-calling terminology, would tell me what was coming. Then I would signal my defensive players.

Our eavesdropping strategy proved even more effective than our usual keys; Cleveland went nowhere the entire first half. Although Paul Brown abandoned his electronic play-calling when he realized our defense was thwarting his plays with surprising frequency, we held on to win anyway by a score of 21–9. A few days later Commissioner Bert Bell decided to bring the experiment to an early end by banning such electronic communication altogether. Our chief spy, Bob Topp, allowed that it was just as well. "If the trend continued," he said, "the Giants number-one draft pick next year would probably have been the valedictorian of MIT."

By midseason Sam Huff established himself as the middle linebacker I needed to make the 4–3 defense work. He learned fast, but then he worked hard at learning. Many weeknights during the season, after supper, I'd call Sam from my apartment in the Excelsior Hotel. "What are you doin' tonight?" I would ask.

"Thought I'd watch a little TV," he would say.

"Well, good. Glad you're not doing anything. Why don't you come down and we can look at some game films of [whoever we were playing the next Sunday]." I don't think Sam got to see much television all season. He spent most evenings watching game films projected on my living room wall while Alicia readied Tom, Jr., and Kitty for bed in the back of the apartment.

The extra work paid off almost immediately. What he learned each week in our film sessions Sam utilized immediately on the field that Sunday. And that commitment to learn, combined with his physical abilities and his competitive intensity, was what made Sam Huff the prototype for the middle linebacker position from that day on. By the time his rookie year ended, he had already established himself as a top NFL player. And the Giants had become a dominant defensive team.

At the same time the final pieces fell into place on my defensive unit, Vince Lombardi's offensive team came of age. Vinnie incorporated the power of Alex Webster with the versatile running and passing skills of Frank Gifford at the other halfback to create a masterful, unpredictable attack that kept opponents constantly off guard and could produce touchdowns from anywhere on the field.

The Giants won the division with an 8–3–1 record, earning the right to face the Chicago Bears for the NFL Championship. We played the game before 56,000 frozen fans on December 30, 1956. The temperature at kickoff time was 18 degrees and dropping. The field itself seemed better suited for ice skating than football.

Fortunately we realized how treacherous the turf was going to be earlier that week. Conditions reminded Wellington Mara of the 1934 championship game against the same Chicago Bears when the old Giants gained a big advantage by coming out to play the second half wearing basketball shoes. He suggested a similar strategy to Jim Lee Howell. So Jim Lee conducted a test. He sent running back Gene Filipski out to run around the field in basketball shoes and defensive back Ed Hughes out in regular football cleats. Ed slid all over the place, but Gene got enough traction to run and cut.

So Wellington and Jim Lee placed a rush order for four dozen pairs of rubber-soled basketball shoes with defensive end Andy Robustelli, who had a sporting goods store on the side. The shoes arrived just in time for the game that would be played on a field as hard and slick as a slab of marble.

Filipski took the kickoff and ran through the slip-sliding Bears for 53 yards. Four plays later Mel Triplett scored on a 17-yard run. Chicago fumbled in their first possession; we capitalized on that mistake with a field goal. And we never looked back. By halftime we led 37–7. The game ended 47–7. The Giants won their first NFL Championship since 1938. And I received a very nice postseason bonus; the winner's share for the championship game came to $3,779.19.

And yet, despite the thrill of winning a World Championship, the accomplishment left me feeling strangely unsettled and unsatisfied.

chapter nine

CROSSROADS:
NEW YORK OR DALLAS?

FOR THIRTY years pro football had struggled along like
a neglected stepchild in an athletic family where professional baseball and collegiate sports elicited a lion's share of
headlines and fan loyalty. I would return to Texas every
winter after my first few professional seasons to have
friends ask, "Where ya been? Haven't seen you for a while!"
Nobody in Texas seemed to follow pro football.

Sometimes the sport drew little more notice in the very
cities where it was played. I recall a time in 1949 when all
three of New York's professional football teams—the Yankees, the Giants, and the old New York Bulldogs—all
scheduled home games the same Sunday afternoon. None
of the games drew more than about six thousand spectators.

While fan interest increased throughout the early
fifties, everything changed during that championship season of 1956. Pro football, the forgotten stepchild, suddenly
came of age in New York City, laying a legitimate claim to
the affections and loyalty of the most important city in the
world.

The Giants became instant heroes. And we all basked
in the unaccustomed glory. At Toots Shor's restaurant and

celebrity hot spot, Giants' players and their wives were shown to the best tables and introduced to numerous legendary stars—from boxer Rocky Marciano to jockey Eddie Arcaro. Alicia and I also tasted the nightlife of New York at places like the Stork Club and the Latin Quarter. Everywhere we went with my teammates and their wives, we received celebrity status, which seemed new and exciting and fun.

Those rabid New York sports fans who filled the house Ruth built to watch baseball all summer and watched their heroes take the baseball World Championship from the Brooklyn Dodgers as Don Larsen hurled the only perfect game in World Series history—those same fans stayed on into that fall of 1956. And they discovered Giants in the land.

You could feel a new atmosphere of electricity in Yankee Stadium on Sunday afternoons. Part of the reason may have been the setting itself. When you walked out onto that field you could almost taste the tradition forged by Ruth, Gehrig, DiMaggio, and Mantle. And when you looked up into the sea of faces in those great upper decks, you couldn't help longing to be a part of the lasting legacy of the place.

But the Giants were also winning. And winning always generates its own electricity.

Yet there was more to what happened to professional football in New York in 1956 and the years that followed than can be explained either by the aura of tradition or the excitement of winning.

Lombardi's flashy, innovative, and star-studded offense seemed perfectly suited to a city accustomed to the excitement and glamour of bright lights and big stars. And the fans began to identify with our defense as well. For the first time in my experience and perhaps for the first time in football history, the crowd would exhort our defensive team on crucial downs by standing and bellowing a cheer that has now become commonplace in football: "Deee-fense! Deee-fense! Deee-fense!" The cheer would resound through that old ballpark, often followed by another chant—"Huff! Huff! Huff! Huff!" And when the defense would trot to the sidelines after holding an opponent, the entire crowd would stand and stomp and cheer and make them feel as much like stars as their offensive counterparts.

Those were heady times for the Giants, with enough acclaim for everyone. And though we became targets for every other team in the league, some of the greatest rivalry we experienced came during practice between our offensive and defensive squads. We became each others' toughest competition.

The friendly nature of the rivalry made it no less intense. Though Vinnie and I became great friends, we each had our own agendas. I'd walk into Jim Lee Howell's office to ask for extra time in practice to work on defense, and Vince would march in five minutes later demanding more time for his offense. On the sideline during the game, whenever the Giants faced a fourth and one, Vince would be begging Jim Lee to "Go for it! Our offense can make it!" I'd be saying, "We should punt! Let them have the ball and give the defense a chance!"

With the exception of the competitive drive we both shared, Vince and I had little in common. He had a loud, aggressive, gregarious, New York Italian personality. I remained a soft-spoken, reserved, shy, rather-generic Texan. Vince screamed at his players, often motivating their performance out of fear. I hardly ever raised my voice when addressing my players, depending on our preparation and knowledge to inspire confidence and motivate them to do their best. Both styles worked, so we made allowances for our differences.

For example, any time his offensive team had a poor game, you could count on Vince being in a foul mood for the next two or three days. If you risked talking to him during that time, he might snap at you or just respond with an angry grunt. But you learned never to take it personally. That was just Vince. The same emotionally volatile personality that gave him a fiery temper also gave him an expressive, warm, and caring nature. When you got to know Vinnie you couldn't help but love the man. His old-world-gentleman style thoroughly charmed Alicia, and we became good friends with Vinnie and his sweet wife Marie, who could handle Vinnie's emotional side like no one else in the world.

I didn't fully appreciate the unique opportunity Vince and I had with the New York Giants until years later. Jim Lee Howell gave us almost total responsibility for our respective squads.

Kyle Rote tells the story of walking down a hallway at training camp one year. First he came to a room where Vince was showing film and working on offense. Then he passed a room on the other side of the hall where I had my projector running, working up the defense. Finally he came to Jim Lee's room to find the head coach with his feet propped up, reading a newspaper.

A gentleman who never had an ego problem, Jim Lee was as quick to defer any credit as he was to delegate responsibility to his assistants. "With Lombardi coaching the offense and Landry coaching the defense," he would say, "all I ever have to do is keep the balls pumped up and enforce curfew." But that statement, like Kyle's story, is a misleading exaggeration.

Not only did he have great public relations skills for handling the New York media, Jim Lee Howell was a strict disciplinarian and a fine football man who always knew what Vince and I were doing. I never for a moment thought he would hesitate to step in if my strategy didn't work or if he had doubts about my coaching. I respected the man and always appreciated his hands-off management style, which allowed his assistant coaches room to learn what it took to become a head coach in the NFL—something I struggled with and didn't do as well when I became a head coach.

The New York fans expected great things of us in 1957. There was some talk the success of '56 could be the beginning of a new dynasty to replace Cleveland's. The trouble with that dream turned out to be Cleveland and their first-round draft pick, Jim Brown.

The big rookie fullback out of Syracuse led the league in rushing and carried the Browns to yet another Eastern Division title. We finished with a respectable 7–5 record and headed into the off-season knowing if we wanted to become champions again, the Browns remained the team to beat.

On March 4, 1958, Alicia gave birth to our third child, a baby girl we named Lisa. This time I was there. And I took several days off from my postseason job selling insurance to help Alicia with the baby and the other two kids. I wanted to make up for missing Tom, Jr.'s, and Kitty's births. But I knew I couldn't. And the reminder of how my football career had so disrupted our family life increased my determination to build another career that would better provide for my family and allow us to live in Texas all year round.

The way the '58 season started in New York, I wished I'd stayed in Texas. Expecting to battle Cleveland once again for the division title, the Giants lost five out of six exhibition games and two out of four to start the regular season. But then we turned it around. Going into the season's final Sunday, at home against Cleveland, our record stood at 8–3. And we trailed Cleveland by only one. A Giants' win would force a playoff rematch to determine the division winner.

A snowstorm on game day threatened to turn the contest into a defensive struggle. But Jim Brown broke out of Sam Huff's grasp and plowed 65 yards for a touchdown on the Cleveland's first possession. The Browns led 10–3 at the half and neither team scored in the third period. Early in the fourth, we recovered a Cleveland fumble and followed the turnover with a daring halfback option pass from Gifford to Rote, who was finally pulled down at the Browns' 6. Two plays later, on another option pass, Giff faked a pass to Rote and hit Bob Schnelker in the end zone for 6. Pat Summerall's extra point tied the game at 10.

The Giants' defense didn't give up another first down

the rest of the game. But we couldn't score either when Summerall missed a field goal from the 25 with five minutes left in the game.

Once more the defense held and a shanked Cleveland punt gave us the ball on their 43 or 44—no one knew for sure. You could no longer see the yard marker on the snow-covered field. Three attempted passes fell incomplete. Fourth and 10. With only two minutes left we couldn't punt; we'd never get the ball back and a tie game would give Cleveland the division title. We had to go for it. At least I thought we did.

Instead, Jim Lee Howell called for Pat Summerall and sent him in to kick a field goal. No one on the sidelines could believe it, including Pat. Not only would this be the longest attempt he'd ever made as a Giant, but from the 50-yard line Pat could barely make out the goalposts through the swirling snow.

Charlie Conerly hurriedly tried to scrape out a clear place on the icy turf to spot the ball. Ray Wietecha snapped it. Conerly got the ball down just before Pat kicked. And the most remarkable field goal I ever witnessed sailed high through the snowstorm to split the uprights. The 13–10 victory tied us with Cleveland and we won a coin toss for the right to host the playoff at Yankee Stadium two weeks later.

The snow had stopped by the time Cleveland came to town again. But the field remained frozen. I had spent two solid weeks studying films, looking for keys to give Sam Huff, and adjusting our 4–3 defense to stop the running of Jim Brown. This time it was the Giants who struck early on another Lombardi-designed razzle-dazzle play. Conerly took the snap and handed off to Alex Webster who gave the ball to Gifford on a double reverse. Giff ran the ball all the way to the 8-yard line where, as he was about to be tackled, he lateraled to Charlie Conerly who loped in for the score. Summerall added a field goal in the second quarter, but one score was all we needed that day. A brilliant performance by the entire Giants' defense held Jim Brown to just 8 yards and shut out the Browns 10–0, the first time Cleveland had been shut out since we beat them 6–0 in 1950 using Steve Owen's famed Umbrella defense. And in what was one of my proudest moments ever in sports, my great defensive lineman, Andy Robustelli, presented me with the game ball.

To top off those two memorable contests with the Browns, we played Johnny Unitas and the Baltimore Colts for the NFL Championship the very next week in Yankee Stadium in what many people have called "the greatest football game ever played." Coach Weeb Ewbank's Colts boasted the most explosive offense in the league with an average of 31.8 points per game by way of the passing prowess of young Johnny Unitas. The stunning nature of the Giants' two straight victories over Cleveland to take the Eastern title had whipped New York fans to a frenzy. And network television coverage suddenly made the 1958 NFL Championship game a national event.

Sixty-four thousand screaming fans at Yankee Stadium and millions of television viewers around the nation watched Johnny U and his air attack dominate the first half, gaining over 200 yards and giving the Colts a 14–3 lead at intermission. We came back with two touchdowns in the second half and led 17–14 with just two minutes to go when the Colts took over the ball on their own 14-yard line.

In desperation we double-teamed Lenny Moore and Raymond Berry. But Unitas coolly directed his team down the field, completing three passes to Berry for a total of 63 yards. That classic drive, in addition to giving birth to the Unitas legend, carried the Colts all the way to our 13-yard line in only a minute and a half of picture-perfect offensive football. From there, with seven seconds left, Colts' kicker Steve Myhra booted the game-tying field goal and the NFL had its first sudden-death overtime championship game in history.

We won the toss and elected to receive the ball to start the overtime. But the Colts held and we had to punt. Baltimore took over on its own 20. This time Unitas and company masterfully mixed an assortment of passing and running plays to move steadily down the field. None of our defensive adjustments could stop what looked from the sidelines to be inevitable. Finally, from the 2-yard line, Alan Ameche plunged into the end zone to give Baltimore a 23–17 victory and the NFL Championship.

Whether or not it was "the greatest pro football game ever played," that championship contest clearly stands as a legendary milestone in the history of the sport. Just as surely as the '56 season marked the time when New York City discovered the Giants, that sudden-death playoff game against Baltimore, by thrilling millions of television viewers, marked the time and the place when America discovered professional football.

Just as so many different factors came together to make the '58 championship game a turning point in pro football history, a number of factors converged during the following off-season to bring me to the most crucial turning point in my own personal history.

From the time as a young kid when I'd begun playing football with my older brother Robert and his friends, athletics had been the arena in which I could measure my own self-worth and establish my identity. Football gave direction to my life by always providing another rung on the ladder leading upward toward success.

Each step had been exciting. The regional championship back at Mission High School. University of Texas football. Three different New Year's Day bowl games. Making it in professional football and living in New York City. Winning All-Pro honors. Becoming an assistant coach. Experiencing a World Championship. Earning national recognition and acclaim as a defensive football coach.

Yet each time I reached the next level of achievement, the resulting excitement and sense of satisfaction was soon replaced by the same sense of restlessness and doubt. *Is that all there is? What now? Am I really good enough? Do I have what it takes to make it at the next level?*

Now, at the age of thirty-three, I'd done everything I'd

ever wanted to do and more in football. And because there was no "next level" I wanted to achieve, I found myself with no clear direction in life, no purpose.

At the same time, I knew I had to do something to provide for my family after football. Since completing my second degree in industrial engineering at Houston in 1952, I had sold big storage tanks for an oil field supply company, dabbled in the real estate business, and tried selling insurance in the off-seasons back in Texas.

It was tough getting established in any new career you could work at only six months of the year. Which was why the insurance business was popular with football players and coaches; it was one of few businesses where you could take off from July to December each year for the football season and be able to come back and take up where you left off. Many times Vince Lombardi, another part-time insurance salesman, and I discussed the difficulty of building any sense of continuity, let alone a solid base for your family's future, when your life was divided into two halves every year.

Like many of my generation, who lived through the depression and the war, I felt a great responsibility to provide for my own family; I wanted my children to have more than I'd had. With three kids, I was more aware than ever of the strain football life placed on Alicia. Both Tom, Jr., and Kitty were in school now, and while they managed the annual, midyear transfer from New York to Texas quite well, they needed the stability of a year-round home. And yet I still wasn't ready to provide a reliable living for my family outside of football. I felt I'd reached a major crossroads in my life, but I didn't have a clue as to which way I should go.

At this point in my life, early in 1959, a friend by the name of Frank Phillips stopped me one day on a street in Dallas and invited me to a men's prayer breakfast. "We meet downtown at the Melrose Hotel every Wednesday morning at 7:30," he said. "It's just a few fellas eating breakfast and studying the Bible together. I think you'd like it. Why don't you come with me this week?"

I wasn't at all interested. But since I couldn't think of a gracious way to decline, I accepted Frank's invitation. And that Wednesday morning when I walked into the dining room of the Melrose Hotel, I was surprised to find four tables full of businessmen—thirty to forty men in all—gathered for that week's Bible study of Jesus' Sermon on the Mount in Matthew 5–7.

Though I had gone to church all my life, I'd never studied the Bible. In fact I had hardly ever read it. Whenever I had tried, my King James Version always seemed confusing and irrelevant. Yet that morning, as we read those chapters and the men around my table began discussing the meaning of Jesus' words, two passages seemed to jump right off the page at me.

The first was Matthew 6:25–34, which said in part—"Therefore I say unto you, Take no thought for your life, what ye shall eat, or what ye shall drink; nor yet for your body, what ye shall put on. Is not the life more than meat, and the body than raiment? . . . But seek ye first the kingdom of God, and his righteousness; and all these things shall be added unto you. Take therefore no thought for the morrow: for the morrow shall take thought for the things of itself."

The second passage that struck me was Matthew 7:24, 25—"Therefore whosoever heareth these sayings of mine, and doeth them, I will liken him unto a wise man, which built his house upon a rock: And the rain descended, and the floods came, and the winds blew, and beat upon that house; and it fell not: for it was founded upon a rock."

Suddenly, in the middle of my personal struggle to find direction and security in my life, here were Bible verses talking about those very issues. I was so surprised and intrigued I went back to that Bible study the next week. And the next. And the next. I wanted to understand what else the Bible had to say.

Using the same sort of scientific, analytical approach

that enabled me to break down and understand an opponent's offenses, I read and studied and discovered the basic keys of the Christian gospel:

That we've all sinned; none of us can measure up to God's standard; and our failure stands between us and God (Rom. 3:23). That God sent Jesus to take the punishment for our failure (John 3:16). That his salvation was a free gift for anyone who accepted it (Rom. 10:13). That we can't do anything to earn it, we just have to believe (Rom. 5:1). And once we come to that belief, God wants us to turn our lives over to him and let him direct us and provide for all our needs (Rom. 12:1, 2).

Then I saw that even though I'd gone to church all my life, I had never understood Christianity. I had been a spectator all my life when God wanted me to be a participant. If I really believed what the Bible said, I needed to be practicing it in my life.

If it was true! That was a big "if."

I had always considered myself a Christian, yet so much of what I now discovered in the Bible went against the grain of the life philosophy I had lived by. I was never much of a drinker, I didn't smoke or even swear; I had always figured I was a pretty good person. Now here was the Bible saying I was as much a sinner as anyone in the world.

I had based my life on the idea that if I could work hard enough I would succeed, if I could learn enough, knowledge would make me a winner. Now here was the Bible saying that it wasn't knowledge or works that made the ultimate difference in life, it was faith. All my life I had made my football career the number-one priority and let it dictate the direction of my life. Now here was the Bible saying I needed to make God and his will first and follow his direction for my life.

Gradually I realized the crossroads I faced in my life was really a spiritual crossroads. I had to decide whether or not I believed what the Bible said. All my other questions hung on that one.

The more of the Bible I read and studied, the more it all

made sense. The more pieces of life fit together. The more I wanted to believe. And yet that analytical part of my nature kept asking questions, trying to dispel all doubt.

One day I came across a short passage of a poem by Robert Browning that said: "You call for faith, I give you doubt, to prove that faith exists. The greater the doubt, the stronger the faith, I say, if faith overcomes doubt."

When I read that, something clicked in me and I began to understand faith in a new light.

I can't point to a specific moment or a specific time when I had a sudden "born-again" experience. For me, coming to my own personal faith in God took place over a period of months in 1959. But I finally reached a point where faith outweighed the doubts, and I was willing to commit my entire life to God.

I can't say that decision made an immediately visible difference in my life. I can't even say it instantly transformed me into a much better person; I had a lot yet to learn—and I still do—about how God wants me to live my life. But what my new Christian experience did do for me was to place football behind the priorities of my faith and my family and give me a sense of confidence and peace about the future—whatever it would be.

A lot had happened in New York during the off-season as well. Tim Mara, the founder of the Giants, had died, leaving the team to Wellington and Jack. Vince had finally gotten a head coaching opportunity and had left New York to take over the Green Bay Packers, who had floundered through a 1–10–1 season the year before.

As the new season began I just had a feeling that it would be my last in New York. As we had in 1958, the family lived in Stamford, Connecticut, and I carpooled into the city every day with three of my defensive players, Andy Robustelli, Ed Hughes, Cliff Livingston, and a talkative young lawyer turned sportscaster by the name of Howard Cosell. At the time Howard primarily covered boxing on radio. Although he wasn't nearly as critical as he later became, he had opinions on everything and didn't hesitate to share them as we drove back and forth from the city.

The Giants' defense played better than ever in 1959, giving up only 170 points all season (and 49 of those in one maddening afternoon against Norm Van Brocklin and Sonny Jurgensen in Philadelphia). Head coach Jim Lee Howell gave me much credit and deflected more media limelight onto me than I ever wanted when, in discussing our defense, he told the press "Tom Landry is the best coach in football." We posted a 10–2 record, the best in the entire NFL. And we defeated the second-place Cleveland Browns twice by the scores of 10–6 and 48–7. In that second game I showed that my new faith had done little if anything to curb my competitive nature. We were 40 points ahead of the Browns late in the game and I was still running along the sidelines yelling at my defensive unit: "Hold 'em! Hold 'em! Don't let 'em score!"

In a rematch of the 1958 championship game, New York played Baltimore again. At the end of the third quarter the Giants led 9–7. Then Unitas exploded for 24 points in the final period, and we lost the championship 31–17.

But my own disappointment at that defeat was overshadowed by an exciting new opportunity that began just one day later.

part three
THE COWBOYS
OF DALLAS

chapter ten
COWBOY BEGINNINGS

THE GIANTS lost the 1959 NFL Championship game on December 27. The next day I got on a plane with Tex Schramm and flew to Dallas. Within minutes after landing, we walked into a press conference at Love Field where Tex introduced me as the new head coach of the Dallas Rangers, the first team to be added to the league since the merger with the All-American Football Conference in 1950. (It wasn't until some weeks later the team's nickname was changed to Cowboys to avoid potential conflict with a defunct Texas League baseball team known as the Rangers.)

Actually, Dallas hadn't officially been granted a franchise at the time I was hired as coach. We were rushing things a bit. But then we had to rush if we were going to field a team for the '60 season.

The NFL's growing popularity in the late fifties had prompted talk of expanding to additional cities. The league's expansion committee, headed by Chicago Bears' owner, George Halas, discussed two new franchises to begin playing in the '61 season—one in Dallas and the other in Houston or Minneapolis.

But then the American Football League got off the

ground. When the AFL's founding father, Lamar Hunt, announced that play would begin for the '60 season in eight cities including Dallas and Houston, Halas pushed for immediate expansion. He didn't want to give a rival league a head start in the Texas markets.

Not all the NFL owners favored expansion, but Papa Bear found financial backing for a Dallas team. Clint Murchison, the thirty-six-year-old heir to one of Texas's biggest family oil fortunes, agreed along with other partners including his brother, John Murchison, Bedford Wynne, Bedford's cousin, Toddie Lee Wynne, and Fritz Hawn to buy an NFL expansion franchise. And even though plans for an immediate start up in Houston never jelled, Halas and the Dallas group pressed on.

Halas knew Clint Murchison and his partners needed an experienced football man. So he put them in touch with Tex Schramm, who had resigned as general manager of the Los Angeles Rams in 1957 to become a CBS executive for television sports. Tex signed on as general manager of the proposed Dallas franchise that fall and immediately began looking for a head coach.

In the meantime, Dallas wasn't my first head coach offer. Texas oilman Bud Adams, owner of the AFL's Houston franchise, had contacted me during the '59 season to ask if I would be interested in the Oilers' job. I agreed to meet with him, more out of courtesy and curiosity than any real interest. We had dinner one night in his suite at a swank Manhattan hotel. He gave me a big sales pitch on the AFL—an exciting new league, a chance to get in on the ground floor, and an opportunity to create football furor in Houston the way the Giants had in New York City. But I had spent ten years in the NFL, my experience in the old AAFC hadn't proved very stable, and I'd pretty much decided it was time to get out of football and into something that would offer more security for my family. I listened, said I would give it some thought, and figured that was the end of it.

A short time later, Wellington Mara called me into his

office to say he'd okayed the Dallas NFL group's plan to approach me about their head coaching position. But he first wanted me to know that when Jim Lee Howell took his planned retirement soon, I'd be first in line to become head coach of the New York Giants. I listened again, but while I felt warm toward my good friend Wellington, and while I appreciated this expression of confidence, Alicia and I had pretty much decided the '59 season would be our last in New York. It was time to take our family home to Texas for good.

Though I had virtually written off two head coaching possibilities, I was curious enough to talk with Tex Schramm about a third. Alicia and I loved Dallas. We had already made it our off-season home and begun a business there.

I knew becoming head coach of a new team wouldn't be a very secure position; it was just a matter of time before I'd be fired. And yet a head coaching job in Dallas, even if it lasted only two, maybe three years, could buy me the time I needed to build my business to the point I could adequately support my family. Plus, a year-round home in Dallas would immediately allow the family the stability I'd been concerned about. So while the position itself didn't look very secure, I realized it could serve as a solid bridge to life beyond football.

That's what I was thinking when Tex first contacted me. And the more we talked, the more interesting the prospect sounded. Tex had a lot of ideas about how a professional football organization needed to be run—good ideas. He would insist on a strong chain-of-command organizational structure in Dallas, having seen some messy personnel problems when he was with the Rams in Los Angeles. As head coach I would report directly to him as general manager, but I would have complete authority over players and the on-field operation of the team. As general manager he would run the business side of the operation and report to the owner. He wanted reporting channels and authority clearly defined so each person could concentrate on his duties with minimal interference and without the distractions of organizational politics.

When we discussed personnel, Tex impressed me with his understanding of scouting—something I knew little about. He seemed confident he and his friend Gil Brandt, who'd worked with him on the Rams, could build a strong scouting system. But he promised the head coach would select his own assistants and have final say in all player personnel decisions.

Everything we talked about sounded good to me. So when Tex officially offered me a five-year contract at $34,500 a year, I took it. That old sense of restlessness and uncertainty I'd felt about the future was suddenly gone. The decision simply felt right to me. At the same time the five-year contract gave me a peaceful sense of security for my family's future, and it allowed me the chance to stay in football a little bit longer.

I knew building a professional football team from scratch wouldn't be an easy job. I said so in that first Dallas press conference. And the other NFL owners made it an even bigger challenge.

Official approval of the Dallas franchise was scheduled for a vote at the January owners' meeting in Miami Beach. A few owners, led by influential George Preston Marshall of the Washington Redskins, still expressed reluctance to rush into expansion. But before the expansion issue could be voted on, the owners had to elect a successor to former commissioner Bert Bell, who'd died during the '59 season.

For seven long days the suspense dragged out in the meeting rooms and corridors of the old Kenilworth Hotel. Through twenty-two ballots the owners remained deadlocked over two candidates for commissioner. George Halas abstained every time for fear of alienating one side or the other and losing their support in the later vote on his expansion proposal.

Finally Cleveland's Paul Brown and Wellington Mara proposed a compromise candidate, the Los Angeles Rams' young general manager and former protégé of Tex Schramm, Pete Rozelle. And on the twenty-third ballot, the NFL had a new commissioner.

The debate over expansion lasted another two days. And if it hadn't been for a song, I might have been out of a job. (No, no one asked me to sing this time.)

It seems a short while before, George Marshall had fired his band director who had composed Washington's official fight song, "Hail to the Redskins." To spite Marshall, the musician sold the copyright for the song to a lawyer who also had some differences with Marshall in the past. And the new owner of the copyright just happened to be one of Clint Murchison's lawyers.

So after two days of haggling over expansion, Marshall, who had always been especially fond of his team's fight song, agreed to vote in favor of the Dallas franchise if Clint's lawyer would give him back the rights to "Hail to the Redskins." An agreement to that effect was quickly drawn up and signed, and Dallas was voted into the NFL on January 28, 1960—Alicia's and my eleventh wedding anniversary.

But voting to give Dallas a team, and helping us get players to fill it, were two separate issues. In an attempt to get a jump on the aggressive AFL, the annual NFL draft of college football players had been held back in November instead of waiting for the end of the season when it was usually scheduled. Since Dallas hadn't had an official team at the time, that meant we didn't have any draft picks at all that first year.

Fortunately George Halas had anticipated such a problem. Halas had encouraged Tex before the college draft to have Clint Murchison sign two college stars from the Southwest to personal service contracts—Don Meredith, a Dallas headliner as a two-time All-American at SMU, and an underrated but impressive running back from the University of New Mexico, Don Perkins. The other NFL owners were informed of Dallas's intentions so they wouldn't draft either player. Just to be sure there would be no dispute later, Halas himself spent a third-round pick in the college draft on the rights to Meredith. Then he traded those rights to Dallas for our third-round pick in the college draft the next year.

Immediately following the draft, Tex had copied some standard NFL player contracts and hired Gil Brandt to barnstorm the country signing up any promising undrafted football players to free-agent contracts with the still nonexistent Dallas team. When the Cowboys began, those two or three dozen undrafted free agents, plus rookies Meredith and Perkins, were all we had. We needed some experienced players.

Halas proposed letting us select a limited number of veteran players off each NFL team's roster. Again the owners proved reluctant. So Tex and I went to the next owners' meeting in Los Angeles in March to plead our own case. No decision had been made when Tex called me into the meeting to make my pitch.

I remember walking into that hotel conference room and looking around that big table at all those unfamiliar faces and thinking, *They don't look very sympathetic*. I never had felt comfortable standing up and making speeches, but I was desperate. In the five minutes they gave me, I told those owners Dallas couldn't possibly be a competitive team unless we had a core of solid, experienced players. I argued that we had to field a decent team if we expected to compete for the Dallas market against Lamar Hunt's AFL team, the Dallas Texans. And I pointed out that everyone in the NFL stood to lose gate receipts and other revenues if our team couldn't play the caliber of professional football the fans would demand.

I felt like I begged. The noncommittal expressions on the owners' faces never changed. And I left the room with no indication that my speech had done any good.

If it did, it didn't do much. What the owners announced a few hours later sounded like precious little. Each team would be allowed to protect twenty-five of the thirty-four men on its roster. Of the nine remaining names, we could pick only three from each team.

That would have been stringent enough. But we couldn't even be sure of getting the best three of those worst nine players on each roster. Because each time we picked a player off the unprotected list, a team could remove another name from that list. And to round out their generosity, the owners gave us all of twenty-four hours to make our selections.

I'd done my homework ahead of that meeting—watching hundreds of hours of game films in an attempt to evaluate players on every team in the league. But you don't see much from the bottom nine guys on a roster in game films. I was allowed to interview the other head coaches about their unprotected players. But sitting down face-to-face with opposing coaches to ask for assessments on players' strengths and weaknesses, their potential, and even their history of injury didn't get me much useful information. I could never be sure whether a coach genuinely wanted to be helpful or was trying to keep me from choosing the best players on his list. Was he saying so many good things about someone just to make it look like he wanted me to take the player so that I would be suspicious and not pick him?

Of course I tried not to be too obvious about which players I was most interested in for fear they would remove my second pick after I'd made my initial selection. The whole process felt like a big bizarre poker game with no sure way to tell who was bluffing whom.

I made the best thirty-six picks I could under the circumstances—trying for a balance of offense and defense and filling as many positions as possible at the same time. My final list had a handful of players I was very glad to have, including Frank Clarke, a talented receiver who had been in Paul Brown's doghouse up at Cleveland; Don Heinrich, a veteran backup quarterback who had been with me on the Giants for years; and Jerry Tubbs, a fine linebacker who had irritated '49ers' coach Red Hickey so many times in contract disputes Red left him unprotected. But as optimistic as I wanted to be, I knew I didn't have a lot of talent to work with.

What we didn't have in the way of quality, we tried to make up for in quantity. At least 193 would-be football players came to our first training camp that summer up in Forest Grove, Oregon. Some days our quarterbacks would be throwing passes to receivers they'd never seen before and never saw again after that practice. Greyhound could have made a killing with a regular route between Forest Grove and the Portland airport. But we were so desperate for people we gave tryouts to anyone we thought had the remotest chance to help the team.

I might have gotten discouraged, but I wasn't. Based on my experience in New York, I felt confident I knew what it took to build a strong defense. And my years of analyzing offenses as a defensive coach had taught me how to construct an offense that could beat a defense. In my own mind, I figured it would take three years to develop a solid, winning program. With a five-year contract I could afford to be patient. I didn't expect to win more than two or three games that first year.

Our two blue-chip rookies provided reason to be optimistic about the future. Don Perkins—a compact back at 5'10", 200 pounds, with an explosive, slashing style—showed flashes of brilliance early in training camp. But not until I'd talked him out of giving up and going home in frustration over his failure to even finish the required mile run—unaffectionately dubbed "The Landry Mile"—in the six-minute time I'd set as the minimal standard of conditioning for my backs.

Meredith too convinced me he had the skill and intelligence to become a good NFL quarterback. But productive quarterbacks take longer to develop than effective running backs; there's just so much to learn about running a pro attack. Which is why we talked Eddie LeBaron, the longtime Redskins' quarterback, out of retiring after the '59 season. Unfortunately, Washington still owned the rights to LeBaron and the Redskins demanded compensation. We had to promise Washington our first-round pick in the '61 college draft, which meant losing our best chance at landing a top young prospect in the next year's draft. But we were willing to pay that price to bring Eddie to Dallas because I believed we needed a cagey veteran like LeBaron, who could help teach Meredith the tricks of his trade and give us some starting experience until Don and the rest of the team matured.

Unfortunately, there weren't many other bright spots in training camp that first year. Unless you want to count Jungle Jamey.

To call Jungle Jamey an eccentric would have been like calling Jim Brown a runner. The word just wasn't adequate. Jamey showed up in Forest Grove the second day of camp with a birthday cake for me. When I told him my birthday wasn't until September, he just shrugged and said he knew that, but he wanted me to have it early. He'd driven into camp in a battered '49 Ford with autographs from stem to stern, steer horns mounted on the hood, and a shank of what he claimed was bear meat hanging from the radio antenna. (It looked like beef to me.) A stocky man, who appeared to be somewhere between thirty and forty, he wore ratty shorts, a football jersey, and a white hunter's hat with a snakeskin band. He went barefoot and walked a large white pet rabbit on a leash.

Jamey had obviously come to stay. He began showing up in the dining hall at mealtime. After workouts he would practice kicking barefoot field goals and give advice to any player or coach who would listen. In the dorm at night he'd regale the players with tales of his many adventures as one of the country's most accomplished gate-crashers.

I'd first met Jungle Jamey when I was with the Giants back in 1956. He had also gone by the name of "Beachcomber Jamey" at that time and had been wandering up and down Broadway with a monkey on his shoulder when Ben Agajanian, the Giants' kicker, took him in, gave him some money, and let him serve as a sort of valet for a time. Jamey had adopted the Giants as his team that year and even played Santa Claus at the Giants' family Christmas party.

Jamey was harmless, though strange. And the players got a kick out of him, so I didn't mind him hanging around camp at Forest Grove. I kind of liked Jamey, even if Tex Schramm didn't.

Actually Jamey didn't think much of Tex either. He claimed Tex had no business at camp since he wasn't a player or a coach. He called Tex a freeloader and even took to calling the white rabbit by the name "Texas Freeloader." Tex wasn't amused. Several times he set out looking for Jamey with the intention of throwing him off the grounds. But the players would sneak him from room to room until Tex finally gave up and let him stay the rest of camp.

After Don Perkins suffered a season-ending injury in the preseason College All-Star game, I spent the entire exhibition season constantly juggling personnel in an attempt to find a lineup combination that wouldn't get us penalized for disgrace of game. I probably expected too much from my players, too soon. The complex defensive and offensive philosophies I wanted to use met with resistance from some of the veterans who resented having to learn such an entirely different system in the twilight of their careers. And the complexity of my system served to thoroughly confuse my rookies.

I remember one time in a preseason game against the Giants, Meredith brought the team to the line of scrimmage and noticed middle linebacker Sam Huff lined up in the exact spot where the play was supposed to go. When Don changed the play by calling an audible, both Huff and defensive lineman Rosey Grier immediately shifted to another gap. So Don audibled another play, and this time the two defensive ends, Robustelli and Jim Katcavage, moved. It was as if the veteran Giants could read Don's mind. He hurriedly tried to think of yet another play to call, stuttered, swore out loud, and disgustedly called, "Time out!" The entire veteran Giants' defense broke out laughing as Don just shook his head in total frustration.

* * *

There was plenty for all of us to be frustrated about when we finally got to Dallas to start the regular season. The coaches and the front office staff of the Dallas Cowboys shared a handful of tiny office cubicles we rented on the second floor of an auto club. While we'd be calling around the league in a continuing attempt to work out trades or find out what players we might use who'd been cut by other teams, excited people downstairs would be mapping out vacation plans.

Our practice facilities proved no more desirable than our cramped office space. The only place in Dallas we could find to work out was Burnett Field, an old, abandoned minor league baseball park. The field itself was fine. But the rats that swarmed the locker room at night chewed up our shoes and a lot of leather pads until we strung wires and hung the equipment up high, out in the middle of the room and away from the walls. The showers never got hot and the building stayed so cold that one winter day someone lit a fire in a trash barrel in the training room to keep warm. When we spotted smoke pouring out from under the stands during the middle of practice, my assistant coaches and I went running to put out the fire. But I think most of the players just stood and watched, hoping maybe the place would burn down.

Perhaps the most encouraging thing about that first season was how few hometown fans came out to see us lose. I remember trotting out onto the field at the Cotton Bowl before one game and wondering if we'd shown up on the wrong date. So few fans came to another home game, that when rain began to fall, the entire crowd moved back under the shelter by the concession stands while we continued to play in what looked from the field to be a completely deserted stadium.

And yet, in spite of everything, that first season was an exciting one. I think everyone connected with the Cowboys felt a sense of adventure to be involved in starting the first expansion team in modern NFL history. Fortunately Tex and Clint hadn't expected much that first year either. So even though we lost week after week after week, we played enough close games for us all to be optimistic about the team's future.

The only true highlight came in the next to last week of the season when we shocked the Giants in New York, battling them to a 31–31 tie. And when we landed back at Dallas's Love Field after that New York game, an overwhelming mob of two fans crowded around the gate to welcome us home. One of them held up a sign that read, "Well done, Cowboys!"

At least we had made progress. But we evidently peaked a little too early, because we lost our final game of the year the next week in Detroit to finish with an 0–11–1 record.

It was the worst record posted by any NFL team in eighteen years.

chapter eleven

LIFE AS LOSERS

EVERYTHING should have been a little easier the second time around. We had a different training camp at St. Olaf College in Northfield, Minnesota. But we still didn't receive the big influx of talent we needed to turn things around in our second season. I remember one recruit, I never knew his name, who took the first lap of the required Landry Mile and ran right off the track, up the hill to the locker room, and disappeared forever. A lot of other players didn't last much longer.

Minnesota, as that year's expansion club, had been given the very first pick in every round of the NFL's '61 college draft, a privilege Dallas hadn't gotten before our first season. We'd also given up our first-round pick in the '61 draft to Washington for the rights to Eddie LeBaron and our third-round pick to the Bears for Halas's favor in selecting Meredith in the previous draft. So we didn't have a lot of good choices in '61 either. But we did draft a young defensive end by the name of Bob Lilly, and we obtained the rights to Chuck Howley, a young linebacker who'd played a few games as a rookie with Chicago back in '59 before an injury sidelined him for a year and a half. With those two new talents to add to middle linebacker, Jerry Tubbs, we at least had the footings for a foundation on which to begin building a decent defense during our '61 training camp.

But I knew I had to concentrate most of my own attention on our offense—for a couple reasons. First, with a solid defense realistically still a few years away, I felt we would have to score big points if we hoped to win any games. Second, we needed to generate some excitement on the field if we wanted to attract fans and compete for the Dallas market with Lamar Hunt's Texans, one of the strongest teams in the AFL.

I had never coached offense and the only offense I'd played in the NFL had been those two games with the Giants when I had been forced to play quarterback. But I'd studied every offense in the league to prepare my Giants' defensive teams. And I knew exactly what an offense needed to do to beat the 4-3 defense, which I'd popularized with the Giants and which more and more teams around the league had begun to use.

My basic idea was this: Since the effectiveness of the 4-3 depends on the defensive team recognizing a formation, knowing what plays can be run from that formation, and then recognizing keys that tell them the likely play or plays to expect, the obvious way to stymie the defense was to cut down on recognition time. The less time a defensive player has to recognize a formation and spot keys before the snap of the ball, the harder it is for him to anticipate the play in time to stop it.

So, to cut down on recognition time, I devised a multiple offense system that incorporated every formation in the book, shifted men around on the line, and often started players moving in the backfield prior to the snap of the ball. Instead of two basic formations with a handful of play options from each, we ran forty or fifty basic plays off eight to ten different formations. And since the formations stayed in flux until just before the snap, the opponent's defense had so little time to anticipate and so many variations to consider that they couldn't anticipate nearly as many plays. Creating even an extra split second of uncertainty in the defense gave our quarterbacks that much more time to execute a handoff or get off a pass. And we needed all the time we could get before the opposing defenses swarmed through our weak offensive line.

After the long ordeal of the first year, the '61 season began with a bang when we beat Pittsburgh 27–24 on a last second field goal for the Cowboys' first-ever, regular-season victory. Our second win came the very next week when we played the expansion Vikings and Don Perkins had his first truly outstanding day as a runner.

Perkins turned out to be the biggest highlight of the year, proving amazingly durable for his size by running for almost 1000 yards. He had to earn most of those the hard way, on his own without blocking, and without another effective running back to help share the ball-carrying load. Don was not only an instinctive ball carrier, he surprised everyone by how quickly he mastered the complex offense system. I could always count on Perkins to be where he was supposed to be on every play. And he gained enough league-wide respect to finish second in the Rookie of the Year vote behind the Bears' tight end Mike Ditka.

Some games I started LeBaron at quarterback, some Meredith. Much of the season I resorted to a quarterback shuttle, alternating the two of them every other play. I wanted to capitalize on Eddie's experience, while getting Meredith some of his own. Using our new offensive system, we finished the '61 season with an improved 4–10 record—though two of the four wins came at the expense of the even more hapless Minnesota Vikings.

We played some exciting, if unpredictable, offensive football in 1962, running up high scores in several games. I continued to use my two-quarterback system, despite the growing public clamor to go with youth and make Meredith my number-one quarterback.

I tried to ignore the critics who called me indecisive, because that wasn't the issue. I knew full well Don Meredith would be the starting quarterback who could make the Cowboys into winners; and he already had the skills needed for the job. But I didn't want to rush him. I didn't want to destroy his confidence and have him begin thinking of himself as a losing quarterback before we could get him the supporting cast of offensive help we needed to become winners. I also didn't want to sacrifice him to psychological abuse from fans, because fans always turn on a quarterback first when a team isn't winning.

And it wasn't just a matter of protecting Don emotionally. I hated to subject him to the kind of physical beating our quarterback had to take playing behind our ineffective offensive line.

Cowboys' quarterbacks had it rough in those early days. One game I noticed Eddie LeBaron stepping up behind the center and raising his right hand before he bent down to take the snap. He did the same thing on the next play. And again the third down. When he came trotting off the field at the end of that offensive series, I asked him, "Eddie, what were you doing out there? Why were you raising your hand like that before you took the snap?"

"Oh," he said, "I thought it might help if I signaled for a fair catch."

That's only a slight exaggeration. For even though our offense scored a lot of points in 1962 and we improved our record to 5–8–1, game films continued to show more mistakes than highlights. We had a lot of lookout blocks. That's where a pass blocker would make an attempt and then yell, "Look out, Eddie! Here he comes!"

Some of our mistakes were pretty bizarre. Like the time we received the longest, costliest penalty in NFL history—99 yards and 9 points.

It came late in a game against Pittsburgh. We'd just intercepted a Bobby Layne pass on our own 1-yard line and thought we would surprise the Steelers with a bomb. LeBaron took the snap, dropped back into the end zone, and sailed the ball far downfield. Frank Clarke, who had beaten his defender, gathered the pass in near midfield and galloped all the way for a 99-yard touchdown—the longest scoring pass in NFL history at that time.

But an official had thrown a penalty flag back at the Cowboys' goal line. One of our linemen had been holding Big Daddy Lipscomb, the Steelers' 6'6", 280-pound defensive tackle. Since the infraction had occurred 2 yards deep in our end zone, referee Emil Heintz not only motioned the play back, he signaled a safety to award Pittsburgh 2 points. Spotting the flag and having such a spectacular play nullified by a penalty was maddening enough. But when the referee's arms went up to signal a safety, I was incredulous. I charged onto the field, screaming in protest, and demanding an explanation from the officials. Players argued. The officials tried to sort out the confusion as the crowd booed for ten straight minutes. (We'd finally found a way to get our fans into the game.)

The referee claimed the rules stated that an offensive penalty occurring in the offensive team's end zone resulted in an automatic safety. I stood right in the man's face, shouting angrily, protesting that I'd never heard such a ridiculous rule. But he held his ground and the rest of the officials backed him up. I still couldn't believe it. Finally frustrated, I turned and stormed off the field, stopping once to shout back bitterly, "You better be right! That's all I can say: You better be right!"

I was so mad. And it just so happened that my minister was at the game to witness both the call and my uncharacteristic outburst. After the game he said to Alicia, "You tell Tom, whatever he said to that official out there, I know God forgives him."

Good thing, too. Because we found out later the referee was right. Though none of my coaches, and none of the Pittsburgh coaches had heard of it, the regulation was there on page 65 of the *Official Rules of Professional Football*: "It is a safety when the offense commits a foul and the spot of enforcement is behind the goal line."

I still don't like that rule. But it remains on the books almost thirty years after that day. It turned a 99-yard touchdown for us into 2 points for the Steelers in a game we went on to lose by just 2 points—30–28.

It seemed even the rules conspired against the Cowboys in those early days. And yet we usually made enough embarrassing mistakes of our own to lose most games.

Like the day against the Browns when Meredith came to the line of scrimmage and called an audible. Our guard Joe Bob Isbell thought he was supposed to pull and trap on the play Don called. And the other guard, Andy Cvercko, thought *he* was to pull. At the snap, both men pulled back from their positions in the line and headed opposite directions, colliding head-on just behind the center and nearly knocking each other out in front of eighty thousand Cleveland fans.

When we showed that play in our film session the next day the entire team howled as if it was the funniest thing they had ever seen in their lives. I think the only ones not laughing were Cvercko and Isbell. And me.

While I can now look back at those days and laugh about many of the crazy things that happened, I have to admit I didn't see much humor at the time. One day in practice, when Cornell Green intercepted a Meredith pass, Don took off and chased Cornell all over the field, waving his helmet over his head like a lethal weapon, the entire Cowboys' team broke up laughing. My response in the next team meeting was the stern announcement: "Gentlemen, nothing funny ever happens on a football field . . . if we can help it."

Because I took football so seriously, it was sometimes difficult to relate to players who didn't. At the top of that category I'd have to put Sam Baker, who kicked for the Cowboys for two seasons. It often seemed like Sam lived to aggravate me.

In training camp one year Sam refused to run the Landry Mile, pointing to the pre-camp letter sent to all players that said "all linemen and backs" would be timed in the mile run at the beginning of camp. He argued that since the letter said nothing about kickers, he didn't have to run. When he finally did consent to take the four laps, he actually ran only the straightaways and walked all the curves to finish with the worst mile time in Cowboys' history.

One day I was lecturing the squad on the need to develop more harmony on a football team, when I heard a resonant "hmm" rising from the back of the room. It was Baker, trying to get the harmony started by giving everyone the right pitch.

He once walked into our locker room in Pittsburgh before a game with the Steelers, carrying a potted orange tree and wearing a goofy grin.

Another time Baker missed the team's charter flight back to training camp after a preseason game in Cleveland, but somehow managed to catch a later commercial flight. It was four o'clock in the morning when his knock on my dorm room door awakened me. As I groggily opened the door, he snapped off a cheerful salute and announced, "Baker reporting for duty, sir!" I informed him he was fined $1000 for missing the plane and went back to bed. And after the second season, I traded him away and found another kicker.

A few years later Baker and I were almost reunited. I had been named to coach in the annual Pro Bowl game and needed to name some special team personnel to my squad. I asked my assistant coach Dick Nolan, "Who was the best kicker in the NFL this year?"

Dick replied, "Sam Baker."

So I asked, "Okay, who's the second best?"

A lot of people over the years have assumed I had similarly frustrating feelings about Don Meredith—that I never really liked or respected him because of his fun-loving, flippant attitude. But that's just not true. I liked Don from the start and he very quickly earned my respect as a football player.

He aggravated me at times, all right. And he deserved his fun-loving image, always trying to lighten things up— making smart remarks in the back of the room during team

meetings, humming honky-tonk tunes in the huddle between plays.

I'm afraid I didn't understand Don as well at the time as
I wish I had. Other people often made such a big deal of the
contrast between Don and me—the irreverent quarterback
without a care in the world and his superserious coach who
never cracks a smile. And at times our differences did create
tension between us.

But looking back with another quarter-century of
experience and insight, I think Don and I were a lot more
alike than either of us realized at the time. He cared just as
much about football and winning as I did. We just showed it
in different ways.

I remember that first Cowboys' win on opening day in
1961. I started Don and played him most of the game until
he threw a second-half interception that Pittsburgh returned
for a go-ahead touchdown. So I pulled him and sent in
LeBaron. Don came to the sidelines, joked a little with his
teammates, and then sat on the bench and cried as Eddie
rallied the team.

There were other incidents, other clues. As much
Maalox as he downed, I should have realized Don was just
hiding his insecurities, his fears, his longings, his real
emotions behind that mask of humor. After all, I concealed
my own feelings behind another kind of mask.

As a coach, I'd very quickly earned a reputation as a
stoic—a stone-faced figure on the sidelines who never lost
his cool. A lot of people assumed I didn't have any feelings.

The explanation for my cool sideline image isn't that I
don't have any emotions, but that I deliberately control
them. By the time I left the football field as a player and
began coaching on the sidelines, I realized that the expression of emotion interfered with my ability to think clearly
and make the complex judgments and snap decisions
needed to coach defense in the NFL. My intense, competitive nature had always come out in the aggressive way I'd
played football. But standing on the sidelines, I had to do

After an injury ended my quarterbacking career, I punted and played fullback on University of Texas Longhorn football teams that won two major bowl games. But the very best thing that happened to me in college was Alicia.

For a couple of transplants fresh from the open spaces of Texas, the chance to play pro ball in New York and live in the world's biggest city seemed like a great family adventure. Here we are in 1955 taking a stroll in Central Park with Tom, Jr., and Kitty, and then later practicing Tom's punting form.

After one year with the New York Yankees of the All-American Football Conference I joined the NFL's New York Giants as a defensive halfback and punter. I soon realized I'd never make it in pro football if I depended on my limited physical skills. My only hope for success was preparation and knowledge. I had to know what my opponent was going to do before he did it. (Right: Giant training camp in 1950.)

The 1941 Mission High School Eagles went 12-0 in our championship season. That autumn of glory, shared with my boyhood friends and teammates, remains perhaps my most meaningful season in fifty years of football. I'm number 88 in the back row; Coach Bob Martin is at the far right in the back. At the age of nineteen I earned my wings in the Army Air Corps and went off to war in Europe as copilot of a B-17 bomber. I'm second from left in row two of the training group photo below.

As player-coach, then full-time assistant coach of the Giant defense, I spent a lot of time drawing up ways to stop the great Cleveland teams and their superstar fullback Jim Brown. I owe my start in coaching to head coach Jim Lee Howell who gave me the defense while turning the offense over to Vince Lombardi. That experience during the Giants' glory years prepared me to become the thirty-five-year-old head coach of the Cowboys in 1960. (Left-Giants' coaches. From left to right, that's Vince and Johnny Dell Isola in front. In back I'm beside Jim Lee Howell and Ken Kavanaugh.)

Here I am (number 49) making a fourth quarter interception in a 14-10 Giants win over the Washington Redskins during the '52 season. Number 45 in the middle of the picture is my Hall of Famer teammate, Emlen Tunnell.

Despite the image many fans have of pregame pep talks, there's little I felt I could do in the locker room other than conduct a last-minute review of the game plan with my quarterbacks. The real preparation takes place on the practice field and in coaches' meetings (above) during the preceding week. Despite my reputation as a mild-mannered stoic, I've disputed my share of questionable calls as I'm doing here (below) for the benefit of official Jerry Markbreit.

I'd never have lasted twenty-nine years without great assistants, many of whom went on to coach other teams. Mike Ditka (not shown) and Danny Reeves (above) were as much like sons as assistants before becoming head coaches in Chicago and Denver. Dick Nolan (top left) played beside me on the Giants and stayed with me till the end, with time out to coach the '49ers and the Saints. Gene Stallings (right) coached with me fourteen years before taking over the Cardinals. And all-time-great receiver Raymond Berry (bottom left) coached with me two years before he coached the Patriots.

I don't think I ever saw a greater natural halfback than Tony Dorsett.

Tony Tomsic/NFL Photos

Tony Tomsic/NFL Photos

Danny White (number 11) never got the credit he deserved as an NFL quarterback; I don't think anyone could have done better following Staubach.

Critics said we wasted our first draft pick in 1969 on a Yale running back; but Calvin Hill proved them wrong.

NFL Photos

The one player who did more than any other to create the image of the Dallas Cowboys as "America's Team" had to be quarterback Roger Staubach. As long as any time remained on the clock, Roger believed we could win the game. And something about his competitive confidence made his teammates believe it, too. Here he is in Super Bowl XII.

I had the great fortune of coaching many fine players in my career. Bob Hayes changed forever the role of speed in NFL offenses.

Mike Ditka played on two Cowboy Super Bowl teams for us.

The Cowboys lost some heartbreakers over the years. One of the most memorable came when Bart Starr pulled a last-second quarterback sneak in the 1967 NFL Championship for a 21-17 Packer win in the "Ice Bowl."

For the first twenty-five years the Dallas Cowboys operated with the same owner, general manager, and coach. The continuity of that alliance was not only unique in the history of professional sports, it provided the foundation on which the Cowboys and our great Cowboy tradition was built. Here I'm standing with minority owner Bedford Wynne, general manager Tex Schramm, and Cowboy owner Clint Murchison, Jr.

The first two players signed by the Dallas Cowboys were two of the best. The University of New Mexico's Don Perkins (above, running into the line) was the Cowboys' running game in our early years. And SMU All-American quarterback Don Meredith (right) courageously hung in there, taking a physical and emotional beating for years before we got him the support he needed to take us to the championship level of the NFL. My 1965 decision to stick with Meredith may have been the most crucial of my career.

Since 1959 when I made a commitment to put God first in my life, I've tried to make my family second and my career third. The greatest benefit of retirement has been the added opportunity to spend time with Alicia and my family. Here's the entire Landry clan today. From left to right, my daughter Lisa and her husband Gary Childress, Alicia, me, Tom, Jr., my daughter Kitty and her husband Eddie Phillips. Our two grandkids, Ryan and Jennifer Phillips, have always lived close enough for regular get-togethers with their proud grandpa. And they sometimes still call me Coach.

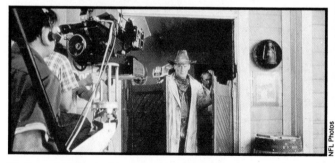

Life away from football has given me more time for golf–a game I've loved since youth(top). In retirement I've also added singing credits to my commercial acting career that began in this American Express spot in 1982(bottom). But one of the biggest highlights of my retirement, along with my election to the Pro Football Hall of Fame, was Tom Landry Day in Dallas(center).

something with all that pent-up intensity. I rechanneled it into a total concentration of focus.

One reason I so seldom reacted to a big Cowboys' play was because I hardly ever saw any of our offensive plays. I always knew what play we had called; I didn't have to watch it. The only uncertainty was how the opposition reacted; it was their defense I needed to watch and analyze so I would know best how to counter it. And once a play ended, I never had time to react, immediately shifting focus to my game plan to decide what play I should send in next.

I'm afraid that same habit of concentration—that ability to maintain an extremely narrow focus—which I found so helpful on the sideline wasn't such a positive trait off the field. I sometimes passed people in the hallway at work without speaking, preoccupied in game plan thoughts or thinking about the text of a luncheon speech. Combined with my reserved personality and an upbringing that made it difficult for me to express emotion, this tendency to tune out everything and everyone around me contributed to the image a lot of people, including many of my players, had: that I was distant, uncaring, and unfriendly.

Today if someone speaks to me in the hall or on a sidewalk, I'm much more apt to notice them. While my tunnel vision can sometimes still cut me off from other people, I think I've improved in this area as the years have passed.

But my power of concentration was just one of the reasons for the unflappable reputation I earned in those early years of frustration and continuing loss. Just as significant was the continuing confidence I had in the system. I kept telling myself and my players that we'd keep on improving; it was just a matter of time, experience, and the right personnel. And our record did improve from no wins in '60, to four in '61, and five in '62.

Another important factor was my new Christian faith. While I'll always have more to learn about applying the Bible's teaching to my daily living, the priorities lesson I'd learned as a new Christian continued to affect me. I saw that

I often let football become more than a career to me—it was sometimes an obsession.

As I began to understand what the Bible taught about loving God and my family, it helped me put football and winning and losing into perspective. While it didn't mean I wanted to win any less, I realized whatever I did or didn't accomplish as coach of the Cowboys wasn't the most important thing in my life. And that helped take some of the pressure off.

And then I had never forgotten what Alicia and I had realized when I took the job: I was bound to get fired sooner or later. I'd already made it to the three-year mark by the end of the '62 season. Any more time was gravy.

The '63 season began with high hopes and expectations. After traveling the northern half of the country like nomads the first three years, the Cowboys finally established a permanent training camp at California Lutheran College in Thousand Oaks, California, where we would return every summer for the rest of my time with the Cowboys.

By this time we had begun building the core of an improving defense, having already added George Andrie, Mike Gaechter, and Cornell Green to the names of Lilly, Howley, and Tubbs. And now in '63 we drafted a promising linebacker out of Alabama by the name of Lee Roy Jordan. The high-octane, multiple offense that had scored so many points in '62 promised to be another year better with several new faces of its own.

Tex Maule, *Sports Illustrated*'s pro football writer, actually picked us to win the Eastern Conference title in his magazine's special fall football issue. Lamar Hunt's Dallas Texan team had left town to become the Kansas City Chiefs; so attendance promised to increase. Everything seemed set for '63 to be a breakthrough year for the Dallas Cowboys.

Then the season started. Other teams seemed better prepared to defend against our varied offensive attack. And we weren't enough better to crank it up another notch. The offense sputtered and struggled all year.

An emotional low point for the Cowboys, the city of Dallas, and the nation came on November 22 when one of our trainers ran out on the practice field during our Friday afternoon workout yelling that President Kennedy had been shot in downtown Dallas, only three miles away. The news stunned everyone; I dismissed practice and we all left to listen to radio broadcasts until the final word came: The president was dead.

The NFL decided not to cancel any of the games that weekend. When we were introduced in Cleveland on Sunday, moments after a silent tribute to the memory of our slain president, the Cowboys of Dallas were booed with a bitterness we had never encountered anywhere before. It was as if the events of that afternoon had suddenly tainted everything having to do with Dallas, Texas. We were booed lustily in every city we visited the rest of that year and into the next.

At home, our own fans had begun to boo for other reasons. They thought four years of losing football was enough. When we finished the '63 season with a disappointing 4–10 mark, a step backwards from the year before, more than a few people were calling for a change in coaches.

While I tried to ignore my critics, I couldn't ignore the disappointing results on the field that season. When I had arrived in Dallas I had confidently announced a five-year plan to make the Cowboys into winners. Privately I had figured it would take three. But now I was heading into my fifth year with no certainty of immediate success. I began wondering if it was time again to start thinking about life after football. Maybe God wanted me to be doing something else. I began to pray for some sense of his direction, some indication of his will for my life.

Through all the Cowboys' early struggles, Clint Murchison had been a wonderfully patient and supportive owner. Because of our organizational chain of command, Tex had a lot more interaction with Clint than I did. So I didn't know him all that well in those early years, but what I had seen of

Clint I liked. Once a 130-pound halfback at MIT, he was
never a physically impressive person. A short man, with
close-cropped hair, his lively eyes took in the world through
horn-rimmed glasses that made him look more like some
conservative professor than the wheeling, dealing business
tycoon he actually was.

Clint enjoyed a reputation as a big practical joker. And
even through the Cowboys' darkest days he maintained a
sense of humor about his football team. One time back in
the '62 season, we experienced engine trouble on the flight
home from a game. Our charter pilot made an emergency
landing in Memphis and pulled the plane to a stop at the
loneliest, farthest gate from the terminal where a three-man
emergency crew waited for us in a jeep. As the players
stood, preparing to deplane, Clint rose from his seat and
bellowed, "Look sharp, men! This may be our biggest
reception yet."

Clint was also an encourager. Several times through the
years, when things looked bleakest, I'd get a note in my
mail, expressing his confidence, offering a word of encouragement or an inspiring or humorous quote. When it came
to management style, Clint claimed to have learned his most
important principle from his father, Clint Murchison, Sr.,
who had been one of the richest and most colorful of Texas's
great oil barons. Clint said his daddy always told him if you
found a man you trusted and believed in, you should give
him a job to do and then leave him alone so he can do it.
And that's just what Clint did with the Cowboys. He gave
Tex Schramm the complete authority he needed to run the
Cowboys as general manager, and that same freedom was
passed on to me as head coach.

So it was that Tex went to Clint to talk about the
growing public criticism I'd received at the end of the '63
season. The fact I was going into the last year of my contract
guaranteed continuing speculation about my future. Tex
told Clint, "We have to do something about all this public
criticism of Landry."

"That's easy enough," Clint replied. "We'll just give

Tom a new ten-year contract. That ought to shut people up."

Ten years! To take effect in 1965 at the end of my first five-year agreement. I couldn't believe it. And neither could anyone else. No coach in any professional major-league sport had ever received an eleven-year commitment. And all I had done to deserve it was to compile a terribly unimpressive record of thirteen wins, thirty-eight losses, and three ties over four straight losing seasons.

I had been praying and asking God for some sort of direction and guidance about my future. And now it seemed I had my answer. I took that remarkable ten-year contract as clear indication of God's will for my life. And I never again doubted that coaching was to be my life's calling.

If I was ever going to have doubts, it might have been that next year. Eddie LeBaron finally left football to practice law and I turned the reins of our offense over completely to Don Meredith for 1964. But Don tore up his knee during the preseason and played the entire year with torn cartilage— perhaps the most courageous and gutsy season any professional quarterback ever played.

What made it worse was that our line couldn't have protected a healthy quarterback, let alone a hobbling one. After watching Don play early in the season, one writer proposed the creation of a new offensive statistic: "Yardage lost attempting to live." Don had to absorb inhuman punishment almost every week, suffering one nagging injury after another all season long. Yet he refused to quit. (We didn't have anyone else and the doctors said there was no danger in waiting till after the season to operate.)

After we had won the last game of the season to finish with a 5–8–1 record, I walked over to Don's locker to congratulate him. He had to shake hands with his left one because he'd injured his right one in the first quarter. "You did a fine job in a tough situation this year," I said. "We're gonna get you more protection next year."

Then, as I moved on to talk to other players, Don grinned and called out after me, "Promise?"

But as I began to think seriously about the next year, I had to face the fact that my five-year plan was over. The system I'd placed so much faith in still hadn't produced a season with more victories than defeats. And I couldn't help wondering how much longer it would take to turn the Cowboys into winners.

chapter twelve
ON THE VERGE OF SUCCESS

IN THOSE first five years I had done everything I knew how to do to shape the Dallas Cowboys into a winning football team. And the Cowboys' front office led by Tex Schramm had proven at least as innovative as I had tried to be on the field. More than just a knowledgeable football executive, Tex was a master organizer who systematically began to build a solid foundation for the Cowboys' franchise. He was also a natural promoter who understood and used the power of public relations to create goodwill and respect for our organization in Dallas and throughout football.

The Dallas Cowboys' organization pioneered the way for professional football to move into the modern computer age. During his network television days in New York, Tex had seen how computers could compile, organize, and analyze seemingly unmanageable amounts of data.

So Tex had decided computers could help us achieve our biggest priority—finding and signing the kind of football players who could help the Cowboys become winners in the shortest possible time. To do that Gil Brandt and the Cowboys' scouting department would begin collect-

ing information on maybe two thousand football players in
their freshman year of college. Each year they would
accumulate more information on these players until we
narrowed the prospects down to maybe five to six hundred
prospects in their senior year. As time approached for the
annual NFL draft of college football players, we would
whittle the list down to the best three hundred. Finally,
those three hundred players had to be ranked from one to
three hundred, in order of our interest in drafting them.
Since it took an hour or more to read and evaluate the
information on each of those three hundred players, there
was no way humanly possible to be objective. The ranking
task just became too exhausting.

What made the process even more uncertain was trying
to compare one scout's evaluation of a runner he saw in
Oregon with another scout's rating of a defensive end in
Georgia. The system relied so much on personal, subjective
bias there could be no real hope of objective comparisons.

So Tex presented this basic problem to the Service
Bureau Corporation, an IBM subsidiary, in 1962. SBC sent
computer whiz Salam Querishi, a native of India, to work
with the Cowboys. While some of my coaches thought the
whole idea a bit crazy, I was glad to try anything that might
help get me more and better football players.

It turned out to be a complicated project—an Indian
who knew nothing about football working with a bunch of
Cowboys' coaches who knew nothing about computers. Or
about Indians for that matter.

It took forever just to try to determine the elements that
made a good football player. To start with we gave Querishi
a total of three hundred variables we looked at in evaluating
football talent. But the most sophisticated computers at the
time could work with only eighty variables, so we had to
refine our list. Querishi helped us organize those into five
basic dimensions we wanted to analyze. To do that we
needed to work through all the semantics to find the key
words to describe what we all wanted to evaluate. Finally
we had the five intangible traits we wanted to analyze:

character, quickness and body control, competitiveness, strength and explosiveness, and mental alertness. (We could physically measure things like height, weight, and speed so we didn't include those.)

Even after we had that framework, we had to have a standard means of accurately measuring those qualities. So Querishi designed a questionnaire for every scout to use in evaluating the variables under each of our five basic traits. Scouts assigned 1–9 scores to each of these variables and those scores were added up to judge each of the five traits. By carefully analyzing the ratings given by each scout, we even refined the system to allow for the individual biases and the differences in scoring that occurred from scout to scout.

While it took a few years to fine-tune the system, we'd begun to use it in 1963. We knew there was no way to be 100 percent accurate when imperfect human beings evaluated other imperfect human beings. But we were looking for any edge we could get over our competition.

It wasn't that we weren't willing to gamble when it came to drafting either. Even at a time when the Cowboys needed all the immediate help we could get, we didn't hesitate to spend a draft pick on a future—a player who wouldn't be available for another year or more down the road. In the '64 draft alone we spent six picks on future prospects, including a seventh-round pick on Bob Hayes, the world champion sprinter who planned to run in the '64 Olympics; a tenth-round pick on Navy quarterback Roger Staubach, who had a four-year military commitment before he could ever hope to play; and a thirteenth-round pick on quarterback Jerry Rhome, who had another year of eligibility left at the University of Tulsa.

When it came to finding football talent, Gil Brandt and the scouting department left no stone unturned. They combed the country to find talented unknowns from small schools and from black colleges. Defensive lineman Jethro Pugh, who came out of Elizabeth City State College in New

Jersey to become a longtime Cowboys' star, is just one such example.

And then there were the many free agents Gil signed, players no one had even bothered to draft. Some of them, like receiver Pete Gent and defensive back Cornell Green, hadn't even played college football. They were merely talented athletes we were willing to take a chance on.

Dick Nolan, our defensive backfield coach when Cornell joined the team, laughs every time he remembers the day in training camp when he noticed the rookie squirming around and acting terribly uncomfortable. When he asked Cornell what was wrong, Cornell said he didn't think his hip pads fit right. Nolan had him drop his pants only to discover he had the pads on completely backwards; the piece designed to protect the tailbone was in front where it painfully pinched Cornell's crotch every time he took a step.

The first time Cornell ever tried to make a tackle in an actual football game was against Paul Hornung and the defending champion Green Bay Packers; Hornung got away from him twice that night. But even though he had a lot to learn, we had time to let him. And the risk paid off when he eventually became an All-Pro player.

Another innovation we introduced with the Cowboys grew out of my industrial engineering background: quality control. Suppose you have a factory that manufactures screws. If you're concerned about your company's success you have to maintain the quality of your product. To make sure you're doing that, you routinely check your product to make sure the screws are of a consistently high quality. If a particular machine isn't producing uniformly consistent screws, you have to make adjustments or perhaps get a new machine.

I thought the same principle could be applied to football: Before you can assure the consistent quality of your product, you have to find where any problems are. So I instituted the foundation of a quality control program at the end of our very first season in Dallas. We took all the game film for the season, cut it apart, and reassembled it by specific plays—all the fullback draw plays together, all the screen passes, all the off-tackle slants—and put it in chronological order for the entire season. Then we could trace the effectiveness of a specific play throughout the season. We could see whether it became more or less effective, what changed, what needed to be changed to make it work better, and whether or not we should even keep it in the playbook for next year.

Eventually we honed our system by hiring a quality control coach whose sole job was to cut apart our films and analyze the effectiveness of each play. And instead of waiting until the end of the year, we did it after every game so we could spot our weaknesses quicker and make mid-course corrections whenever possible. The advent of video tape made our quality control efforts even easier and the computerized controls of more recent video editing technology made it possible to splice together action in an infinite number of variations—not just by specific plays, but by situation (second down and long yardage, third and short), or by player so we could show a player what he specifically did to make a certain play succeed or fail. Under the direction of long-term Cowboy cameraman Bob Friedman we not only filmed every down of every game, but every day's practice as well.

Yet another innovation in our Cowboys' system actually began during the off-season in 1965. Realizing that my original five-year plan hadn't paid off with a winning-caliber football team, I took another page out of my industrial engineering book and brought in Dr. Ray Fletcher, industrial psychologist, to help make us better managers for the future.

He helped us articulate our offensive and defensive philosophies in short, understandable statements. He showed us how to then establish goals that would allow us to implement that philosophy. He taught us that every goal needed to be reasonable, attainable, and measurable.

Then, using a pyramid-type approach, we developed an overall team goal, followed by subordinate offensive and

defensive goals that would enable us to achieve the team
goal. Position coaches added their own goals under the
broader defensive or offensive goals. Finally we would
establish individual goals for each player.

Once we agreed on our philosophy and goals, we
began deciding what specific steps we'd use to achieve
them. I don't think all my assistants bought into this sort of
goalsetting at first; none of us felt particularly comfortable
with the initial exercise. We got better at it only as we used it
year after year. But from its beginning in 1965, it gave the
staff and our players a sense of common direction. Everyone
knew what was expected of them.

My confidence in 1965 got an additional boost from the
talented bunch of rookies I saw in training camp. With
Meredith suffering so many injuries the year before, we had
drafted quarterback Craig Morton as extra insurance. Both
he and our future pick from the previous draft, Jerry
Rhome, looked like they had NFL potential. Malcolm
Walker seemed like a strong candidate at center, and
defensive tackle Jethro Pugh was an absolute steal as an
eleventh-round pick. Ralph Neely would obviously become
a fine lineman. A free-agent quarterback out of South
Carolina by the name of Dan Reeves didn't have the skills to
compete with all the other talent at that position, but his
determination, intelligence, adaptability, and most of all, his
character, impressed me so much we kept moving him
around until we found him a spot on the roster as a running
back and flanker.

And then there was Bobby Hayes. I'd never been a big
proponent of track men who played football. But Bobby
turned out to be a football player who happened to have run
track. Watching him execute his first post pattern was all it
took to convince me he deserved the title of "World's Fastest
Human." He could blow by a defensive man so far, so fast,
my sudden concern was whether our quarterbacks could
throw the ball far enough to reach him before he ran right
out of the stadium. What an offensive weapon!

I was just as encouraged on defense. I had shifted Bob Lilly from his original position of defensive end into the tackle spot midway through 1963. He was already beginning to show the kind of dominance that was to make him the best ever to play his position.

Having introduced the multiple offense as a means of defeating the old 4-3 defense, a number of other teams had begun to copy our basic attack. So we had adjusted on defense and developed a variation of the 4-3, which I termed the Flex and had introduced for the '64 season. With a year to get familiar with it, the Flex promised to be more effective in '65.

We turned in a very inconsistent preseason—winning impressively over powerful Green Bay one week and getting blown out by the Minnesota Vikings the following week by a score of 57–17. I gave all three of my quarterbacks playing time. Meredith had some typical early-season soreness in his throwing arm. Of the two rookies, Rhome looked the most impressive; Morton seemed to be struggling a bit with the complexity of the offense.

Clint Murchison had never made a personnel suggestion to me in our five years together. So I had to laugh at the note he sent me before our final preseason game against the Chicago Bears that was scheduled to be played up in Tulsa, where Clint had a major investment in the cement business and where Jerry Rhome just happened to have been the hometown college football hero for the past three years. Clint's note said, "You know I wouldn't ever try to influence your decision about who to play at quarterback this week. But do you know how hard it would be to move a cement plant?"

Meredith and Rhome alternated quarters with Jerry having the best night—10 for 17 passing and three touchdowns in a strong Cowboys' win. An impressive enough showing to spark speculation that the Cowboys might have a battle for the starting quarterback spot.

But I hadn't forgotten the performance Don Meredith had turned in the previous season—playing hurt all year, getting beaten up week after week. I felt he deserved a chance to show what he could do on two legs behind an improved line.

We came out of the blocks fast, winning home games handily over New York and Washington. Attendance for just those two home games was more than the entire season's attendance in 1960. It looked like professional football had finally arrived in Dallas, Texas.

But Meredith hadn't passed well in either win. And over the next three games—all losses—he slumped so badly I began shuttling between Rhome and Morton. The rookies both did well. But when Don looked a little better during our fourth straight loss, I named him to start the next game in Pittsburgh. With so many young players on the offensive unit, I thought we needed as much experience as possible in the quarterback spot. If Don could produce, it wasn't too late to turn the season around.

But in Pittsburgh Don had a terrible day, hitting only twelve of thirty-four passes in a 22–13 loss to a clearly inferior team. When I walked into the locker room after the game, no one looked up. I stood in the middle of the room, groping for words. I told the team that in the six years I had been with the Cowboys, this was the first time I'd been truly ashamed of the team's performance. Still no one looked up.

After a minute I said, "I'm sorry. Maybe the problem is with our system, with the approach we . . ." My voice broke and I coughed as tears dribbled down my cheeks. I don't know who was more embarrassed, me or the players.

Meredith stood up and said it was his fault. That he was sorry he'd played so poorly. That he'd been trying his hardest. But he was going to work even harder and we could start winning again.

No one else said anything.

I walked into the coaches' locker room, closed the door, and cried. Everything had looked so good for this year. How could it have gone so bad?

When I finally came out of the locker room to give my postgame interviews, the press naturally wanted to know who I planned to start at quarterback the next week. I said, "I haven't decided that yet. But after today it's safe to say I'm going to be reevaluating our quarterback situation."

That Monday and Tuesday were two of the worst days of my coaching career. Everyone—public and press alike—had turned on Meredith. With good reason. He had only completed an embarrassing 38 percent of his passes all season. We couldn't possibly win with that kind of performance. I had to go with one or both of the rookies.

And yet that decision went against everything I had ever believed about bringing quarterbacks along slowly. We desperately needed experience and Don was the only one who had it.

I tossed and turned for two miserable nights. I prayed for wisdom to make the right decision. But there seemed to be no right decision.

Finally I called Meredith into my office. He sat down, his face somber, ready for the blow he knew had to be coming. When I looked at him and said, "Don, I believe in you. You're my starting quarterback the rest of this year," Don began to cry. Then we both cried.

On Wednesday, at my weekly noontime press conference, I made the announcement and explained my reasoning. I felt our biggest need at the quarterback position in 1965 was experience. Don had it. He'd proved his ability to withstand hardship the year before, and I believed he was the quarterback who could get the Cowboys back on track.

That may have been the toughest decision I ever made as a coach. And certainly one of the most important of my career. Don came through, rallied us to win five out of our last seven games and conclude the season at 7–7, our first break-even season in history.

Our .500 performance was good enough for second place behind Cleveland that year in a weak Eastern Conference. That meant we had won our first postseason opportunity and would play in the annual "Playoff Bowl" in Miami against the Baltimore Colts. Most teams disdained what was sometimes called the NFL's "Loser's Bowl" between the two conference runners-up. And it wasn't truly a playoff because neither team could advance any further. But for us it was an exciting milestone. Over two thousand Dallas fans made the long trip to see us soundly whipped by the Colts by the score of 35–3.

Asked after the game to assess the reason for the embarrassing loss, I could only shrug and reply, "It was a team effort."

But I saw more reason than ever to hope for better things next year. Finally, after six grueling seasons of struggle, I knew the Dallas Cowboys were on the verge of success.

chapter thirteen

THE COLD BLOW
OF THE ICE BOWL

PRO FOOTBALL was also on the verge—of a historic agreement.

On June 8, 1966, at a press conference in New York, the NFL and the AFL announced an agreement to merge. The two leagues had been warring bitterly for years with escalating player contracts, attempted raids of each other's personnel, and more than a few lawsuits. Ironically, the chief negotiators for the two sides, who had been meeting secretly for months, were the Cowboys' Tex Schramm and Lamar Hunt, owner of the Kansas City Chiefs (formerly the Dallas Texans). The two men had been opposing commanders during the Battle for Dallas, which had served as the opening salvo of the football wars back in 1960–62. Now they sat together on either side of Pete Rozelle, smiling at the prospect of peace and announcing the first competition between the leagues. Starting after the '66 season, the AFL champion and the NFL champion were to meet in an annual postseason showdown Lamar Hunt thought should be called a "Super Bowl."

But as I went into the summer of 1966 I was more concerned about the Cowboys' preseason than I was the postseason. Usually I viewed the exhibition season as a chance to experiment with procedures and personnel; we didn't worry much about final scores. This year would be different.

I knew we'd taken a big step forward to finish '65 with a break-even 7–7 record. But after so many losing seasons, I felt it crucial to establish a winning pattern in the preseason. I wanted my players to get used to the emotional feel of winning.

Hoping to add an outside running threat to complement Don Perkins' inside rushing ability, I switched speedy Mel Renfro from defensive back to halfback where he turned in some very impressive performances in the preseason. But after he sustained some injuries I decided not to risk the possibility of losing Mel and his invaluable athletic skills. I moved him back to defensive back where he could be the hitter instead of the hittee.

The next man in line for the halfback spot, Dan Reeves, didn't have Mel's speed. But he ran smart, turned in a superb preseason of his own, and gave our outside running game an added wrinkle. An old college quarterback, Dan could throw the halfback option pass like no one I'd seen since Frank Gifford back in my Giants' days.

The '66 draft had brought us offensive guard John Niland, defensive lineman Willie Townes, and two promising backs—Les Shy and Walt Garrison. Garrison, a rodeo competitor and real-life cowboy whose contract called for a new horse trailer rather than cash as a signing bonus, looked especially good as a backup for Don Perkins at fullback.

We took the first two preseason games out in California against the '49ers and the Rams. Public excitement over the Cowboys ran so high the Cotton Bowl actually sold out for our annual exhibition game with the Packers. As was our custom every August when Green Bay came to town, Alicia and I went out to eat with Vince and Marie Lombardi the night before the game. That was our chance to forget our rivalry for a few hours and get caught up on old friendships.

The next night the Cowboys played an outstanding all-round game in soundly defeating the Packers, 21–3. After the game, as Vince and I headed off the field together, he smiled and said, "You have a damn good team, Tom."

"Thanks," I replied. "I hope you're right."

We went on to win all five of our exhibition games. And as the regular season opened, my greatest reason for optimism was also my greatest reason for concern: our youth. We obviously had the makings of a fine football team; but were we there yet?

We opened the season with a big offensive bang, averaging 45.7 points in winning our first four games before tying St. Louis and losing to Cleveland. From there we bounced back to finish with a 10–3–1 record for the season. And when we flew back to Dallas from New York late in the season after clinching the Eastern Conference title, over ten thousand joyous fans thronged the airport to welcome us home.

The Flex defense had worked to perfection; the Cowboys gave up fewer yards rushing than any defense in the league. And our multiple formation offense ran up over 31 points per game. Now that the Cowboys finally had the personnel, the system worked like I had always believed it would.

Meredith won the prestigious Bert Bell award as MVP of the league. Four other Cowboys—Lilly, Howley, Green, and Hayes—were named All-Pro. And I received Coach of the Year honors from AP, UPI, and the *Sporting News* for the first time in my career.

But the most exciting result of our performance was that it earned us the right to host defending champion Green Bay at the Cotton Bowl for the NFL Championship on January 1, 1967. That game got off to a disastrous start when the Packers took the kickoff and marched 76 yards for a TD on their opening drive. Then Renfro fumbled the kickoff, and Green Bay's Jim Grabowski picked up the ball and ran it for another touchdown. We trailed 14–0 before our offense ever got onto the field.

We rallied to tie the game at 14–14 before finally falling behind again 34–20 late in the game. Then Meredith completed a 68-yard touchdown bomb with just over four minutes to play. Our defense held and we got the ball back on a squibbed punt at the Green Bay 47 with just 2:11 left. Don completed a pass to the 26. And two plays later a Green Bay defender interfered to break up a certain touchdown play and we had a first down on the 2. A touchdown would send us into overtime; you could feel our momentum building. We were going to win.

We ran inside the 1. Just two feet to go in three plays. Then one of our linemen jumped offside and the 5-yard penalty made it second and goal on the 6. Meredith threw to a wide-open Reeves, but Dan, who'd had his eye scratched on the preceding play, saw two footballs sailing toward him and didn't catch either one. On third down Meredith underthrew a wide-open Pettis Norman, who dove back to catch it at the 2. None of us noticed on fourth and 1 that Bob Hayes was still in the game; all year we had substituted Frank Clarke, a better blocker than Bobby, on short yardage situations. Meredith rolled out looking to pass, but the Packers' big outside linebacker charged right past the smaller Hayes and grabbed Meredith, forcing a wild toss that was intercepted.

So the Packers won the NFL title and the chance to play the Kansas City Chiefs in the very first Super Bowl in January of 1967. But the upstart Cowboys who almost pulled off an upset were the talk of the league. We were the youngest team ever to play an NFL title game. Everyone knew Dallas would be back.

Repeating our success the next season turned out tougher than most observers imagined. In a series of mishaps, Meredith suffered two cracked ribs, one twisted knee, a broken nose, and lost 20 pounds in a less than a week with a case of pneumonia that sidelined him for a month. Craig Morton filled in admirably for Don, but it seemed every win was an all-out battle.

For so many years the Cowboys had been a soft spot in everyone's schedule. Our Eastern Conference Championship in '66 changed all that. Now every team in the league geared up for their games with us.

One person who evidently took the Cowboys very seriously was George Allen. He had taken over as coach of the Los Angeles Rams in 1966 to lead them to their first winning season in nine years. During a Cowboys' workout toward the end of the week the Rams were scheduled to play in Dallas, we spotted a strange car parked just outside the cyclone fence around our practice field. When we sent someone out to check on it, the driver raced away. But not before we got the license number and traced it to a rental car company that had leased the vehicle to Johnny Sanders, a Ram scout.

Tex Schramm protested to commissioner Pete Rozelle, but George Allen denied the spying charges. When he arrived in Dallas he even tried to deflect the accusations by raising some of his own. George insisted someone had been spotted up in a tree overlooking the Rams' practice facilities in California that same week. He implied it might have been the Cowboys' chief scout, Bucko Kilroy; but the man had scrambled down and gotten away before he could be questioned.

We could only laugh at the absurdity of that story. Bucko Kilroy, the old Eagles' defensive man, weighed some 300 pounds at the time. If he'd been up in any tree, it must have been a California redwood.

George Allen always tried to get a psychological edge wherever he could find it. And whether or not his spy got anything helpful watching our practices that week, the Rams did get the best of us on the field with a convincing 35–13 win.

Despite George and our injury-riddled season we finished with a 9–5 record at the top of the new Capitol Division of the NFL's Eastern Conference. That meant we hosted Cleveland in a playoff game on Christmas Eve for the right to play the winner of the Western Conference matchup between Green Bay and Los Angeles for the NFL Championship.

Meredith opened the playoffs in spectacular fashion, completing ten of his first twelve passes as we jumped to a 24–0 lead over the Browns. When I finally pulled him from the game at the beginning of the fourth quarter, Don shook hands with each of his linemen and walked off the field to a standing ovation from the Dallas fans who had ridden him so hard for so many years. Our 52–14 pasting of Cleveland may have been the best performance of Don's professional career.

We flew to Green Bay for the championship, wary of weather reports calling for cold. But when we worked out on Lambeau Field the day before the game, we felt encouraged by its condition. Even with temperatures holding in the teens, the ground offered pretty good footing. Forecasts for the game day promised much of the same. And Vince Lombardi, who had spent $80,000 before the season on a new underground heating system for the field, smiled confidently as he assured us and reporters: "Gentlemen, the field will not be frozen."

The night before the game, the Cowboys stayed at a motel in nearby Appleton, Wisconsin. But I didn't get much sleep. Rabid Green Bay fans kept phoning our rooms until the wee hours of the morning, despite our continued instructions to the motel switchboard not to put through any outside calls. So Alicia, in an attempt to give me a few extra minutes of rest, took the wake-up call from the motel operator the next morning. She was the one who first heard those chilling, cheerful words, "Good morning. It's eight A.M. and the temperature is now sixteen degrees below zero."

The real shock came when we stepped outside the room to walk to the hotel dining room and got the first inkling of what it was going to be like to play football on the coldest December 31 in Green Bay, Wisconsin, history. The mood during our pregame meal seemed quiet and somber. But we had come north prepared for cold weather, and we hoped Vince's heating system would keep the field in decent shape despite the unpredicted drop in temperature.

Equipment manager Jack Eskridge had all the extra sweatshirts, socks, and gloves we could possibly wear laid out when we walked into the toasty warm visitors' locker room at Lambeau Field. He had even cut two slits in the front of Meredith's jersey so that between plays Don could slip his hands into the pockets of a fleece-lined sweatshirt he would wear under his uniform.

Taking one look at me in a long winter overcoat and my usual felt hat, Eskridge gave me extra pairs of long underwear and then bundled me up in minority owner Toddie Lee Wynne's long fur coat with a matching fur hunter's cap to pull down over the hood of my sweater. Though I moved like a polar bear with arthritis, I remained optimistic until we trotted out onto the field for our pregame drills; it was then I first felt the brunt of the brutally cold wind.

I'd tried to encourage the players in the locker room by assuring them, "The Packers are going to be playing in the same weather we are." But we all knew Green Bay's basic, gut-it-out style of football was far better suited for these conditions. Our wide-open attack that depended so much on speed and deceptive motion would be severely hampered by an icy field. As would our man-to-man pass coverage.

So I knew the weather gave Green Bay a decided edge. And when I saw Vince standing on the far sidelines before the game, grinning and holding his hands down near the turf as if to warm them with his underground heating system, I knew Vince realized his advantage as well.

We won the toss and elected to receive. But our offense could go nowhere. By early in the second quarter Green Bay had mounted a 14–0 lead and we looked to be in serious trouble. Then our defense came through. Defensive end George Andrie recovered a fumble and went slipsliding in for a touchdown. We converted a second fumble into a field goal to close the gap to 14–10 by the end of the second quarter.

At least the team got to go into the locker room for a few minutes of warmth at the half. The band scheduled as halftime entertainment couldn't perform because their instruments had frozen. Alicia and Tex Schramm's wife, Marty, endured the entire game sitting out in the open stands where their eyes watered and their eyelashes froze. They might have suffered severe frostbite if it hadn't been for the kindness and generosity of nearby Packers' fans who gave them heavy plastic bags to wrap around their legs and feet.

Incredibly, the temperature dropped all through the second half, finally reaching 20 below with a wind chill factor more than 40 below. There's just no way to describe adequately what it was like to try to play football in that cold.

The weirdest sensation for me was never being able to find an assistant or a player when I wanted one. I'd turn to say something and no one would be there; I felt like an arctic explorer lost and all alone at the South Pole. Everyone else had retreated from the sidelines to huddle in front of the butane heaters back under a makeshift shelter of tarps and plastic the grounds crew had erected as a windbreak over the benches.

Our offense warmed up enough to launch a couple decent third-quarter drives, though the first ended with a Meredith fumble and the second with a missed field goal. On the first play of the fourth quarter we surprised Green Bay by running Danny Reeves on what looked like a sweep to the left, before he stopped suddenly and threw a 50-yard touchdown pass to a wide-open Lance Rentzel to give us a 17–14 lead.

And that's the way the score remained, until Green Bay took over on their own 32 with 4:50 left in the game. The plummeting temperatures had finally neutralized the underground heating system; the turf now quickly turned to frozen tundra.

The Packers hadn't been able to advance the ball more than 14 yards in any of their last ten possessions. But this time the icy field helped Bart Starr launch a drive. The first down came on a short pass to Packer halfback Donny Anderson that went for a big gain when Cowboys' linebacker Chuck Howley's feet went out from under him as he moved to break up the play. After our linebacker Dave Edwards fell on another play, the Packers had another first down on our 30. With just a minute and a half left, Green Bay's fullback broke through a hole for 19 yards when yet another Cowboys' defender slipped and fell on the ice. First down on the 11. George Andrie fell down on the next play and Green Bay ran through the hole to the 3. Another run moved them to the 1. First and goal.

Green Bay ran for a foot. On the second play their halfback slipped and got nothing. Starr called time out with sixteen seconds left and the ball well inside the 1-yard line. As he hurried to the sidelines to confer with his coach, Cowboys' linemen Bob Lilly and Jethro Pugh pounded at the ground with their shoes, trying desperately, but in vain, to chip away enough ice to create some kind of foothold on the line of scrimmage.

In one of the most talked about calls in the history of pro football, Lombardi instructed Starr to keep the ball on a quarterback sneak. If they didn't make it, the game was over. They'd never get the pile untangled in time to run a fourth-down play. So from a percentage standpoint, it was a terrible call. That's what made it so brilliant; no one expected it. The simplest, most basic play in football won the championship when Green Bay's guard Jerry Kramer opened just enough of a hole for Starr to fall across the goal line.

So it was that we did again on the last day of 1967 what we'd done on the first: We lost the NFL title to the Green Bay Packers in the final seconds of another heartbreaking championship game. Several Cowboys' players had to be treated for frostbite after the game; our medical people said some of our defensive players might have lost their fingers if Green Bay had gone for a field goal and sent the game into overtime.

But the physical numbness inflicted by the excruciating cold was nothing compared to what that loss did to our spirits. Don Meredith took the loss so hard that he talked with me on the flight back to Dallas about the possibility of retiring from football. I told him he was being too hard on himself for his performance under such dreadful conditions.

However, Don still assumed the blame for our offensive failure in the game. And he pretty accurately summed up the entire team's discouragement when he told the press, "It's most disappointing to have this happen twice in a row. I guess we can do everything except win the big one."

He had no idea how many times those words would come back to haunt the Cowboys over the next few years.

chapter fourteen

STILL LOSING
THE BIG ONES

THE COWBOYS looked to be in the best physical shape ever starting the '68 training camp. We had bolstered our special teams with the acquisition of kicker Mike Clark and punter Ron Widby in off-season trades. Offensive guard Blaine Nye and defensive lineman Larry Cole looked like solid draft picks. We moved Rayfield Wright in from tight end to tackle where he was to become a superstar. And the core of remaining veterans on our still youthful team all returned.

Everything pointed to an excellent year. Yet I wondered what lasting psychological effect the two last-minute losses to the Packers would have on the team. My worry seemed groundless when I saw the commitment the entire team showed during preseason. We coasted through the first six games of the season before losing our first game of the year to a struggling Green Bay team. Then we won all but one of the remaining seven games to finish the season with our best record yet, 12–2. Perkins, in his final year as a Cowboy, ran for 836 yards, with an excellent 4.4 yards-per-carry average. Meredith had another sterling year, barely losing the NFL's passing title because of a subpar performance in the last game of the season, a meaningless contest against the Giants, in which Craig Morton came on to wrap up the Cowboys' win.

We played Cleveland again in the playoffs, the same Cleveland team we'd annihilated 52–14 the year before and had beaten handily (28–7) earlier in the '68 season. But the dreary gray day on the chilly shores of Lake Erie proved a fitting setting for one of the worst days in Cowboys' history. Meredith threw poorly and the entire offense floundered, though we clung to a 10–10 tie at the half. When Don threw back-to-back interceptions leading to two quick Cleveland TDs in the third quarter, I made the decision to pull him and go with Craig Morton. The interceptions weren't entirely Don's fault; one had bounced off a Cowboys' receiver, and the other was picked off by an out-of-position defender. However, the entire Cowboys' team had been playing so poorly the whole game I felt I had to do something to try to jump start our offense.

Morton did direct a late touchdown drive. But our comeback fell short and Cleveland beat us 31–20.

Meredith felt so upset he skipped the team charter flight home and flew to New York instead. I didn't have the heart to fine him. I would have liked to skip that flight myself. It was a long, grim trip back to Dallas.

During the final minutes of the game, Tex Schramm had walked over to Meredith on the sidelines, thrown his arms around the first Cowboy he'd signed back in 1959, and shared a good cry. And on the plane home Tex summed up everyone's frustration saying, "A whole year, shot in two and a half hours!"

In my postgame press conference I admitted, "This is my most disappointing day as a coach." And I had never felt any lower personally than I did walking off that plane when it landed in Dallas. And yet two days later I was back at work in good spirits—preparing for one more visit to the NFL Playoff Bowl in Miami and already thinking about next year.

Some of the beat writers who covered the Cowboys wrote about the surprising way I bounced back from such a bitter disppointment. And the truth was, I surprised myself. The only explanation I could offer was the sense of strength and equilibrium I found in my faith.

In the nearly ten years since I'd made my personal commitment to God, I had looked for ways to incorporate my faith into my daily work and life. Soon after taking over as head coach of the Cowboys, I appointed Christian players to lead voluntary chapel programs and to invite guest speakers for a short morning service before our Sunday games. I also encouraged the beginning of a weekly husband/wife Bible study for Cowboys' players as a means of building spiritual and family values. While some of my assistant coaches and their wives joined the players at the weekly Bible studies, I didn't attend them for the same reason I didn't lead or speak at (though I did attend) the team chapel services: I wanted to be careful not to abuse my authority as head coach to push my own beliefs down the throats of my players.

At the same time, I never tried to hide what I believed. I regularly shared appropriate Bible verses in talks during team meetings. And every year at training camp when I met with incoming rookies for the first time, I would share the story of my own spiritual pilgrimage, including what I'd learned about priorities.

The first time Bob Lilly heard me say that as a Christian I believed my relationship with God and my responsibility to my family came before football, his first reaction was to think I'd mispoken myself and gotten the order mixed up. When he realized I'd meant what I said, he'd thought, *Oh, no! We're never gonna win a football game!* Bob went on to make his own commitment to the Lord after he retired from the Cowboys, but when he joined us, he didn't understand how I could say such a thing.

I'm sure many other players never understood. And some who did couldn't agree with my beliefs. Yet it was as important for me to tell my players what I believed as it was to try to live it.

When it came to actually putting what the Bible said into practice in my everyday life, I confess to sometimes being a slow learner. And the job of head football coach in the NFL can eat you alive if you're not careful. If you're the kind of perfectionist I am, there's always something else to plan, another game film to look at, or perhaps the same film to be analyzed yet another time. The job is never done; there's always more you can do to be better prepared for next Sunday or next season.

I found the only way to make my family the priority I wanted it to be was to give it priority in my regular routine. Football season did do a lot to dictate family schedules. June was always family month, a time when we usually traveled or vacationed with our children, something that was out of the question from July through December. But I always felt pro football had to be much less disruptive for family life than other pro sports. Training camp lasted several weeks, but during the season we never had to take extended trips away from home. Even when we played road games, we'd practice at home all week, fly out on Saturday, and come home Sunday after the game. I was always able to go to see Tom, Jr. play high school football and watch Kitty and Lisa do their cheerleading on Thursday or Friday nights.

Alicia and I went out alone together one night every week. I tried to eat breakfast with my children every day before they left for school. And no matter what was going on at the office, no matter how much preparation remained to be done before Sunday, I always came home for dinner with the family. A lot of nights after dinner I disappeared into my den to watch more game film, but whenever one of my daughters knocked on the door and asked, "Are you busy, Daddy?" I'd turn off the projector and say, "I'm never too busy for you, Sweetheart."

I don't mean to give the idea I was a perfect husband and father. I certainly wasn't. But I do know I was a much better person to live with than I would have been if God hadn't shown me the need to reorder the things in my life I counted as most important. Fortunately God was as patient with me as my wife and kids were when I would succumb to a serious case of tunnel vision and temporarily lose sight of everything but football.

Another important factor in my life throughout the sixties, and ever since, was my introduction to the Fellowship of Christian Athletes. FCA is a national organization aimed at presenting athletes and coaches—junior high through college—with the message and biblical teaching of Christ and challenging them to put those life-changing values into practice in their own lives.

The very first time I spoke at an FCA National Conference in Estes Park, Colorado, back in the early sixties, I looked into the faces of fourteen hundred young athletes and coaches and immediately realized this was my calling, my niche. Here was where as a coach I could have the most impact on the lives and values of others—by sharing my own spiritual life experience through FCA. And it had been that sense of purpose and direction that had made that ten-year contract Clint Murchison gave me in 1964 all the more exciting. Because I knew even then my role as coach of the Dallas Cowboys would enable me to do more than direct a team of professional athletes, it would provide me with a platform to speak to thousands of young athletes about their physical and spiritual needs.

Besides addressing FCA camps and programs around the country, I soon received other invitations to talk about my faith. Billy Graham first asked me and Cowboys' receiver Frank Clarke to speak at his San Antonio Crusade in 1966. And I've gladly helped out Dr. Graham many times since, often going into a city and speaking at a kick-off rally to help get a crusade organized.

My exposure during my early Cowboys' days to the great people working in Christian organizations like FCA and the Billy Graham Evangelistic Association provided an invaluable spiritual boost for me. The more experienced Christians I met there inspired and challenged me to grow

spiritually and to become more consistent in applying Jesus'
teaching to my life. It was through the influence of these
people that I became convinced of the importance of
establishing the habit of setting aside a daily time for Bible
reading and prayer.

So by the time the Cowboys had suffered through all
those losing seasons and then the disappointing playoff
losses to Green Bay and now to Cleveland, my ten-year-old
faith provided me with the strength to go on, even in the
wake of my "most disappointing day" as a coach.

For example, I now knew that the apostle Paul writing
in Romans 5:3–4 says Christians should rejoice even in
difficult times because we know that suffering produces
perseverance, and perseverance builds character, and out of
character comes hope. It was my belief in that kind of
biblical truth, which isn't just good religion but also good
psychology, that enabled me to climb out of the depths of
discouragement.

And when that old complaint cropped up again—"The
Cowboys can't win the big one"—I tried to shrug it off. Just
as I tried to shrug off the speculation from some quarters
that the reason the Cowboys couldn't win the big one might
be my own emotionless coaching style. Or that my Christianity made me too soft and therefore the Cowboys just
weren't mean enough to win.

After three straight playoff losses, there seemed to be no
stopping the second-guessing. And when we made an Ivy
League running back from Yale our number-one pick in the
draft that spring, a lot of people decided maybe the
Cowboys couldn't draft a big one either. Despite what Gil
Brandt's scouting department told us, few football fans had
heard of Calvin Hill.

But public dismay over the Cowboys' draft had hardly
begun to settle when Don Meredith dropped his own
bombshell. In a tearful July 5 press conference, just a few
weeks before the opening of training camp, Don announced
his retirement. He had come to see me just the day before to

say he wasn't sure he wanted to play football anymore. I knew he was tired of the hassles and boos of the Cotton Bowl crowds. He'd been deeply hurt when I pulled him from the Cleveland game. And he, more than anyone else, had shouldered the heavy weight of those charges that the Cowboys always choked in big games.

If that had been all there was to it, I probably would have tried to talk him out of his decision. Going into his tenth year, Don was in the prime of his career. I believed he had some great years left in him.

But football wasn't the only consideration. When Don finished telling me about the various family concerns facing him at the time, I sadly told him, "If that's the way you feel, retiring is probably the right decision." To me it sounded like a matter of priorities; his family needed to come before an extension of his football career.

The hastily called press conference in the dining room of the Central Expressway Towers where our Cowboys' offices were located, turned into an emotional scene for Don and for me. We'd been through a lot together. He said some very warm and generous things, even surprising me when he looked my way and told the gathered reporters, "I've come to love this man."

Then it was my turn to talk about Don. In addition to expressing the personal loss I felt at his retirement I told the press, ". . . I firmly believe that my decision in 1965 to stick with Don was the most important decision made in this club's history and led directly to our conference championships in 1966 and 1967."

From the Cowboys' perspective, Don's retirement couldn't have been more poorly timed. While backup quarterback Craig Morton certainly seemed capable to take over for Don, we had only weeks before accommodated Jerry Rhome's wish to be traded. Now that Craig moved up to number one, the only backup quarterback we had was rookie Roger Staubach.

At twenty-seven years of age, Roger wasn't your

average rookie. But after spending four years' service in the Navy, no one knew for sure if he could recapture the potential he had shown during his career at Annapolis when he'd won college football's highest honor, the Heisman Trophy.

Roger had spent a couple weeks of leave time at the Cowboys' training camp in '67 and '68. I had seen enough during those workouts to be impressed by his athletic ability and his arm. I'd even made an exception to one of my strictest policies and let him take a Cowboys' playbook to study one year when he had to return to active duty. We had also sent him some extra footballs when he was stationed in Vietnam so he could keep his arm in shape. But he was still a question mark. I would rather have had someone with two or three years of NFL experience as a backup to my new starting quarterback.

Morton's apprenticeship had served him well. He looked good in the preseason. And Calvin Hill's spectacular showing at halfback silenced his critics once and for all.

Another valuable addition came in an off-season trade with Philadelphia for former All-Pro tight end, Mike Ditka, who had been sent from the Bears to the Eagles a couple years before after angering George Halas by considering a jump to the rival AFL. To be perfectly honest, when Mike came to the Cowboys, he wasn't worth shooting. His knees were bad, his legs gone. But he worked diligently with our weight coach to build his legs back up to the point where he made a valuable contribution to the Cowboys' offense for the next several years. Mike immediately proved he was not only a smart player, he was a tough competitor who wouldn't let anything keep him from playing.

Just over a week before the season opener, an automobile accident left Ditka shaken and badly bruised, knocking four of his front teeth loose. A dentist told Mike he should sit out a few weeks and allow the teeth time to tighten back up.

Mike just looked at the man and said, "Pull them." The dentist decided to fit him with a special rubber mouthpiece instead. And Mike played his first game as a Cowboy the next week.

Rookie halfback Calvin Hill threw a touchdown pass in a season-opening win and broke the Cowboys' single-game rushing record with 138 yards and two touchdowns in the second game. By the time the season ended, our unknown rookie, who some observers had thought was a wasted draft pick, had done nothing less than tie Jim Brown's all-time rookie rushing totals and play a leading role in an 11–2–1 Cowboys' season. Walt Garrison filled in admirably for the retired Don Perkins. And Craig Morton proved himself as an NFL quarterback while playing in pain most of the season with a separated shoulder.

Once again we captured our division title and the chance to face the Browns for the Eastern Conference Championship. This time we played in Dallas rather than Cleveland. But the weather and our play were just as lousy. Morton completed only three passes in the first half while Hill and Garrison, the league's best pair of running backs all season, could gain only 22 yards in seven carries. We trailed at the intermission 17–0 and things only got worse in the third quarter. We'd fallen behind 31–7 in the fourth quarter when the Browns intercepted a Morton pass and ran it back for an 88-yard TD. That's when I sent in Staubach, who passed for the final score in a game ending 38–14.

Four years' experience giving press conferences after losing playoff games didn't make this one any easier. I didn't know what to say. "I guess we'll have a complete reevaluation. When you finish first in the league offensively and third defensively and then it all comes down to nothing, you have to reevaluate. I just don't know where we'll start."

We obviously had great talent. The offensive and defensive systems worked all year. But we had lost another big one. Perhaps there was a reason, something I should have seen but overlooked. But I couldn't begin to explain it.

I'd only thought I felt bad the year before on that long plane flight home from Cleveland. This time the short drive home from the Cotton Bowl seemed even worse.

As I walked in the front door of my house, the phone rang. Alicia answered. It was Don Meredith.

"Is Tom home yet?" he asked. When she said we'd just gotten home, he said, "I'm coming right over."

Don arrived a few minutes later and stayed with us an hour or more. He just wanted to tell me how sorry he was and to let us both know he cared. He even told me I ought to get out of this "rotten football business" and give myself a chance to enjoy life.

In years to come Don would achieve television stardom as the colorful partner of Frank Gifford and Howard Cosell on ABC's *Monday Night Football*. He would say some critical things about me and crack a few jokes at my expense—the funniest line being a comparison between me and stoic Minnesota coach Bud Grant: "In a personality contest between Tom Landry and Bud Grant, there would be no winner." But Alicia and I never forgot Don's compassionate gesture of friendship and support on that most discouraging Sunday afternoon.

Despite Don's advice I wasn't ready to give up coaching just yet. While I braced myself for another round of critical speculation about the reasons for our loss of yet another "big one," Clint Murchison remained his usual, upbeat, and wonderfully supportive self.

He told the press: "No one has mentioned any unhappiness with Tom to me, and I suggest they not. We had an 11–2–1 season which is not too bad. We've won a conference or division title the last four years.

"I like to win football games, but I don't intend to cut my throat if we don't. . . . I'm looking forward to the seventies, the decade of the Cowboys."

I only hoped the Cowboys and I could justify Clint's patience.

chapter fifteen
SUPER WIN, SURLY STAR

WHEN Lamar Hunt's Kansas City Chiefs beat Minnesota in Super Bowl IV, many of our Dallas critics said it looked like the wrong team had left town. It was easy to feel defensive and point out the Cowboys had a better record than any team in football except Baltimore over the preceding three years.

However, the fact remained: We hadn't even gotten to the Super Bowl. As I searched my mind for a possible explanation for our string of playoff losses, I came to some conclusions.

The toughest championship to win is the first one. Once you do win, you have the psychological advantage of knowing you can. It gives you confidence. That's how success breeds success.

If we'd have won that first game against the Packers in 1966, we very possibly could have won the next three championships. But the Packers had the advantage over us in maturity and in winning experience. And after we'd lost the second championship to the Packers, we carried the big psychological weight of failing twice. And failure, like success, has a carryover effect.

After losing the two Green Bay championships in a row, our chances of winning that first game against Cleveland were worse. And they'd been even worse in 1969 when we'd lost the second time to Cleveland.

Despite the physical nature of the sport, I believe football is mostly a mental game. And the more I thought through the four years we had just been through, the more convinced I became that our problems on the Cowboys were primarily psychological.

If that was true, our fourth straight year of playoff disappointment would make winning even more difficult the next year. Unless we did something to turn the team around, to rebuild a sense of confidence. But what?

Since one of my biggest concerns was the emotional strength of the team, the first thing we did was try to find out just how the players felt. To do that we sent out an anonymous survey asking everyone on the team to evaluate every aspect of the Cowboys' organization, including our training and practice routines; our coaching; our offensive and defensive philosophies; our team discipline; our team spirit; our game plans; and much more. We asked players to define commitment and mental toughness, to tell us what they thought we needed to change to win a championship, to say what they thought went wrong in our big Cleveland losses. We even asked for their comments on the emotional tone, or lack of emotional tone, set by the head coach.

I never would have thought of sending out a survey like that when I began coaching the Cowboys in 1960. But a lot had happened during the past decade. As tumultuous and trying as the sixties were in America, as difficult as they sometimes seemed for my generation to accept and understand, those years underscored a very healthy concept: the value of the individual. Those of us who grew up in the Depression and lived through the military experience of a world war got used to being lumped together in a group and having our personal desires and opinions subjugated to that of the group; individuals just didn't matter.

I think a lot of us who had grown up with that kind of

example automatically brought that kind of thinking into our own leadership roles. In that sense the sixties provided a course correction by forcing society and its authority figures to recognize the worth of every individual.

This societal trend paralleled some spiritual lessons I was learning. I had begun to understand what the Bible says about the importance of every individual in God's sight. And then there was Jesus' teaching on the value of putting the needs of others ahead of our own—a difficult lesson especially for those in my generation who came out of the Depression and war years motivated by a materialistic, sometimes selfish drive for personal security.

To overcome the huge psychological hurdle that now loomed between the Cowboys and a championship, some basic attitudes needed to change. It obviously wasn't enough for me to sell the team on my strategy for a winning season, they had to buy it for themselves. Which meant they had to feel more involved. So the player survey gave the team not only a chance to have a say, but to watch the coaching staff respond to their feedback.

We spent hours compiling and considering every response to every question. Some players complained about cliques on the team; some felt we overprepared for games; while still others believed we needed to be more physical and not just finesse the other team. Players expressed concern about our training program, our will to win, and some even offered criticism of the coaching staff.

I spent days reviewing the survey, trying to weigh all the different opinions. And I made a number of changes. I brought in former Olympic weightlifting coach Alvin Roy to serve as a strength coach and develop a new weight training program. And we made other adjustments in our practice and training routines.

In an attempt to improve communication and under-standing between coaches and players, I rearranged some of my assistants' assignments and appointed Dan Reeves as player/coach of the backfield. At the age of only twenty-six,

Danny was greatly respected by players and my coaching staff for his football intelligence and his character.

The great majority of players felt our basic approach and philosophy worked. But in response to some of the opinions expressed I decided we ought to depend less on big plays and incorporate a tougher, grind-it-out dimension into our attack. And because a number of players raised the issue of the team's emotional commitment to excellence, I decided to take a tougher, more demanding approach in that area as well.

In my pretraining camp letter to the team I announced some of the changes and warned the players that none of the starters were assured of a job. The coaching staff would design performance standards for every player, and those who didn't show a complete dedication to meeting those standards and to improving as a football player would be replaced by someone who did. I wanted the team to understand I was ready to make whatever changes had to be made to win that year, even if I had to shake things up to do it.

Our '70 draft shook some things up all by itself. After our first pick in '69, Calvin Hill, won Rookie of the Year honors at halfback, we surprised observers by spending our first pick in the next draft on another player for the same position.

I remember sitting at the draft table, watching the board where we recorded the other teams' selections, waiting to see which of the top players might be available when we got our initial chance. As a first-round playoff loser we had the twenty-third pick. The one consolation for having to wait so long was realizing the twenty-two teams ahead of you all had worse records than you did the year before.

While I waited I asked our scout Red Hickey to tell me about Duane Thomas one more time. I'd read the report carefully. He was a 6'2", 220-pound back out of West Texas State—intelligent and fast. Our computer ranking rated him as one of the top three players in the draft, but as our turn approached, no one had taken him.

Red went over all the positives again, pointing out the only negative was a potential attitude problem. Thomas sometimes argued and swore at his coach, but he worked hard in practice and did everything he was assigned to do. Finally Red said, "He's the best running back in the country without exception."

"You think we should draft him?"

"Tom, if he's there when we pick, you should take him if you think you can handle him."

"You're convinced he's better than Calvin?"

"He'll be your starting halfback."

"Okay, Red," I said. "I think I'll try to handle him."

That '70 draft resulted in one of our best rookie crops ever. In addition to Thomas we drafted defensive backs Charlie Waters and Mark Washington, plus offensive lineman John Fitzgerald, who all eventually became Cowboys' starters. An unknown free agent by the name of Cliff Harris, from little Ouachita College, walked right onto the field and began hitting people so hard he not only made the team but earned a starting role as safety by the time the regular season started. Several other rookies—defensive linemen Pat Toomay and Steve Kiner, running back Joe Williams, and Pete Athas—showed promise and later became starters on other teams when we traded them. The arrival of all that rookie talent, plus the addition of former All-Pro cornerback Herb Adderley from Green Bay convinced the returning veterans they had to fight for their jobs.

Roger Staubach especially wanted to play. In one of our quarterback meetings I talked about the importance of experience, pointing out that there wasn't a quarterback in the league who'd ever won a championship with less than three years of experience. Even Joe Namath was in his fourth year before he won the Super Bowl.

At that Roger exploded. "How can you judge every individual by the same yardstick? If you do that, I don't have a chance to start because I'm only in my second year. You've got to judge every individual separately!"

A little taken aback by his outburst, I said, "Roger, see me after the meeting."

Then after everyone else left, I tried to explain my feelings about developing quarterbacks: How the mental knowledge of the game is so crucial in the pros. How I felt so many quarterbacks had been ruined and lost the confidence so essential to a good quarterback because they were sent in before they had the understanding needed to succeed against NFL defenses.

Roger wasn't convinced. "Coach," he said, "I feel I can physically make up for any mental shortcomings."

I wished Roger could be more patient. I had no doubts the necessary knowledge was going to come in time. He was not only intelligent, but one of the most dedicated athletes I've ever known. If he gave his all, he knew he could succeed.

Unfortunately, Craig Morton's recovery from the off-season shoulder surgery didn't proceed as quickly as we'd hoped. So Roger started the first two games of the season, winning both, but not playing particularly well. So I replaced him in the third game with Craig, who once again became the starter.

We had struggled to a 5–3 record, two full games behind the Cardinals, when St. Louis came to the Cotton Bowl for a crucial Monday night game. The Cowboys had to win to have any reasonable hope of capturing our division title and making the playoffs.

Playing on our home field, in front of millions of viewers around the nation, the Cardinals humiliated us by a score of 38–0. No one could do anything right the entire game. When the crowd finally tired of booing Craig Morton's performance, they turned and chanted toward ABC's broadcast booth, "We want Meredith! We want Meredith!"

Afterwards I told the team, "I've never been through anything like this. This game was embarrassing to us all.

You guys didn't really want to win. Maybe it was my fault, I don't know, but it was the worst performance of a Cowboys' team I've ever seen."

That was it. Our record stood at 5–4. We'd fallen three games behind St. Louis with only five to play. The season looked to be over.

The next day at practice I decided we'd tried everything else, and we might as well loosen up. So I told the team, "We're just gonna go out today and play touch football."

We didn't worry about who played what position. We just had fun. That next week we beat the Redskins 45–21.

The Cardinals fell apart, we won all the remaining regular season games, and we captured the division title in what was the most remarkable turnaround I had ever been a part of. The defense went twenty-three straight quarters without giving up a touchdown. We beat the Lions 5–0 in the first round of the playoffs and then downed the San Francisco '49ers, coached by my old assistant Dick Nolan, by a score of 17–10 in the NFL Championship game.

Super Bowl V. We'd finally made it.

Sports Illustrated called us the "team without a quarterback" because Craig's continuing arm trouble had forced us to depend on our outstanding defense. But we felt our defense would be dominant enough to defeat the Baltimore Colts.

For a time it looked like we would dominate as we took a 6–0 lead and the defense shut down Johnny Unitas, intercepting him twice. But just before Unitas retired to the bench with a game-ending injury, he managed a Baltimore score on a fluke pass that bounced off one Colts' receiver to another who raced for a TD. The play wouldn't have been legal except an official ruled one of our defenders had tipped the ball before the second Baltimore receiver caught it. We bounced back to lead at the half 13–6.

When the Colts fumbled the second-half kickoff, we appeared ready to ice the game. On second and goal on the 1, Duane Thomas fumbled. The game film clearly showed that Cowboys' center Dave Manders recovered the ball, but the official was screened from the play and when Colts' tackle Billy Ray Smith jumped up and pointed downfield shouting, "Our ball! Our ball," the official signaled a Baltimore possession.

I ran down the sideline screaming to the officials. But my protests made no difference. The Colts eventually tied the game on a drive with yet another tipped pass completion.

The score remained tied until late in the game. We had the ball with 1:09 left, when Craig threw a pass that bounced off Danny Reeves' hands. It was intercepted by Colts linebacker Mike Curtis who ran the ball all the way back to our 28-yard line. From there, with five seconds left on the clock, Colts' rookie Jim O'Brien kicked a 32-yard field goal and we lost 16–13.

The second that football passed over the goalpost crossbar, a frustrated Bob Lilly ripped off his helmet and flung it half the length of the football field. I knew exactly how he felt. For the Dallas Cowboys it hadn't been enough just to make the Super Bowl. We'd lost again.

Yet I saw reason for hope. The way the team pulled together at the end of the '70 season had been the most rewarding experience I'd ever had as a coach. When someone made a mistake, everyone else on the team worked even harder. Because no one else believed we had a chance—not the writers, not our fans—our players realized they had to believe in themselves. We had won seven straight big games just to make it to the Super Bowl. So despite the loss to Baltimore, I thought maybe, just maybe, we'd broken through the mental barrier that had kept us from becoming champions. If so, I believed 1971 would be our year.

The year did not start well. Craig Morton had another off-season operation. While recovering from his shoulder operation the year before, he had evidently altered his throw and damaged his throwing elbow. The doctors felt the problem was correctable, but after two seasons with a bad arm, you had to wonder about a pattern of injury.

Duane Thomas, after his brilliant rookie season, wanted to renegotiate his contract. When Tex refused to do that, Duane went off in a huff to Los Angeles and didn't report for the opening of training camp. Over a week late he finally arrived at Thousand Oaks with a friend wearing a dashiki, insisting his friend stay in camp with him and be given a tryout. When we refused, he left again.

This time he headed for Dallas and held a press conference in which he demanded a bigger salary; he said the Cowboys had never gotten to the Super Bowl before he joined the team and wouldn't do it again if he didn't play. He complained he was being mistreated because he was black. And he angrily attacked me, Gil Brandt, and Tex Schramm. He called me "a plastic man, actually no man at all." He called Gil a "liar" and said Tex was "sick, demented, and completely dishonest."

Tex's reaction was to laugh and respond, "That's pretty good. He got two out of three."

When reporters wanted my reaction I tried to shrug it off by saying, "Everyone is entitled to his own opinion." I didn't want to burn any bridges or make too big a deal out of it. My experience has been that football players are like other people; they sometimes react angrily and say something in the heat of a moment that they often regret and want to apologize for later. I figured that would be the case with Duane.

However, as the weeks passed and he still didn't report to camp, I gave the okay for a trade with New England for running back Carl Garrett and a number-one draft pick. But Duane himself fouled those plans. First, he refused to take a blood test and a urinalysis as part of the complete physical the Patriots required. And second, he walked away from a New England practice rather than take a stance the way a Patriots' coach suggested. New England got the trade nullified, and we had to send Garrett back to them.

Still no Thomas in our training camp. Which would

have been worse if Calvin Hill hadn't been running true to his rookie form once again.

I had to try to forget the Thomas uncertainty and concentrate on my quarterback situation. Craig was back throwing well and Roger had made great progress in his ability to read defenses. So I gave them both an equal shot at the starting role by splitting their time during the preseason. I planned to evaluate both players' performances before the season began and give the nod to whichever one had the best stats at that time.

The week before the opener I still hadn't decided. Morton and Staubach had both thrown well. Neither of them had clearly won or lost the job. So in my regular mid-week press conference I announced that for the time being, we were a two-quarterback team. Until Craig or Roger clearly established himself as our quarterback for the future, I was going to let one of them start one week and the other the next.

Craig started the first game and Roger started the second. (Though Craig did relieve Roger after he was knocked unconscious early in the second game.) We won both games. Craig started the third game and we lost to Coach George Allen's Washington team.

The quarterback controversy got overshadowed the fourth week when Duane Thomas showed up for practice and indicated he was ready to rejoin the team. I had no idea how soon he'd be ready to play, but that next Sunday in our home game against the Giants, Calvin went down with an injury in the second half and I decided to give Duane a try. Despite having had only a couple workouts, he ran nine times for 60 yards.

I told the press after the game, "Duane is just an amazing fellow. He is a great natural runner and just doesn't make mistakes."

I wanted to talk to Roger Staubach after that game. But he was angry that I'd pulled him at halftime when we led 13–6, and let Craig finish the game. When I walked up to him in the locker room, he exploded, "Coach, just don't say anything. You'll never understand me! What you did by pulling me out of the game was uncalled for! You'll just never understand me!''

On the one hand I admired Roger's will to play. I just wished he'd be less vocal in his disagreement with me. But a player like Roger, who said more than I wanted to hear, was easier to deal with than someone like Duane Thomas, who had evidently decided not to communicate with anyone at all. He wouldn't say one word to any member of the press and on some days wouldn't even speak to his teammates.

Duane had been a bit resistant to authority his first year, but not any more than a lot of players coming out of college after the "do your own thing" freedom of the sixties. Now suddenly he refused to cooperate.

We had a club rule everyone had to wear a coat and tie on trips. Duane would show up wearing a jacket and have the tie just draped over his shoulders. He refused to answer roll call, and he wore a wool stocking cap at all times.

I called Duane into my office time and again to let him know what I expected of him and try to learn what the problem was. But each time I felt as if I was holding a conversation with a statue. I would talk about the positives first, his hard work in practice and his excellent running during the games. I'd let him know what a valuable contribution he was making to the team. Then I would move into areas of concern, explaining what needed to change. Each time I paused, waiting for him to respond, he'd just sit there staring at me, not saying a word until I would finally dismiss him.

In 1971, I hadn't had any exposure to the effect of drugs on a player's personality or I might have suspected Duane of using drugs. But at that time his mood swings and his drastic change in behavior simply baffled me. He would sit in meetings, never opening his playbook, his stocking cap pulled down over his eyes as if he wasn't paying a bit of attention; then we would walk out on the field and he'd do exactly what I had been talking about as if he had memorized everything I had said. He refused to do warm-up calisthenics with the team. Instead he would walk down to the far end of the field by himself and go through the most incredibly rigorous exercise routine.

I didn't know what to do with him. As disruptive as his behavior was, he did the job on the field and made a valuable contribution to our offense.

That wouldn't have been enough for me to put up with him a few years before. But another thing my Christian faith had done was to make me a more patient and tolerant person. When you believe God loves a person despite his faults, just as he loves you despite your shortcomings, it's harder to simply write that person off. And it's easier to separate the person from his actions. Even if I didn't care for the way Duane was acting, I cared about Duane. He was obviously a troubled young man. I wanted to help him just as much as I wanted him to help the team.

Some of the other players weren't happy about the double standard treatment I gave Duane. I think they had as much trouble relating to him as I did. You just never knew from day to day whether he would walk into the locker room and be civil toward you or if he'd be ready to bite your head off. Yet his teammates tolerated Duane because he gained crucial yardage every week.

Meanwhile, both Roger and Craig continued to play as our newest Dallas quarterback controversy raged on. Even Don Meredith, who'd been in the middle of our earlier quarterback dilemmas, voiced his opinion during a Monday night football game when he said, "It's Landry's responsibility as a head coach to pick a quarterback. Now after all this time, if he still has no idea which one is the best, then get another coach. I'm somewhat disappointed but I'm sure not nearly as disappointed as Morton and Staubach, not to mention the other thirty-eight players who are involved in this wishy-washy decision."

I actually alternated Craig and Roger on every other play during a loss against Chicago. The shuttle system got us an impressive 480 total yards in that game. But the ongoing controversy surrounding the quarterback situation practically demanded I make a decision, just so we could concentrate on the business of playing football.

Still neither player had gained a clear edge over the other. So I agonized over the choice, studying their stats, praying for insight and good judgment.

Finally, on the Tuesday evening after the Bears' game, I called Roger at his home to say, "I've made a decision, Roger. You're going to be the starting quarterback for the rest of the year."

Obviously thrilled, he thanked me and promised, "I won't let you down, Coach."

And he didn't.

We didn't lose another game the rest of the season. Roger led the NFL in passing percentage (60 percent) and averaged over 8 yards a carry. Thomas and Garrison—plus Hill when he returned—gave us the best ground game in football. And the Doomsday defense did a number on almost everyone we played as the Cowboys finished with an 11–3 record.

We downed the Vikings 20–9 in the first playoff round before finishing off the '49ers again, 14–3, for the NFL title and the right to return to the Super Bowl. But after neither playoff victory was there any celebration in the Cowboys' locker room. It was as if those games didn't matter; everyone was looking toward the Super Bowl.

This time the Cowboys were not to be denied. You could feel the confidence build during practice. You could see it in players' eyes. By the time we took the field in New Orleans' old Sugar Bowl, I had no doubt we'd crossed that last psychological hurdle.

The game wasn't even close. Roger completed twelve out of nineteen passes. Our backfield trio rushed for a Super Bowl record 250 yards and the defense held the frustrated Miami Dolphins to just 185 total yards in our 24–3 win.

In the dressing room afterwards as the veteran players whooped and celebrated the victory that had been so long coming, Clint Murchison, Jr., grinned as he announced, "This is a very successful culmination of our twelve-year plan."

I couldn't seem to stop smiling for days.

chapter sixteen
THE COMEBACK COWBOYS

ANY HOPE I had that the '72 Cowboys could take right up where the '71 team left off and become a football dynasty dimmed immediately that next summer. We lost the services of our two most potent offensive weapons before the preseason ended.

When Duane Thomas showed up at training camp four days late, I called him into my office and had another one of our weird, one-sided talks. I told him we couldn't go through another season like we had the year before. This season there would be one set of rules for everyone; if he couldn't abide by them, he would be gone. I couldn't expect the rest of the players to put up with his disruptive behavior again. I also let him know I believed if he cooperated, and utilized his tremendous ability, he could become one of football's greats.

Duane didn't say a word. I guess he listened to the conditions because he went along with them. At least for a few weeks.

Not that he suddenly became a model citizen. He still didn't talk with his teammates. He'd show up for meals—sometimes climbing in through a dining room window—

load his pockets with fruit, and head back to his room to eat alone. He'd lost weight on his new vegetarian diet and didn't look strong in practice. But at least he was playing hard. I assumed we'd get him in shape by the end of training camp.

Then one day he missed a meeting and failed to show for practice. Assistant Coach Ray Renfro went to check on him. Duane wouldn't talk to him. When Ray reported back to me, I walked over to the dorm myself.

Knocking on his dorm room door I said, "Duane, are you in there? This is Coach Landry."

He opened the door. "Yeah. How can I help you?"

"Well, I came to check on you because you weren't at practice."

He shrugged. "I didn't feel like it."

I slipped past him into his room, saying, "Duane, we have to talk." At least I had to talk. I had to try to reach him one last time. I wanted to give him one last chance. But he didn't want to take it.

When I finally walked out of Duane's room, I went to find Tex Schramm. "That's it," I told him. "We have to trade Thomas."

Tex got on the phone and in no time had an unconditional deal with San Diego: Duane Thomas for running back Mike Montgomery and receiver Billy Parks. The next morning I announced the trade in a squad meeting, explaining I'd spent hours with Duane talking about what he had to do to become part of the team but that he refused. "I had no choice but to trade him."

But having no choice didn't keep me from feeling sick about it. Here was one of the greatest running talents I'd ever seen come into professional football. What bothered me even more than his wasted talent was the fact that Duane was obviously a troubled young man. He needed help. And I hadn't been able to get through to him.

The second crucial loss to the Cowboys came when Roger Staubach separated a shoulder during a preseason game. The doctors elected to operate, which meant Roger was done for most of the season.

On the bright side, Calvin Hill stepped into Thomas's halfback slot and became the first Cowboys' rusher in history to gain over 1000 yards in one season. And Craig Morton took over at quarterback to guide the team to a solid 10–4 season record.

The high point of the season came in our playoff game against the '49ers in San Francisco, though it started like a game we'd want to forget. We had fallen behind by 15 points late in the third quarter when I finally replaced Morton with Staubach. I expected Roger would be rusty; he'd been out all season since his shoulder injury. But I thought we needed some kind of change to spark the team. It didn't happen immediately.

With 1:53 left in the game, we had the ball on our own 45-yard line, down by 12 points. One of the San Francisco linebackers, recalling the frustration of losing to us in the last two playoffs, taunted our offense: "Now you guys know how it feels to lose a game like this!"

Suddenly Roger's passing began to click. The hurry-up offense moved down the field until, with 1:30 left, Roger connected with Billy Parks for a touchdown that brought us to within five, 28–23. Everyone in Candlestick Park knew we had to try an onsides kick. The '49ers put all their best pass receivers up on the line to field the kick.

Our kicker, Toni Fritsch, an Austrian soccer star we'd signed a couple years earlier during a Kicking Karavan tryout tour of Europe, knew what he had to do. At least we hoped he knew. Toni didn't understand English very well those first few years.

Toni approached the ball on the run, stepped past it, and crazy-kicked it sideways with his trailing foot. The football caromed diagonally toward the '49ers on the right side of the field. San Francisco's receiver Preston Riley grabbed for it and was hit immediately by Cowboys' rookie Ralph Coleman. The football popped loose and Mel Renfro recovered for us on the 50-yard line.

Roger faked a pass and ran for 21 yards. Then he hit Parks again for 19. From the 10, with time running out and the '49ers blitzing in his face, Staubach lofted a pass to Ron Sellers in the end zone and we won 30–28. Two touchdowns in the final minute and a half. Our team went crazy on the sidelines. Lineman Larry Cole turned summersaults. It was one of the most exciting and remarkable endings to a football game I'd ever seen, just the sort of Staubach-engineered comeback that was to become a Cowboys' trademark in the years to follow.

We lost the NFC Championship game the following week against Coach George Allen's Washington Redskins. Yet we went into the '73 season feeling optimistic, despite a sizable turnover in the team with Chuck Howley, George Andrie, Lance Alworth, and Mike Ditka all retiring. We'd drafted Robert Newhouse and Jean Fugett in '72 and our rookie crop of '73 included Billy Joe Dupree, Harvey Martin, Golden Richards, and a free agent by the name of Drew Pearson.

With Staubach recovered from his shoulder injury, I had to decide once and for all whether Roger or Craig Morton would be the Cowboys' quarterback. I believed they were both fine quarterbacks, each with his own strengths.

I settled on Roger. He took us to another 10–4 season and led the league in passing as he'd done in 1971. We beat Los Angeles in the playoffs on the strength of an 83-yard touchdown pass from Staubach to rookie Drew Pearson. But with Calvin Hill out with a dislocated elbow, Walt Garrison playing with a broken clavicle, and Roger throwing four interceptions, we again came up short. We lost the NFC Championship game to Fran Tarkenton and the Minnesota Vikings 27–10, missing our third straight Super Bowl by one game.

The '74 season turned out to be a tumultuous and crazy one. A players' strike kept the veterans out of training camp until August 14. The new World Football League announced the signing of Calvin Hill to a contract for the '75 season, making him a lame-duck Cowboy. Toni Fritsch injured his knee. And we struggled through an 8–6 season that prompted a lot of experts to speculate that age had caught up with the Cowboys, as it had Green Bay in the late sixties. They predicted we would soon slip back into middle-of-the-pack mediocrity.

Though we missed the playoffs for the first time in nine years, 1974 offered one memorable highlight when we beat George Allen's Redskins on national television Thanksgiving afternoon. It wasn't so much that the Cowboys won, but how we won.

Washington led 9–3 in the third quarter when a Redskins' tackler knocked Roger Staubach out of the game. Having traded away Craig Morton at his request just weeks before, I sent in our only backup, rookie quarterback Clint Longley.

Clint didn't have enough experience to be able to read and adjust to the Washington defense. All he could do was look for an open man and throw. So he surprised me and everyone else in Texas Stadium by leading the team down the field for a touchdown, giving us a lead. In the fourth quarter, Duane Thomas, who had never played more than a game or two in San Diego before the Redskins put him on their roster in '84, ran for a 19-yard TD and put the Skins back in the lead.

With 1:45 left on the clock our offense took over for one final possession. Longley moved the ball to midfield. Only 35 seconds remained and we'd used our last time-out. George Allen had his team in a Nickel or Prevent defense, with an extra back in the game just to make sure we couldn't throw long.

I decided we should throw to Drew Pearson on a crossing pattern in front of Washington's zone coverage and hope he could find an opening to run through. But in the huddle, Drew told Longley he was going to fake in, as if to cut across the middle, and when the defense committed he would turn and go deep to try to beat the two men covering him.

That's what he did. When he faked inside, the first defender bit and Drew cut back past him and had a footrace with the second man for the goal line. Longley heaved the ball as far as he could, and Drew gathered it in for the game winner.

Another impossible Cowboys' comeback! This time the hero was a rookie quarterback who hadn't taken a snap since the preseason. He threw a 50-yard TD pass over Washington's famed Nickel defense to win the game as time ran out. As the Cowboys' bench went wild, I looked across the field at the silent Washington sideline. I'll never forget the expression of complete disbelief and disgust on George Allen's face.

It was a very sweet win in a sour season. Cowboys' lineman Blaine Nye, marveling at Longley's performance, called it "a triumph of the uncluttered mind." But it added to the Cowboys' growing reputation for making a big play in the clutch.

Unfortunately, Clint Longley never got another chance at Cowboys' heroics. Two summers later, after starting a fight in which he slugged Roger Staubach, Clint fled training camp and the Dallas Cowboys forever.

I'm not sure my family really minded missing the '74 playoffs. We were finally able to use the Christmas holidays for family time. We each selected just one of the packages under our tree to open on a Christmas week ski trip to Crested Butte, Colorado. We all learned to ski, went caroling in the snow on Christmas Eve, and enjoyed one of our most memorable holiday seasons ever.

Those observers who sounded the death knell for the Cowboys during the '74 season dug a hole and were all set to bury us in '75 when Bob Lilly, Cornell Green, and Walt Garrison all retired and we traded away Bobby Hayes. Everyone just assumed the Cowboys wouldn't be Eastern Conference contenders that year.

What no one foresaw was the incredible college draft we got that year. By the time we finished training camp I knew we had landed the kind of talent we needed to keep us near the top of the heap for years to come. The rookies that year were the hardest-hitting bunch of kids we ever brought into Thousand Oaks. When they scrimmaged or ran contact drills you could hear the pads popping all the way to the other end of the practice fields.

Twelve first-year men made the 1975 team. Someone dubbed them the Dirty Dozen. Their names: Randy White, Burton Lawless, Thomas Henderson, Bob Bruenig, Rolly Woolsey, Pat Donovan, Kyle Davis, Randy Hughes, Mike Hegman, Herb Scott, Mitch Hoopes, and Scott Laidlaw. Nine of them eventually became Cowboys' starters. Five of them were named to the Pro-Bowl in later years. Even the veterans watched the encouraging level of rookie talent with interest. And just before the season started we made another addition when we picked up veteran back Preston Pearson after the Steelers cut him from their team.

Another change that year was the introduction of the Spread or Shotgun formation in obvious passing situations. Red Hickey had first used it as his primary formation at San Francisco in the early sixties. I had wanted to try it back in the mid-sixties, but Don Meredith never felt comfortable with it.

Yet it made sense to me, especially on downs where everyone knows you're going to pass anyway. Instead of snapping the ball to the quarterback up under center, then have him drop back 5 to 7 yards to set up and pass, why not put the quarterback 5 yards deep and snap the ball to him there? It gives him more time and a better look at the defense as it develops.

Roger loved the formation. It looked strange and drew some criticism at first. But most teams in the NFL now include the formation in their repertoire.

Since no one expected us to have a good year in 1975, our young team didn't feel much pressure. All they did was go out and win, managing a 10–4 record and a wild card spot in the playoffs.

For a while it looked like the Cowboys would be

finished in the first-round game against the Vikings up in Minnesota. With the score 14–10, the Minnesota crowd started for the exits signaling "We're Number One!" even as we began a fourth down and 16 play from our own 25-yard line with forty-four seconds left in the game. Staubach threw to Drew Pearson who grabbed the pass and stepped out of bounds at the 50-yard line to stop the clock. After two incomplete passes we remained at the 50 with twenty-four seconds left. Then, with Roger back in the Shotgun formation, Pearson lined up on the right. After Drew faked to the middle he broke straight down the right sideline. Roger threw deep and as the ball came down, Drew and Vikings' defender Nate Wright slowed and collided at about the 5-yard line. Wright fell, Drew turned, and when the ball came down he pinned it somehow between his right arm and his right hip, clutching it there as he trotted in for the touchdown.

After the game Roger told reporters that was his "Hail Mary Pass." The term became part of football lore and added yet another unforgettable comeback episode to the Cowboys' still-growing legend.

The week after the Minnesota shocker we played the Rams in Los Angeles for the NFC Championship. Roger completed sixteen out of twenty-six passes for four touchdowns, three of which were caught by Preston Pearson, the man no one else had wanted when we claimed him off the waiver wire before the season started. The game was never close as we drubbed the Rams 37–7 to win the right to go to Super Bowl X in Miami to play the defending Super Bowl champion Steelers.

We scored first in the Super Bowl and still led 10–7 going into the fourth quarter. But that changed. And with 3:02 left in the game, Terry Bradshaw connected on a 59-yard TD to Lynn Swann to give the Steelers what looked like an insurmountable lead of 21–10. Cowboys' defensive back Charlie Waters hit Bradshaw and knocked him out just as he released the ball; Terry didn't know he'd thrown a touchdown until he came to in the Pittsburgh dressing room.

Roger then took the Cowboys 80 yards in five plays in just over a minute to make the score 21–17. And when we held the Steelers on downs and forced them to punt, we got the ball back and moved to the Pittsburgh 38-yard line. On the last play of the game, Roger went for another miracle in the end zone, but a Steelers' defender intercepted and raced back upfield as time ran out.

That's how we lost what many people called "the most exciting Super Bowl ever." The near comeback seemed only to add to that Cowboys' mystique. The fact we'd made the Super Bowl in what was supposed to have been a rebuilding year served notice to the entire league that Dallas remained the team to beat.

I received a surprising phone call sometime before our training camp started the next summer. It was Duane Thomas. He'd played a little for the World Football League's Hawaii team during the '75 season. But the WFL had folded and Duane wondered if I'd give him a tryout with the Cowboys. He admitted, "I made mistakes. But I've learned. A man grows."

I believed him. And when he came to camp I rooted for him. I think everyone did. He seemed a step or two slower than he had been five years earlier. He injured a hamstring and missed a lot of training camp. When the preseason ended, he didn't make the final cut. But when Duane Thomas walked out of the Cowboys' locker room for the last time, he came by my office where we chatted cordially for a few minutes, shook hands, and wished each other well. While I still felt sad, that last parting seemed so much better than our first.

We started fast in 1976 but the running game suffered from injuries to Preston Pearson and Robert Newhouse. Then, in the seventh game of the year, someone stepped on Roger Staubach's hand, chipping a bone. With rookie Danny White as our only backup quarterback, Roger played out the year and we finished with a fine 11–3 record. But our passing game suffered and we just didn't show much offensive punch the last half of the season. We lost to the Rams in the first round of the playoffs.

Even with a healthy Roger Staubach, we needed more offensive firepower, a dominant runner. Yet it's hard for a winning team to get a blue-chip player like that the way the NFL operates its draft: Each year your team's turn to select college players is determined by the preceding year's records—the teams with the worst records picking first and those teams with the best records choosing last. With our good marks, the only way we could get a high enough pick to be assured of a top quality player was to trade for it.

So that's what Gil Brandt did in the '77 draft. We gave Seattle our first-round pick, number twenty-five, and three second-round picks for the Seahawks' spot in the first round, the number two choice. As soon as Tampa Bay made USC's Ricky Bell the number-one pick in the entire draft, we selected Heisman Trophy winner Tony Dorsett.

Even with veterans like Blaine Nye and Lee Roy Jordan retiring, we won eight straight games to start the '77 season. We lost the next two and then won our last four to end the year with an impressive 12–2 record. We beat the Bears 37–7 and the Vikings 23–6 to reach Super Bowl XII in New Orleans against the Denver Broncos, led by none other than veteran quarterback Craig Morton.

But the Cowboys' defense dismantled the Broncos that day. Two of our defensive linemen, Randy White and Harvey Martin, were named Co-MVPs for the game, which we won handily 27–10. The victory tied us with Green Bay, Miami, and Pittsburgh with two Super Bowl wins apiece.

chapter seventeen
AMERICA'S TEAM

AS A FOOTBALL coach, I had a constantly changing cast of players. For example, only three of my starters in Super Bowl XII had been starters when we won Super Bowl VI. Every year there would be new positions to fill, new questions to ask, new problems to solve. Even though we made the playoffs year after year, the jigsaw pieces never fit together the same way twice in the changing picture of the Dallas Cowboys. That constant change, that uncertainty I felt going into training camp every summer, provided the coaching challenge I loved.

Yet there's also a comfortable sameness to the annual routine. The seasons may change. The players come and go. But football is still football. And when you love coaching it as much as I did, years would go by without my ever stopping to think about the passage of time.

At thirty-five years of age, I'd been the youngest head coach in football when Tex Schramm hired me to coach the Cowboys in 1960. When Paul Brown retired as coach of the Cincinnati Bengals in 1976, I became the dean of NFL coaches, starting my seventeenth season at the age of fifty-two.

However, it wasn't as much the changing seasons of my public life in football, which reminded me of my mortality as it was the events of my personal life. As parents we often measure time by the ages of our children; mine had suddenly grown up. It really hit me when I walked my oldest daughter down the aisle to be married in the spring of 1976; Kitty married former University of Texas quarterback, Eddie Phillips, in a beautiful ceremony in a small chapel at our church. But it was when my own parents died that it really hit me—this awareness of the shortness of life.

My mother passed away in 1975 at the age of seventy-six. After fifty-five years of marriage, Dad had a hard adjustment to life alone. He had a debilitating stroke, but he'd battled back to the point where he could live alone and take care of himself. He had even come to New Orleans for Super Bowl XII, had a wonderful time, and entertained half the town with his stories when he got back home to Mission. Then on October 10, 1978, while mowing his lawn, Dad suffered a massive stroke and died.

It seemed most of Mission crowded into that little Methodist church for the service. Afterwards, instead of going straight to the cemetery, the funeral procession wound through the familiar palm-lined streets of Mission, past the house on Dougherty Street, past the fire department and the school, past the "Ray Landry Park," which the town had already named in his honor. Everywhere the procession went, people poured out of their homes and businesses to stand on sidewalks and line the curb in silent tribute to my father.

Dad never was very expressive about his feelings. Still I knew what so many friends and relatives told me after the funeral was true: "Your dad was always so proud of you, Tom." I wished I had told him how proud I was of him.

One of the greatest honors I ever received came in 1971 after the Cowboys had lost our first Super Bowl. The Mission town council proclaimed a Tom Landry Day and named me Mission's "Man of the Year." It meant a lot to me to be remembered by old friends and neighbors and to be able to share those proud moments with my mom and dad.

But I think what gave me the most pride was knowing that when the town had first come up with the idea of having an annual Mission "Man of the Year" award, the very first citizen they had ever honored with the title had been Ray Landry. I was just walking in my dad's footsteps; his shoes always seemed such big ones to fill.

The Cowboys began the '78 season with a solid 6–2 record before our offense bogged down and we lost two in a row. Then Staubach began hitting receivers, Dorsett's running took off, and our defense tightened to hold our opponents to 10 points or less in six straight wins as we finished the season 12–4 and captured the Eastern Division title for the tenth time. In the playoffs we downed Atlanta 27–20 and Los Angeles 28–0 to make the Super Bowl against the Pittsburgh Steelers once again.

There had been no love lost between the Cowboys and Steelers after Super Bowl X when the tough, physical Steel Curtain defense had constantly battered our receivers without drawing a single penalty all day. This time the Cowboys sought revenge. Both teams wanted to become the first NFL team ever to win three Super Bowls.

So feelings were already running high that week in Miami when Thomas "Hollywood" Henderson further fanned the flames by insulting Terry Bradshaw's intelligence: "The guy couldn't spell cat if you spotted him the c and the a." I cringed when I heard that. The last thing I wanted to do was rile a competitor like Bradshaw and give him added motivation in a big game.

For a time that Super Sunday I wondered if we would even get a chance to play. The Cowboys' bus left our hotel in plenty of time to get us to the stadium a full two hours before the game. But traffic around the Orange Bowl slowed to a crawl. When we finally pulled off the street into the parking area, a traffic cop refused to let us turn right and pull directly to the gate we were supposed to enter. In spite of our driver's explanation, the officer motioned us to the left with all the other traffic, forcing us to drive completely around the stadium to get to our gate. It took us another thirty to forty-five maddening minutes to maneuver that big bus through the throngs of people in the parking area. Much of that time our way was blocked by Steelers' fans who not only refused to give way, but shouted insults as they pounded loudly on the outside of the bus and even rocked it.

Once the game started, so did Terry Bradshaw. He broke Bart Starr's Super Bowl record of 253 passing yards by late in the second quarter. Yet we trailed only 21–14 at the half. Midway through the third period, we had third down and 3 on the Pittsburgh 10-yard line.

Roger threw the ball to reserve tight end Jackie Smith in the end zone for a sure TD that would have tied the score. Seeing there wasn't a defensive man within five yards of Smith, Roger pulled the string and tried to float a soft pass to him. When the ball unexpectedly dropped a little short, Jackie reached for it, and it bounced out of his hands and onto the ground.

We settled for a field goal that brought us to within 4. The Steelers scored next on a Franco Harris run and followed that by recovering our fumble on the ensuing kickoff. Then Bradshaw hit Swann on an 18-yard TD pass— the second Pittsburgh touchdown within nineteen seconds. That made it 35–17, Steelers.

The Cowboys weren't through yet. We mounted an eight-play, 89-yard drive, which ended with a Staubach to Billy Joe Dupree touchdown pass with 2:23 left in the game. When we recovered the onsides kick Roger passed us right down the field again to hit Butch Johnson for the TD with 22 seconds left. Only 4 points down.

That's when we ran out of miracles. Pittsburgh's Rocky Bleier recovered the second onsides attempt and the ball game ended in a 35–31 Dallas loss. But once again Roger Staubach and the Cowboys had made a valiant comeback at the end, only to fall a little short.

I never saw a more despondent player than Jackie Smith in the locker room following Super Bowl XIII. After a fine career with the Cardinals he'd finally made it to the Super Bowl only to drop a wide open touchdown pass he wouldn't miss again in a thousand tries. Jackie felt absolutely sick. And I felt for him.

When Bob Ryan, the editor of NFL Films, put together the Cowboys' 1978 highlight film, he couldn't seem to come up with a suitable title. He said, "What I was looking for was something that would serve as a hook to build the highlights around, something a little different. Then I noticed that in all the research that had been done, all the games I'd been to, and in all the films I'd seen, the kids across the league were wearing Roger Staubach's and Dallas Cowboys' jerseys.

"Dallas was on *Monday Night Football* all the time and the second game of just about every Sunday doubleheader. I think during the sixteen-game schedule they were on national TV twelve times. Obviously they were popular nationwide.

"I decided they were like the Montreal Canadians in hockey and Notre Dame in football. They were, in truth, a national team. So I began playing around with a title along those lines. First I thought of something like 'The Dallas Cowboys—National Team.' That lacked the ring I wanted. Then I thought about 'America's Team,' and decided that was what it should be."

America's Team. The moment I heard it I thought, *Oh, no! Everybody's really gonna be gunnin' for us now.* I don't know anyone on the Cowboys who liked that label to start with. So many newspapers picked up on it that other teams used it as a motivational tool against us. However, what seemed so presumptuous at first eventually became part of the proud Cowboys' tradition.

So many great and colorful players aroused and attracted the widespread affection that made the Dallas Cowboys into America's Team. Yet the one player who did

more than any other to create the image of "America's
Team" had to be Roger Staubach. The combination of his
military background and his penchant for game-ending
heroics earned him the nickname of "Captain America."
While he didn't like that moniker any better than the other
Cowboys' players liked "America's Team," both names
stuck because they fit. A closer look at the Cowboy who
wore number 12 shows why.

In the course of his professional career, Roger Staubach
brought the Cowboys from behind to win twenty-three
times. Fourteen times he did it in the last two minutes. And
while no one kept such statistics, I'm sure most of those
comebacks occurred on national television broadcasts—
earning him renown as one of the greatest clutch performers
in sports history. As long as any time remained on the clock,
Roger believed he could win the game. And something
about his competitive confidence made his teammates
believe it, too.

It wasn't just his great athletic ability or even his gift of
leadership that made Roger Staubach great. In all my years
of coaching, I never knew a more dedicated athlete, never
had a player who worked any harder to do what I asked of
him than he did.

That didn't mean Roger and I always saw eye to eye.
From those early days when he argued with me about how
many years of experience a quarterback needed to reach
championship caliber, Roger never hesitated to disagree
with me. For years we had a running conflict over the issue
of play calling.

When Roger first established himself as the Cowboys'
number-one quarterback, I let him call his own plays on the
field. But during the '73 season, I reassumed play-calling
duties, shuttling the plays in with a substitute on every
play. While I didn't explain my reasons at the time, I made
the decision in part as an attempt to take some of the
emotional pressure off Roger during the time his mother
was dying of cancer. But the fact was I always preferred
calling the plays from the sideline.

The next year I continued the practice because the system had worked so well. I believed it allowed the quarterback to concentrate on execution without having to be thinking two or three downs ahead, without trying to watch the defense's response in order to decide what to do on the next play. I knew Roger didn't like my play-calling system. He felt it restricted his freedom to adapt to what he saw on the field. Yet he knew he could change the play at the line of scrimmage, and did more times than I thought he should. So there always seemed to be at least a little tension between us on the subject.

I remember one game in '78 when I called a short pass to fullback Robert Newhouse. But instead of dumping the ball off short, Roger sent Drew Pearson deep on a post pattern. Just as he released the ball, a blitzing linebacker rang Roger's bell, splitting his lip, and ending his play for the day with a dizzying concussion. The pass fell incomplete and Danny White had to come in and finish the game. Afterwards in the locker room, I walked over to check on Roger and his bleeding lip. "You know, Roger," I said, trying not to smile, "for a while, every time you look in the mirror to shave you're gonna have a reminder *not* to change my plays."

But Roger got his digs in, too. One day as he came off the field following an interception I met him at the sidelines asking, "Why did you throw that pass? The defensive man had him covered."

Roger snapped right back, "Why did you call such a ridiculous play?"

We lived with this underlying tension between us for so long that we could joke about it. I remember an interviewer on a radio show asking about my play-calling policy and any plans I had for retirement. I told him, "I plan to coach as long as Roger lets *me* call the plays."

Another time Roger and I both took part in a big fund-raising dinner for the Fellowship of Christian Athletes. Roger coached half the audience and I coached the other half in a contest to see which side could reach its goal in pledges first. Roger's side was about $25,000 short of the goal when he announced, "If Coach Landry will let me call the plays next year, I will cover the rest of the contributions."

The whole audience laughed. Though not nearly as hard as Alicia did. Afterwards I cornered Roger and told him, "I've never been so tempted in all my life."

We had a system that worked so well I didn't want to change it. Despite Roger's opinion, I don't think his career suffered too much from it. Since he always had the last word in the huddle, he knew he could always surprise me—as he often did.

I think his most amazing day as a Cowboy came during the '79 season, his last year of play, in a regular season game against the Washington Redskins at Texas Stadium. The winner of the game would claim the Eastern Conference Championship.

Redskins' quarterback Joe Theismann led Washington to a 17–0 lead. We came back with three touchdowns to lead 21–17 before they scored 17 straight points to lead 34–21. And Washington had possession of the ball with just four minutes to go in the game. Then Cliff Harris forced a fumble, which Randy White recovered for us. The offense hurried onto the field and Roger quickly rifled a 26-yard TD pass to Ron Springs to bring us back to 34–28.

Washington took over, threatening to run out the clock. On third down and 2, they handed off to big John Riggins who had already rushed for more than 150 yards in the game. But somehow Cowboys' defensive end Larry Cole broke through and incredibly from behind tackled Riggins in the backfield for a 2-yard loss. The Redskins had to punt.

With 1:46 on the clock, the Cowboys' offense took over on our own 25. After Roger made up a pass play to Tony Hill for 20, two more big completions put us on the Washington 8-yard line with forty-five seconds remaining.

We called a pass for tight end Billy Joe Dupree, but just before the huddle broke, Roger told wide receiver Tony Hill to be ready. If the Redskins blitzed he was going to throw quick, an alley oop into the corner of the end zone. Washington did blitz with their linebackers and Roger barely had time to lob a high, arching pass into the corner where Tony Hill was waiting. Rafael Septien kicked the extra point and we won the Eastern Conference Championship by a final score of 35–34 in a game in which Roger Staubach brought the Cowboys back not once, but twice— first from 17 points down and then at the end from 13 back to win with only thirty-nine seconds left in the game.

We finished the season with an 11–5 record before the Rams beat us in the playoffs 21–19 on a 50-yard touchdown pass with two minutes to go in the game. Los Angeles went on to the Super Bowl and we lost out on a rematch with the Steelers, missing a shot at an unprecedented sixth Super Bowl appearance in ten years, and a chance to supplant Pittsburgh as the "team of the seventies."

Even so, the Cowboys' second decade hadn't been a bad one. Five Super Bowls, two World Championships, nine out of ten years in the playoffs, and more victories than any other professional football team from 1970–79.

America's Team. It had a nice ring to it.

When Roger Staubach announced his retirement from the Cowboys after the '79 season, his press conference made the national evening news. A Dallas newspaper printed a special retirement section on Roger. NFL Films compiled its first-ever highlight film for an individual player. And the experts once again predicted the imminent demise of the Dallas Cowboys.

But it didn't happen. In 1980 Danny White replaced Staubach and led the Cowboys to a 12–4 regular season record. We scored a league-leading 454 points as Danny passed for 3,287 yards and Tony Dorsett ran for 1,185 yards.

After we crushed the Rams 34–13 in the Wild Card game of the playoffs, Danny White pulled off a miracle of his own in the divisional playoff game against the Atlanta Falcons. We trailed 24–10 going into the last quarter and remained 10 points down at 27–17 with four minutes to go.

The offense kicked into gear and marched down the field to score on a White pass to Drew Pearson, which brought us within 3 with 3:40 to play. Our defense held and we got the ball back for one last time, on our own 29, with 1:48 on the clock. The Falcons dropped back into a prevent defense, but Danny hit Butch Johnson at midfield and completed another pass to Preston Pearson on the 36. A screen to Dorsett got us to the 24. And from there, with forty-nine seconds left in the game, Danny threw to Drew Pearson, who went up between two defenders and came down with the ball for the winning TD. We may have had a new Cowboys' quarterback, but it was the familiar Cowboys' miracle comeback. And the excitement of that win helped ease our disappointment the next week when our Cinderella season ended with a 20–7 loss to the Philadelphia Eagles—one game short of another Super Bowl.

The biggest highlight of 1980 came with the birth of my first grandson, Ryan. Alicia and I waited at the hospital for word about Kitty and the baby. Within minutes of the time Ryan was born, the nurses came to announce his arrival and bring me hospital scrubs so I could go into the newborn nursery and hold the little bundle of joy the staff had already dressed in a little Cowboy jumper. One look and I knew that boy had made my team.

In 1981 we again won the division with a 12–4 record as Danny White turned in a Pro-Bowl season and Tony Dorsett ran for 1,646 yards to become the first player ever to rush for more than 1000 yards in each of his first five seasons in the NFL.

We routed Tampa Bay in the first round of the playoffs by a score of 38–0. Then our season ended again in the NFC Championship game when '49ers' quarterback Joe Montana managed his own last-minute miracle drive. Receiver Dwight Clark made a circus catch in the end zone to give Bill Walsh's San Francisco team a 28–27 victory and their first shot at the Super Bowl.

We finished 6–3 in the strike-shortened '82 season. Then we beat Tampa Bay and Green Bay in the playoffs before losing to the Redskins in the NFC Championship by a score of 31–17.

But the most memorable moment from that '82 season summed up for me all the previous years of the Cowboys' success. I coached the NFC squad in the Pro Bowl that year. Down late in the game, I yelled out to my quarterback Danny White, "Come on, Danny! Let's go. We gotta score!"

Jeff Van Note, longtime great Atlanta Falcons' center, stood beside me on the sidelines. "Don't worry, Coach," he said. "You Cowboys always pull it out in the end." Indeed Danny threw an 11-yard TD pass with thirty-five seconds left as the NFC beat the AFC, 20–19.

"You Cowboys always pull it out in the end." Even the opposition believed in Dallas's winning tradition. That's what made us America's Team, a title the Cowboys eventually wore with pride.

chapter eighteen

THE COWBOY IMAGE

FROM THE beginnings of the franchise in 1960, we had tried to create a different kind of image. To compete with the Dallas Texans and to compensate for our own weak defense, we introduced a wide-open, exciting style of multiple offense that soon became synonymous with the Dallas Cowboys. Over the years we signed a host of colorful, exciting, entertaining, and talented football players.

One network executive said, "We have a rule we go by when planning NFL telecasts: Give people the best game possible, and when in doubt give 'em the Cowboys."

The big play, the come-from-behind finishes, the long winning tradition—these trademarks earned the Cowboys the image of "America's Team."

But there was always a lot more to the image *Newsweek* once called "Cowboy Cool" than what happened on the football field. While I spent my time focusing on the X's and O's of coaching the Cowboys, Tex Schramm forged an organization respected, emulated, and sometimes envied throughout the sports world.

New football franchises coming into the league looked to Dallas to see how the Cowboys did things. Even the U.S.

Army visited Thousand Oaks one year to see how the Cowboys conducted training camp.

Tex and Gil Brandt both worked the power of PR to benefit the team and strengthen the Cowboy image. Gil may have had more friends among the ranks of college coaches than any other professional sports executive in the country—a great advantage in scouting college talent and in signing those undrafted free agents who could go anywhere they wanted. We also fostered the goodwill of college coaches by inviting many of them to visit our training camp out at Thousand Oaks and supplying the children of half the college coaches in the country with Cowboys' souvenir shirts, hats, posters, and other paraphernalia.

Under Tex's leadership the Dallas Cowboys became the most prestigious organization in the NFL. We had the largest radio network of any team in professional sports with weekly coverage on almost two hundred stations in fourteen states. In addition we had the NFL's first foreign-language network with sixteen Spanish-speaking stations in seven states. The *Dallas Cowboy Weekly*, a tabloid publication the team began in the mid-seventies, grew to a paid circulation exceeding 100,000, with subscribers in every state in the United States and numerous foreign countries. According to NFL Properties, the licensing organization for league-endorsed souvenirs, the Cowboys outsold every other team, some years accounting for as much as 30 percent of the entire league's licensed sales.

We even became the first professional sports team in history to have a commercial airliner painted in team colors and sporting our team logo. When the 727 wasn't used to charter the Cowboys on trips, Braniff flew it as part of its regularly scheduled service.

Tex believed nothing was too good for the Cowboys. Our first-class training facilities out at Thousand Oaks were one example. Texas Stadium was another; built in 1971, Tex helped fashion what has become a model for many newer stadiums. He equipped the stadium with high-priced skyboxes, inspiring the concept of luxury boxes now standard in stadiums coast to coast.

Another Tex Schramm brainchild, the Dallas Cowboy Cheerleaders, transformed sideline entertainment not only in professional football but in other sports as well. The Cowboy Cheerleaders became a tradition in themselves— not just at Cowboys' games but with charity appearances around the country and even USO tours overseas. Yet I always had reservations about the Cowboy Cheerleaders' revealing attire, feeling it sexually exploited the young women by pandering to the baser instincts of men. I said as much to Tex. But he disagreed and he was in charge.

Tex saw the cheerleaders as just another part of the entertaining and glamorous Dallas Cowboys' image that he, as general manager, carefully built and fostered. A high-profile image of style, flair, and maximum visibility.

Somewhere along the line I developed an image all my own. I didn't campaign for the title of "the man in the hat." But I got it.

It all started back in New York, actually. As an assistant coach of the Giants, with plans to go into business after football, I decided I should try to look successful and businesslike along the sideline. It can get cold in New York during football season, and hats were in fashion at the time, so a nice fedora seemed like the finishing touch in my working wardrobe.

When I came to Dallas our first Cowboys' teams were so bad I felt it was even more important to at least look successful. A lot of people suggested I switch to a cowboy hat, but that seemed too trite. I stuck with my traditional sideline attire.

I suspect my "man in the hat" image really solidified when hats went out of style. I became something of an endangered species and a hero to hat companies at the same time. Resistol Hats of Dallas, one of the biggest hatmaking companies in the world, began sending me a selection of new hats every year in a variety of colors and styles. They even established a "Tom Landry Signature Line" of hats. It was never a big success, however, and fedoras never made a great fashion comeback.

My hats *did* give me an identity. In fact, if I had a dollar for every time someone has seen me bareheaded and said, "I almost didn't recognize you without your hat on," I could have bought the Cowboys myself.

It happened so often Alicia used to laugh and say I'd make the perfect American Express spokesman: "People don't always recognize me without a hat on, which is why I carry an American Express card." Then one day, American Express did call and ask if I'd be interested in doing a commercial.

I told them no. I've never done much in the way of endorsements. I always felt too busy during football seasons and I tried to protect what time I had during the off-season for my family and for speaking to FCA groups. But during the strike in 1982, American Express called to ask again. I had some unexpected free time, and Alicia and I had joked about the possibility for so long that I figured it would be fun.

Alicia had a previous engagement on the day of the shoot, so I flew out to Arizona alone. I packed a few fedoras, assuming they would do something with hats. When I got there and read the script I was surprised to discover they wanted me to dress up like an old cowpoke and ride on horseback down the deserted street of an old western ghost town. I'd walk into an unfriendly saloon where I'd deliver my straight-faced line: "Do you know me? I'm one of the best known cowboys in Texas. A lot of people don't recognize me in this cowboy hat. That's why I carry my American Express card." Suddenly surrounded by Washington Redskins in uniform as I ambled toward the door, I nonchalantly sent them all reeling with the swinging saloon doors as I walked out at the end of the commercial.

It seemed simple enough. But we shot the whole thing so many times I nearly wore myself out climbing off and on the horse. I hate to admit it, but after a while some thoughtful assistant actually brought me a short stepladder. All in all, it proved to be a lot of fun.

And since it was such a different scenario from the one Alicia and I had always joked about, I wouldn't tell her anything about it when I got home. "You'll just have to wait till you see it," I said.

Sure enough, a few weeks later we were sitting and watching TV when the commercial came on. I didn't say anything; I just waited for Alicia's reaction. There I was on the screen, riding down the street on horseback, wearing a worn cowboy hat and an old full-length longrider's coat. I pulled up and dismounted in front of the saloon. Then I climbed the steps and headed into the saloon.

Finally Alicia shrieked, "Tommy! That's you! That's the commercial." She thought the Redskins' bit was hysterical. And I thought it was pretty funny that my own wife hadn't recognized me on TV because I hadn't been wearing the hat she and half the country expected to see me in. I knew then I'd never be able to shake the image.

I won't complain though, because the image and the public visibility I had for so long as the coach of the Cowboys provided me with a world of opportunities. One of the greatest has been the interesting mix of people I've gotten to know.

My football schedule never left me as much time for leisure reading as I would have liked. But Louis L'Amour, the great western writer, was always one of my favorites. So when he and I both attended an annual American Academy of Achievement weekend one year, I made a point to meet him. We developed an ongoing friendship.

One time when we were in Southern California we asked the L'Amours to join us for dinner at the Hollywood restaurant, Chasen's. We also invited another Los Angeles couple, a newspaper publisher and his wife, who had once been neighbors of ours in Dallas.

When we made the invitations we explained to Louis and Kathy who our other friends were. I just assumed a

well-informed newspaperman would know who Louis
L'Amour was.

When we met at the restaurant we introduced the two
couples. My newspaperman friend said to Louis, "I understand you're a writer. What do you write?"

"Oh," replied Louis, "mostly I write western novels."

"Have you written very many?"

"I think it's about seventy-some now," Louis answered.

Noting our friend's surprised, almost disbelieving look,
Alicia and I could hardly keep a straight face when he asked,
"Do western novels sell very well?"

Matter-of-factly Louis said, "I think each of mine has
sold over a million copies."

In a short, sudden silence at the table you could almost
hear our stunned publisher friend trying to calculate the
royalties in his head. Alicia and I began to laugh. Louis
seemed to get a kick out of it, too. Even our journalist
friend, when he got over his embarrassment, had to laugh at
the irony. Here was a publishing mogul who had no idea he
was talking to one of the world's best-selling authors.

I remember another surprise introduction I made to a couple
of my players.

I'd first met Gerald Ford when he'd been a Michigan
congressman, and had run into him at various political and
public events over the years. When President Ford came to
Dallas during the '76 election campaign, I invited him to
visit the Cowboys' headquarters. We arrived just before a
scheduled quarterback strategy session, so I left the president in the hall and hurried into the meeting with Roger
Staubach and Danny White.

"Fellas," I told them, "we've just picked up another
quarterback for the Cowboys and I'd like you to meet him."

Danny and Roger got these uncertain expressions as I
walked to the door. When I opened it, there stood the
president of the United States with a big grin on his face and
holding a football. My quarterbacks almost fell out of their

chairs. Roger, old Navy man that he was, looked as if he didn't know whether to shake hands or salute.

Of course I knew President Ford had played college football, so I expected him to be a football fan. But I was sometimes surprised to learn just who did consider themselves Dallas Cowboys' fans.

After Dallas won Super Bowl XII against Denver in 1978, Alicia and I received numerous invitations to special events, including one to Nelson Rockefeller's seventieth birthday celebration. We presented the former vice president with a football autographed by the World Champion Cowboys and thoroughly enjoyed our evening, especially the tour of the Rockefeller family's remarkable estate in upstate New York.

It was during the Rockefellers' party, as we mingled and chatted with the other guests, that someone introduced me to former Secretary of State Henry Kissinger who admitted he was a big Cowboys' fan. With his European background I figured him to be a soccer fan, but I told him I had never heard that he followed professional football. "Oh, yes," he said, "I enjoy watching football and when I do, I always try to analyze a team's strategy. Usually by the second quarter I can figure out the offensive pattern. But when I watch the Cowboys I never know what your offense is going to do."

I laughed and told him if he ever did, I hoped he wouldn't tell the Washington Redskins. But the conversation reminded me just how far the image of professional football had come in the time since I'd begun as a player back in the days of the Truman administration. Here was a world-renowned intellect like Henry Kissinger wanting to understand the fine points of football strategy.

Interesting people. My role as coach of the Dallas Cowboys enabled me to meet a lot of them. It's also provided me with many unique experiences.

One of the most memorable occurred a few years ago when the Blue Angels, the U.S. Navy's precision flying team, performed in Dallas. To generate a little advance publicity for their show, they invited me to take a short test flight in one of the jets. In the middle of preparation for our spring quarterback school, my first reaction was, "I don't really have time right now." But Alicia and my secretary Barbara Goodman helped convince me I'd always regret the decision if I didn't do it. As an old bomber pilot who had gotten a civilian license in recent years, the idea did intrigue me. So I agreed.

Buckling myself in and looking around the cockpit of that A-4 jet reminded me how much military aviation has advanced since the days of the Flying Fortress, the B-17s I used to fly. But it was on takeoff that I really felt the difference. My pilot pointed the plane's nose into the sky, gave it power, and we shot up to five thousand feet in seconds. After he had demonstrated a few loops and rolls, he told me to take over the controls.

I couldn't believe how easily the jet handled. Flying a B-17 had been a lot like handling a huge old truck. Even my own single-engine Cessna required the coordination of feet and hands to simultaneously work the stick and the tail rudder. But just the slightest movement of the control stick was all it took to climb, dive, loop, or roll that Navy aircraft.

When we returned to the field a few minutes later, the pilot warned me he was going to take one fly-by and then circle around to land. "Here goes," he said. "Hang on. We're gonna make a little turn." As the plane banked and accelerated the sudden G-force caused me to black out and the next thing I knew we were approaching the field again on our final descent.

When we climbed out of the plane I told the pilot what had happened and asked him how he kept from blacking out and losing control. He grinned and admitted, "We have to take it easy at first. You get used to it."

What an exhilarating experience to ride in one of those modern jets!

Yet my flight in the Blue Angels' jet that afternoon didn't compare to the power I witnessed on another ride I took a few years before. The same day I tried to recruit President Ford to play quarterback for the Cowboys, he invited me to ride along with him in his limousine to one of his campaign events. As usual, wherever the president goes, police blocked off his route. So we sped down an absolutely deserted Central Expressway, the main arterial highway leading into the heart of downtown Dallas.

As a loyal American citizen, I admit feeling excited and proud to have been invited to the White House and to have attended several State Dinners over the years. But the most dazzling display of presidential power was to ride in that presidential motorcade down Dallas's busiest highway, during rush hour, without another car in sight. I'd have loved to have the Secret Service running that kind of interference for my Cowboys' running backs.

Especially in more recent years, when America's Team could have used a little more help.

part four

THE COWBOYS
CHANGE REINS

chapter nineteen
THE FIRST SALE OF
THE COWBOYS

GOING into the '83 season, I faced the makings of yet another quarterback controversy. Because we'd lost out in three straight NFC Championship games, and because Danny White had upset some of his lower-paid teammates by not being supportive of the players' strike in 1982, some people questioned whether he had the ability or the confidence of the team to rally the Cowboys to a championship.

I did worry for a while about Danny's ability to win back the confidence and support of his teammates, which is why I gave Gary Hogeboom a shot at the top quarterback spot. I figured in the battle to regain his number-one role, Danny would prove himself to his teammates as well. And that is eventually what happened.

I don't know of any quarterback who could have replaced a Roger Staubach and done a better job. After we lost in the '80 and '81 playoffs, I think Danny and the Cowboys ran into the same sort of psychological barrier the early Cowboys did after those Green Bay losses. If we had just managed to hang on and win that 28–27 loss to San Francisco in the 1981 NFC Championship game, we'd have made the Super Bowl again and might well have gone a few more times after that.

Not many people realize what a fine quarterback Danny White was. He threw more touchdown passes during his Cowboys' career than either Staubach or Meredith. And in 1983 he had the best statistical year a Cowboys' quarterback ever had when he set club season records for 3,980 passing yards and twenty-nine touchdown passes. It was hardly his fault we couldn't get our ground game going in the first-round playoff game against the Los Angeles Rams. Danny threw a record fifty-three passes in that game, completing thirty-two of them, as we lost 24–17.

Two personal family milestones took place during 1983.

During training camp that year Kitty gave birth again— this time to my first granddaughter Jennifer. I was more than a thousand miles away and couldn't hold Jenny in the hospital nursery like I had Ryan. But Alicia got a nurse to snap a Polaroid picture and took the photo to the Cowboy offices to be shipped to Thousand Oaks in the team's daily overnight trunk. So I had my very own portrait of my gorgeous little granddaughter just hours after she was born.

A few months earlier our youngest daughter Lisa had been married in a formal wedding at Highland Park United Methodist Church. While that was certainly a happy family occasion, I have to admit giving away my baby girl in marriage did more to make me feel my age than trying to run on my 60-year-old bum knee.

The very first people to greet Alicia and me when we walked out the back door of the church after the ceremony were Roger and Marianne Staubach. The next week at a public social event a mutual friend laughingly explained the reason the Staubachs were waiting right outside the church was because Roger had gotten lost and they'd actually gotten there too late to come in for the ceremony. Alicia jokingly responded, "Roger got lost? No wonder Tommy had to call the plays for him."

A local reporter happened to overhear that conversation and Alicia's response appeared in the paper the next day. She felt mortified that she might have embarrassed Roger. But I thought it was pretty funny and served Roger right for changing so many of my plays.

Losing one more playoff game was nothing in comparison to the sense of loss I felt a couple months later when Clint Murchison announced he was selling the Dallas Cowboys to a group of investors led by Bum Bright. However, the sale came as no surprise.

The Murchison business empire had begun to crumble. Clint's brother John had died and John's heirs were pressing Clint to liquefy the Murchison assets to settle the estate. On top of all the financial pressure, Clint had developed a degenerative nerve condition that would eventually kill him.

A year or two before, on a team charter flight, I'd seen Clint stand up in the aisle, lose his balance, and almost fall down. That was the first indication I had that Clint wasn't a well man.

By 1983 Clint's financial and .physical condition had deteriorated to the point he informed Tex he had no choice but to sell the Cowboys. Clint authorized Tex to find a buyer, in essence charging Tex with the task of finding his own boss—Clint's one stipulation being that whoever bought the team should be committed to continuing the Cowboys' history of hands' off ownership.

Tex kept me informed, but I played no active role in the owner hunt. I didn't worry about any threat to my job because I understood Clint wanted to protect everyone in the organization and preserve the Cowboys' tradition. In the end, when the sale was completed, Clint did much more than protect my job. He gave me, along with Tex and Gil Brandt, huge financial bonuses to express his thanks for our twenty-five years of service to the Dallas Cowboys and to him as owner. In typical low-key Murchison style, Clint didn't tell me about the bonus; he let Tex do that. When Tex came by the house to tell us Clint's intentions, I was stunned. As soon as he left, I told Alicia and we decided to go over to Clint's house immediately to thank him. His wife Anne had Clint propped up in a sitting room chair when we got there. His speech sounded slurred, but he seemed happy and surprised to see us. And when we thanked him for his overwhelming generosity, Clint acted almost embarrassed by our gratitude.

The spring 1984 press conference officially announcing the sale of the Cowboys was the first press conference Clint had called in twenty years—since he announced he was giving me that ten-year contract. This time he promised the press and the people of Dallas that the Cowboys' tradition would continue under new management. Bum Bright assured everyone of those same intentions. In fact, he said he wanted to be even more low-key than Clint; he intended to be downright invisible.

Bright said, "What Clint Murchison and his people did with the organization in the first twenty-five years was incredible. They built the Dallas Cowboys into the finest sports operation in the country. What we hope to do is see that things run the same for the next twenty-five years."

At the same time Tex and Bum Bright assured everyone there would be few noticeable changes in our organization, they pointed to new developments that promised an even brighter Cowboys' future. We began a new state-of-the-art training center and Cowboys' corporate headquarters at Valley Ranch, a project Clint had planned for years. After its completion, plans called for a unique two-hundred-acre development next to the headquarters called "Cowboys' Center." It would include a hotel and conference and retail center, a sports arena, and a large residential development. All of this would center around Tex's dream, the Dallas Cowboys' Show Place—a museum and theater where Cowboys' fans could come and see multimedia presentations and films highlighting Cowboys' teams and the history of the Cowboys' organization.

But as excited as everyone seemed to be about the Cowboys' future, the day Clint Murchison sold the Cowboys marked the sad end of an era. For twenty-five years the Dallas Cowboys had operated with the same owner, general manager, and coach. The continuity of that alliance was not only unique in the history of professional sports, it provided the foundation on which the Cowboys' 20-year winning streak and our great Cowboys' tradition was built. None of what we accomplished on the football field or in the phenomenal success of the Cowboys' corporate organization would have happened without the management style, quiet wisdom, and patience of Clint Murchison.

I think Tex and I both realized, no matter what exciting things lay ahead, the Cowboys could never be the same again.

When we ended the '84 season with a 9–7 record and missed the playoffs for the first time in ten years, I realized age and attrition were taking a toll on our team. And the NFL's parity system, deliberately designed to handicap the best teams and help the worst, finally became a factor. Not only do winning teams draw a tougher schedule in the year ahead, but those with the best records get last pick in the draft and therefore have the hardest time getting the top-caliber players they need to keep winning.

For a period of ten years or so from the early seventies through the early eighties, we averaged the twenty-second pick in each round of the draft. And as all the teams followed the Cowboys' example with more computerized information on prospects, everyone else's scouting system became as sophisticated as ours. When almost all the clubs joined cooperative-style combines that brought the top prospects together in one place to be tested and to work out in front of large groups of scouts representing many different teams, everyone had the same information. So it became harder and harder to find great unknown players like Rayfield Wright or Jethro Pugh playing in small-college obscurity. And a lot of clubs began to catch up with us in terms of talent.

We made mistakes by passing up some good players in

the draft because we thought we needed more help in other areas. For example, we felt pretty strong at quarterback in '79, so we passed on the chance to take a guy by the name of Joe Montana in the third round. We didn't know at the time '79 would be Roger Staubach's last season, and we felt pretty confident with backups Danny White and Glenn Carrano. We didn't draft Dan Marino in 1983 either when we had the chance. But then it's a lot easier in retrospect to see who has become a star and know whom you should have taken.

Unfortunately, a number of the players we did draft just didn't work out and some promising ones suffered early career-ending injuries. By 1985 we had only fourteen players from the preceding eight drafts still on the squad.

We desperately needed a "dirty dozen" draft like we'd had in 1975. Unless we got an outstanding crop or two of rookies right away, it looked like the Cowboys would get worse before we got better.

That's why we surprised so many people in '85. We played some terrible games including a 44–0 shellacking at the hands of the Chicago Bears. Yet the team never quit battling and we ended up the season with a 10–6 record, beating out New York and Washington—both of whom had stronger football teams—for the Eastern Division title. As proud as I was of that squad's showing, I realized we weren't as good as our record. And the Los Angeles Rams confirmed that fact by shutting us out in the opening round of the playoffs by a score of 20–0.

The end of that '85 season would have been a logical time to retire. We'd won the division in a year when no one expected us to do anything. We'd had a record twenty straight winning seasons. I had just turned sixty-one years old.

Yet I wasn't ready to pack it up and go golfing just yet. I felt strong and healthy. And I hated to leave the Dallas Cowboys at a point when I felt we had started a downward slide.

I know Tex wanted to be ready when I did retire. In fact, he had expressed concern after the '84 season that all my younger assistant coaches had gone elsewhere to become head coaches: Mike Ditka had gone to the Chicago Bears, Dan Reeves to the Denver Broncos, and John Mackovich to the Kansas City Chiefs. Since the remainder of my coaching staff averaged about fifty-four years of age, Tex had suggested I hire some young men. He didn't want me to fire anyone, just shift responsibilities around and bring in some younger blood.

I had told Tex I didn't think I'd be around long enough to train any new coaches in our Cowboys' system, that I would rather go with the experienced coaches I had. Which is what we did in 1985.

But Tex brought the subject up again at the end of that year. I realized Tex had to be thinking about the future. When I did retire he would have to pick my successor. If he was leaning toward bringing in a new, young coach eventually, it seemed a lot less disruptive to bring someone on gradually. I had never paid much attention to assistant coaches on other staffs around the league, so I listened to Tex's suggestion that I hire a sharp young assistant of Bill Walsh's out in San Francisco—Paul Hackett. I interviewed Paul and signed him on as coordinator of our passing game.

That decision created immediate conflict. Jim Shofner, the man who had been coach of our passing game, resigned rather than accept other duties. That upset my other assistants because everyone liked Jim and felt Tex had undermined my authority by forcing me to hire Hackett. I didn't try to explain that those weren't my feelings until the press started reporting the unrest. Then I said, "As far as anybody in the organization digging a tunnel under me, running in their own coaches and all, that's simply not true. I have final say in all members of my staff, and everything to do with the football aspects of the organization. I always will. No, I don't feel anybody is trying to undermine me. . . .

"I've reached the point, with my longevity, that I'm not

going to coach a lot longer. Tex needs to be in a position to take an active role in looking at what is available and what will happen if I step down. There will be a transition period. I don't know how long it will be, but I'm a Cowboy and interested in what the team is going to do when I leave. It's important that Tex be in a position to do that. He hasn't interviewed or hired a coach in a long time.

"We're trying to improve ourselves in every area. After all these years, we need a fresh look."

I meant what I said. I intended to be open-minded. I would listen and try to incorporate Paul Hackett's fresh ideas on offense. But doing that created another conflict—a conflict of philosophy.

There was nothing wrong with Paul's ideas; he was a fine coach. The problem was that he came from the Bill Walsh/'49ers' school of offense, a system diametrically opposed to the one we'd used with the Cowboys since 1960.

The foundation of our Cowboys' system is recognition; the quarterback reads the defensive alignment and coverage. Based on what he sees the defense doing, he knows which receiver should be open.

The '49ers' system doesn't try to attack a particular defense. The quarterback has one list of plays and he runs them no matter what the defense does. The adjustment comes when he looks for his primary receiver. If the man is covered he looks to his secondary receiver. And if that man is covered he looks to still another man. If everyone is covered the quarterback steps out of the pocket created by his blockers and tries to buy time for one of his receivers to adjust and break open.

There's obviously nothing wrong with the system. Bill Walsh had remarkable success with it in San Francisco. Its primary goal is the same as our multiple offense we used with the Cowboys: the object is to prevent the defense from recognizing a play soon enough to react and stop it. But it is different—fundamentally different—from the system we'd used successfully for twenty-five years.

With an experienced and intelligent quarterback like

Danny White, I figured we could combine the two systems and utilize the strengths of each. That experiment worked for a while. We had a solid mid-season record of 6–2 and looked to be heading back to the playoffs when Danny White broke his throwing wrist against the Giants. Our young backup quarterback, Steve Pelleur, hadn't had enough experience to master our old Cowboys' offense, and the new system just proved too complicated for him. Additional injuries decimated our running game and we lost seven of our last eight games to finish 7–9, our first losing season since '64.

The Cowboys' unprecedented twenty-year winning streak had ended.

I lost much more than a winning streak that spring when Clint Murchison died at the age of 64. I lost a friend.

He'd been a financially and physically beleaguered man in the years before he died. Creditors circled like vultures as his companies were sold off.

For many months he'd been confined to a wheelchair. Eventually his disease robbed him of the ability to speak. Yet even then, when Alicia and I went to the Murchisons' home to visit Clint and his wife, Anne, you could still see that fun-loving sparkle in his eyes. He could still laugh and enjoyed being kidded.

He loved for us to recount those rough early days with the Cowboys. I ribbed him about the play he had once suggested to me—a reverse to Bobby Hayes. We practiced that reverse and actually ran it in the next exhibition game—losing 10 yards. What I never did tell him was that I'd purposefully left out two key blocks; so Hayes got stopped before the play ever got started. Which is why I had never had to worry about him suggesting a play again.

Since his death, a number of critical things have been said and written about Clint and the wild, profligate life he supposedly lived. I don't know how much, if any, of that is true. I never saw that side of Clint. What I do know is that in the final years before his death Clint Murchison, through

the influence of his wife Anne, became a born-again
Christian, found forgiveness for the wrongs of his past,
committed his life to God, and found great joy and
contentment in his new faith.

The last time I saw Clint, just shortly before his death,
Tex and I went together to visit him in the hospital. Anne
had warned us he was slipping and no longer responding at
all to visitors. But when we walked into that hospital room,
a light seemed to come into his eyes. "He recognizes you
two," Anne told us with a smile.

We didn't stay long. It wasn't easy carrying on a one-
sided conversation. As Tex and I chatted with Clint and
Anne so many memories raced through my mind: the
painfully long charter flights home after playoff losses; the
encouraging and funny notes he sent me; his vote of
confidence in giving me that ten-year contract; fishing
together off his island in the Bahamas; that Super Bowl
locker room in 1972 when he finally held the World
Championship trophy in his hands.

It hurt to see a friend who had lived such an active,
vital life, a man who always had such a quick wit, reduced
to a shell of a human being who could no longer move or
speak or even laugh. Yet there was a sense of peace with
Clint and Anne in that hospital room.

I remembered Alicia saying to me, "Isn't it sad that just
after Clint becomes a Christian, he comes down with this
terrible disease."

I agreed it was sad, and had added, "But isn't it great
that before he had to go through this, Clint came to God and
found the peace and strength he needs to face it." That
sense of inner peace and strength was there in Clint's
eyes—you could see it—till the end.

After we said our good-byes to Clint, Anne thanked us
for coming, and Tex and I walked out of the hospital room
together. Neither of us said much on the way back to the
office. We didn't have to.

Clint died a few days later. For me, a big part of the
Dallas Cowboys and the Cowboys' tradition died with him.

chapter twenty

TROUBLES THROUGH
THE FINAL SEASON

I HAD never worried about a contract or negotiated one. Clint and Tex had always assured me I could coach as long as I wanted. When one of my contracts ran out Tex would come and tell me what he could do on the next one. He was always more than fair; we never quibbled about any of the terms.

One day early in 1987 when Tex and I were talking about the future I just came right out and said, "I need a three-year contract, Tex." After the '86 season I felt it could take a few seasons to turn the club around. However, I was willing to make a commitment to do it.

I hadn't intended to talk contract when Tex came into my office that day. The thought just crossed my mind and I verbalized it. I had no idea why.

Tex said, "Okay, Tom." And that was that.

It wasn't until much later I recognized the significance of that conversation and could see that God was way out in front of me, taking care of my future.

* * *

Unfortunately, the troubles of 1986 had been only a small foreshadowing of 1987—a season brimming with conflict and controversy.

To start with we brought on two new staff people, a new special teams coach and a new offensive line coach, to replace Jim Myers, my longtime assistant head coach and friend who was retiring. Even though I made the final hiring decision, Tex had some input. And that rekindled some of the same hard feelings that came up the year before over the Hackett hiring.

That season also brought the most bitter players' strike in pro football history. Coaches often feel caught in the middle in any conflict between players and management. The owners' plan to field replacement teams to play the scheduled games made this strike even more awkward for me. And Tex's leadership role in the owners' hard-nosed strategy made Cowboys' management the brunt of a lot of hard feelings on the part of union officials, players around the league, and even fans.

Tempers ran hot for the duration of the strike. Even after the union finally caved in just prior to the third replacement game, an aura of bitterness hung over the team like a dark cloud for the remainder of the season.

Then there was the Herschel Walker–Tony Dorsett controversy. That one actually started in the 1986 training camp and requires a little background.

Herschel had left college after winning the Heisman Trophy his sophomore season to sign with Donald Trump's New Jersey Generals in the rival United States Football League. In 1984, the year Herschel would have been a senior and became eligible for the college football draft, the Cowboys gambled a fifth-round draft pick to take his NFL rights. Although he already had a valid, long-term contract with the USFL, we would have the right to sign him if anything happened and he ever came into the NFL.

When the USFL folded, the long shot paid off in a big way. Herschel signed with the Cowboys just a month before the opening of the '86 season and we suddenly had an exciting new dimension in our offense. We also had a big controversy because Herschel's five-year, $5 million contract made him the highest paid Cowboy. That infuriated Tony Dorsett, who bitterly complained to the media that all his great years of running for the Cowboys evidently weren't appreciated.

Tony's reaction was unfortunate and untrue. Just the year before the Cowboys had helped him out of serious financial trouble with the IRS. Tex had renegotiated his contract, even though he had three years to go on an old one that stipulated it would not be renegotiated. The Cowboys brought in financial experts to help restructure a new contract so Tony could pay his debts and have an adequate salary left over.

Tony eventually apologized. And we had spent most of the '86 season trying to figure out ways to use both Tony and Herschel on the field at the same time. Tony had played his usual halfback spot most of the season. Herschel played halfback when Tony was out with a knee injury; we also used Walker at fullback, flanker, and even tried him at tight end.

By the time we started the '87 season, I had concluded we could utilize Herschel best out of the halfback position. But since that was the only position Tony could play, I decided to try to use them both.

We couldn't just interchange them, however. They were very different runners. Each was great in his own way.

I don't know that I've ever seen a greater natural halfback than Tony Dorsett. No one could hit a hole quicker. And once he broke into the open field, his running instincts were a wonder to watch. In his eleven years as a Cowboy, he gained 12,036 yards.

Tony and I didn't always agree on our offensive system. Feeling we never ran enough of his plays, he publicly complained that the Cowboys didn't utilize him to carry more of the offensive load. While I'd rather he had been less vocal in his disagreement, I understood his frustration. You don't get to be the caliber of football player Tony was solely on physical talent; it takes pride and an intensely competitive nature. I knew he wanted to lead the league in running every year and he felt the only reason he couldn't was because I didn't run him twenty-five or thirty times a game like Walter Payton and Eric Dickerson did in Chicago and Los Angeles.

I didn't think Tony could take that kind of physical pounding game after game, though. He didn't have the size of a Dickerson or the strength of a Payton. He wasn't their kind of runner either; he had his own style. In '86 and '87 he may even have shortened his career a year or two by altering his style and trying to be more like Herschel.

What Herschel had was an awesome combination of speed and power. While he never had the sheer running ability of Tony Dorsett, he had enough physical strength to run right through a tackler and then break away. He could block well. And what we didn't know until he came to the Cowboys was what a fine receiver Herschel was.

On top of all that, Herschel was a rare individual. A superstar with true humility; bright and likable; the kind of person his coaches and teammates loved. And what an attitude: Herschel always sat in the front row of meetings to make sure he didn't miss anything.

While I felt Tony at the age of thirty-three had another productive season or two left in his great career, Herschel was only twenty-five. The future of the Cowboys' running game clearly rested with Herschel. If we designed an offense to capitalize on his strengths, I felt Herschel could play a huge role in the rebuilding of the Cowboys. I would never have willingly traded him.

As I began to use Herschel more and more, Tony made it very clear he would not play second fiddle to anyone. In essence he said, "I'm not going to share the halfback position, so choose one or the other of us." When I chose Herschel, Tony demanded to me and to Tex that he be traded—a request we would honor after the '87 season.

While all this would have been controversy enough for any season, there was more.

After starting the season with a 3–1 record, we floundered. Danny White's wrist still hampered his throwing. Without Danny, the new combined systems of offense we'd introduced the year before just didn't seem to work. So I began going more and more with the old Cowboys' system. We managed to win only two games over the next nine-week period, guaranteeing our second losing season in a row.

For the first time in my head coaching career, I came under fire from management. It began early in November with Tex after a particularly galling loss to Detroit, a team that had won only one game all season before they beat us 27–17. On his regular Monday night radio show, Tex vented his frustration saying, "Some of the things we're doing are frankly mystifying. It's very seldom I put myself in a position of giving the players a reason for losing, but I'm not sure it's all on the players. When things aren't working and you continue to see the same things [being tried], it shakes your confidence. . . . There's an old saying, 'If the teacher doesn't teach, the students don't learn.'"

And a few weeks later after a 21–10 loss at home to Atlanta, a team with the worst record in the NFC at the time, Bum Bright spouted off in front of a television camera saying the Cowboys' play-calling "horrified me. . . . It doesn't seem like we've got anybody in charge who knows what he's doing, other than Tex." Bum went on to complain that we weren't using Herschel Walker enough considering how much we were paying him.

I tried to shrug off the criticism. But I'm human; it hurt. It was easier to discount Bright's comments because he knew nothing about football. He had a reputation as a bottom-line businessman and his bottom line wasn't doing well. Word on the financial pages was that he'd lost almost $40 million in the recent stock market crash, and his personal fortune had shrunk from $600 million to some $300 million in the wake of the Texas real estate crunch and the savings and loan crisis. Only forty thousand people had shown up at Texas Stadium to see the game we lost to Atlanta; even his football business had turned sour.

Tex's comments hurt more. But he's an emotional person. And he'd been frustrated. He'd stuck by me and defended me for twenty-eight years. I could forgive him, even if he hadn't apologized in the press, saying: "This is an emotional game, and those things were said under stressful circumstances. I wish I hadn't said them, because they created a misimpression. Obviously, I don't have any criticism of Tom's coaching today any more than I've had in past years."

Fortunately, the season ended on a more hopeful note. We won our last two games of the season with the defense playing a solid game, Steve Pelleur executing the old Cowboys' offense, and Herschel Walker running for over 100 yards in each game. Even though we finished with a 7–8 record, I felt we were back on track and we knew what to do to improve the following year.

But things were to be worse in 1988.

I decided to take back total control of the offense. I'd never felt comfortable calling the plays in the mixed-philosophy offense we'd tried in '86 and '87. I couldn't make the split-second decisions in the new offense with the same confidence I could in the system I'd used for more than twenty-five years. If I had two more years to try to turn the Cowboys around, I simply concluded I would have to go with what I knew best.

I planned a simpler, basic offense better suited to a young team and an inexperienced quarterback. Herschel would become a focal point for our offense. I went into the season encouraged by a team I knew was green, but had shown me a willingness to work throughout one of the toughest, most demanding training camps the Cowboys had in years.

But after winning two of our first four games, the roof caved in. The week after George Bush defeated Michael

Dukakis for the presidency of the United States, the Cowboys lost their seventh game in a row. Last time that had happened, Eisenhower lived in the White House.

A particularly painful loss came in Philadelphia where we blew a 20-point lead to lose on an interference call in the final seconds. I took a public roasting over the late-game developments after that one.

We still clung to a 6-point lead with two minutes left—third and 2, deep in Eagles' territory. Three points would have clinched a victory; we were within normal field goal range. However, our kicker had been so inconsistent there seemed to be no such thing as a "normal" field goal. To make matters worse, we were in the windy end of the Philadelphia stadium. The only sure way I saw to ice the game was a first down.

Instead of a conservative running play that would have set up a field goal on fourth down if it didn't get us a first, I called a pass play. An official flagged quarterback Steve Pelleur for intentionally grounding the ball, and the resulting penalty put us so far out of field goal range we had no choice but to punt. The Eagles promptly marched 85 yards to win at the final gun.

In my postgame press conference, reporters naturally wanted to know about that crucial call. I said I hadn't been comfortable going for a field goal with the ball on the 30-yard line. Actually it had been on the 23, which would have meant we'd have had to kick from about the 30, plus the 10 yards in the end zone, making for a 40-yard field goal.

I was surprised that night watching the TV news when a sports commentator made a big issue out of my confusion about the actual location of the ball before the controversial call. As far as I was concerned, the line of scrimmage had never mattered because I still hadn't wanted to risk a field goal. We needed a first down.

But the big story in the newspapers throughout the week was that I'd lost track of where the Cowboys were and my memory lapse had cost us the game. The implication being made all over Dallas was that I must be slipping, age had caught up with me, and it was obviously time I hobbled off to the nearest porch rocker. The newspapers conducted public opinion surveys on whether or not my coaching days should be over; one poll said yes, the other no. My most vocal critic among local sports columnists called me "senile."

Senility would have helped me ignore the rage of criticism that rose around me. I hadn't seen or heard so much flak since those World War II bombing runs over Germany. Just as then, I had to set my mind on the task and press on.

I didn't try to defend myself, but then I didn't have to. I had plenty of friends in football who jumped to my defense. And then there was Alicia. The "senile" charge really riled her. She thought the whole attack reeked of age discrimination and told reporters so. In spite of the din of criticism and calls for my retirement, she said she wouldn't try to influence me to quit.

She told the press she believed that "sports is a lot like politics, if you can't stand the critics you need to get out . . . [sometimes] life is difficult but once you know it, it isn't so difficult anymore."

When it came to criticism she said she'd learned to consider the source. "Everyone who knows anything about the game still thinks he's doing a great job. . . . I know Tommy can coach. He's proved that, hasn't he?"

With that kind of support and confidence from a woman who had attended nearly every Dallas Cowboys' game, home and away, in the team's twenty-nine-year history, I figured I could withstand anything.

I remained convinced the Cowboys were a better club than we had been for a couple years, even though our losing streak stretched to ten games. We lost a half dozen games in the last minute when we couldn't seem to make the big play on defense to hold a lead, or else we fell just short in trying to push the ball over the goal line. That to me was a sign of our immaturity and inexperience, which wasn't surprising on a team with twenty-nine players who had less than three years in the league.

What the team did have was character. Even when we lost one demoralizing heartbreaker after another, the players never quit. Morale stayed high and they continued to play their hearts out, battling to the finish week after week. The team's reaction to adversity gave me real reason for hope for the future. Experience would come, and with it, improvement.

Other people didn't share my confidence. I knew Tex had to be feeling the pressure from a management trying to sell the team; but he wasn't voicing his frustration out loud to the media. Bum Bright was preoccupied trying to salvage his financial empire, so he didn't complain the way he had in 1987.

Yet, there's seldom a shortage of critics when you lose. Cowboys' minority owner Ed Smith quickly jumped in the breach. His knowledge of football seemed mostly to consist of what he'd learned in five years attending Cowboys' games. He and his wife would sit a few rows ahead of Alicia and me on team charter flights, and during our long losing streak, you could hear him venturing his opinions on what was wrong with the Cowboys. He'd even wander back to try to engage players and assistant coaches in conversations about what needed to be done to correct the problems. But he never bothered talking to me.

Smith, who owned 27 percent of the Cowboys, eventually announced his intentions to make an offer to buy the club from Bright. And after we lost our tenth straight game, a 3-point loss to Cleveland in which we had two field goals nullified by penalties, he made clear his plans to clean house if he took over. He wondered if a sixty-four-year-old coach could still pull the trigger, even though he obviously believed as a prospective owner in his seventies that he still had the right stuff. In a television interview he finally told the public what he'd been implying in the plane all year. I had to go. "We don't have any leadership. We haven't had any for three, four, five years. I think you have to blame the coaching staff."

Fortunately Ed Smith's deal to purchase the Cowboys fell through, but he still rode the team plane to our game in Washington the following week, sitting right there in front of Tex and me in his usual spot. He even joined the team celebration in the locker room after we ended our losing streak with a 24–17 victory that eliminated the defending Super Bowl Champion Redskins from the 1988 playoff picture.

The joyous locker-room scene reminded me of earlier Super Bowl wins. To these gutsy kids it seemed just as big. So I wasn't surprised when they decided to make a special game ball presentation right there in the locker room. (Coaches usually award honorary game balls the day following a game, after they've reviewed and graded the films to see what offensive, defensive, and special teams' players most deserve recognition. It had been thirteen years since the Cowboys' last such spontaneous locker-room presentation.)

I figured they'd give the ball to Michael Irvin for his three great touchdown catches. I was surprised and moved when my old center, Tom Rafferty, called me to the front.

This big 6'3", 265-pound veteran, one of four remaining Cowboys who'd been on that last Super Bowl championship team back in 1975, cried as he said, "This is for the guy who stuck by us when we were 2–12, and he's taken a lot of [bleep]." Then he handed me the ball and I nearly cried as the entire team began an in-cadence chant of my initials: "TL! TL! TL!"

I'd had many more important wins in my twenty-nine-year career. But none more memorable than that one that turned out to be my very last.

We lost the final game of the season the next week.

What I needed most after that long, painful 3–13 season was a nice long vacation away from newspapers, television, and questions about football. That's just what I got when Alicia and I accepted an invitation for a long Caribbean cruise with our friends, Dallas real estate developer Trammell Crow and his wife.

I returned from vacation feeling rejuvenated and positive about the final year on my contract and what I fully expected to be my last year coaching the Cowboys. With another year of improvement and the very first pick in the draft, a luxury we'd had only one other time in club history, I felt we could realistically hope for a .500 season in 1989.

Aware that some critics were still calling for my scalp, and concerned about everyones'—including my players'—perception of me as a lame duck coach, I told the press out at Valley Ranch one day that I definitely planned to coach next season. In fact, I felt so good I might even coach right into the nineties.

Just a couple weeks later Jerry Jones came to town.

chapter twenty-one

AFTERMATH OF
THE FIRING

I LAY in bed that Saturday night thinking not so much about the past, or even about the meeting I'd had a few hours before with Tex and Jerry Jones. I fell asleep mulling over the difficult tasks I knew had to be done in the next two days.

As soon as we landed at Love Field in Dallas and unloaded the plane, Alicia drove home and I headed directly to Valley Ranch. I saw only a few cars in the parking lot at the Cowboys' headquarters when I got there. So I had the place pretty much to myself as I began cleaning out my office.

It's amazing how much stuff you accumulate in twenty-nine years. I tried to sort through some of the files to decide what should be kept and what I could pitch. But there was too much to go through carefully.

As the hours dragged on and the cardboard boxes began to fill up, some members of the media wandered in. I don't know how they knew I was there, but the press always finds you. A photographer asked permission to take pictures as I worked. A Channel 8 TV crew arrived. Both the reporter and the cameraman had tears in their eyes when they left; I always had a lot of good friends in the media.

The reporters who stopped by the office that afternoon wanted to know how I felt and if I was surprised by what happened. I told them it had been pretty clear that if Bum Bright finalized the deal with Jones, he was going to bring in Johnson.

"It was just a matter of whether the deal came to a conclusion. Once it did, I was out of a job. . . .

"I'm not bitter. I knew what I was doing when I tried to bring this club back. I could have very easily quit three years ago, but I felt pretty strongly about the team and the direction it was going. I don't regret it.

"People say you have to know when to retire, which is a dumb thing to say. If you want to go out on top, yeah, it becomes important when you quit. Or if you're afraid to get into the situation we've been in the last two or three years. But I wasn't afraid of that. And I wasn't worried about getting fired. I knew the risk.

"To me it's not an ego thing. I enjoy coaching. I enjoy helping people achieve something. . . . I always measured how the team was playing, and as long as the team played for me the way they have the last three years, then I decided I would stick with them as long as I could. If the team had fallen flat on its face at the end of last year, I would have said, 'Hey, I can't help them.' But they didn't. They kept fighting back.

"I was really looking forward to this year. I thought it was going to be a tremendous challenge and an interesting one. But it's all over with now. And I can't worry about things over which I have no control.

"I'm going to miss the players and my coaches. That's going to be my greatest loss."

Tex stopped by to say again how sorry he was. And the two of us talked alone a few minutes about the past and the future. I assured him I would be fine. I wasn't so sure about

Tex. The Cowboys had been his entire life for twenty-nine years.

He said he planned to stay on. But we both knew that was going to be hard because so much would be different. Just how different had been made obvious in Jerry Jones's televised press conference the night before.

All the principals in the Cowboys' sale had gathered at Valley Ranch for an official announcement. It had been carried live on all three television network affiliates in Dallas and picked up by radio and TV stations around Texas.

Tex had been there along with Bright and Jones. But his only real role had been to walk to the microphone in front of the gathered media and say, "I want to introduce you to Jerry Jones, the new owner of the Dallas Cowboys." When he'd done that, he went to sit back down beside Bum Bright, only to find that Ed Smith, who had retained his minority interest in the new ownership, had slipped in and planted himself in Tex's chair. Tex spent the rest of the press conference standing on the back edge of the platform, his head lowered, as he listened to Jerry Jones excitedly promise to be the kind of owner who was involved in every aspect of the organization, every decision.

When Jones was asked about Tex's role in the new organization, he acknowledged that Tex had played an invaluable role in the Cowboys' success; he wanted to learn all he could from Tex, but as owner, he expected to be in charge. Looking over his shoulder, he added, "Tex is standing a little behind tonight."

Jones's plan was vastly different from the ownership philosophy Clint had established in the beginning. I think Tex knew it would be impossible for him to live with it. But he said he was going to try.

My secretary Barbara Goodman came in to help me finish packing up. Together we took the pictures and plaques off the wall, removed the books from my shelves, and cleared the assorted memorabilia off my desk and credenza.

I studied that first Super Bowl trophy that had stood on

my office shelf for seventeen years. But it belonged to the Cowboys. The second one sat in Tex's office.

Then I looked at the office door I'd brought with me when the Cowboys moved to Valley Ranch.

After we won Super Bowl VI, a Cowboys' fan by the name of Sam Wing, whose company made wooden window shutters, had commissioned a woodcarver to create a door for my old office over in Expressway Towers. The mahogany door stood eight feet tall and was divided into three panels. In one panel was the carving of a Dallas Cowboys' football helmet, in a second was the Super Bowl trophy, and in the third was an aerial view of Texas Stadium.

I decided to remove the door and take it with me.

The daylight outside the glass wall of my office had turned to dusk by the time we finished. Six hours had passed as I'd packed up the last remnants of my Cowboys' career.

As I sat looking over the stack of cartons in the middle of my darkened office, the sound of noisy laughter carried in from the hall. A jubilant group of Jerry Jones's friends and relatives passed by my office door on their first guided tour of the Cowboys' headquarters.

When they were gone I carried the boxes containing twenty-nine years worth of memories out into the parking lot and loaded them into my car. Driving home I realized an even more emotional task lay ahead.

By the time I kissed Alicia good-bye and left to drive to the office one last time on Monday morning, I knew what I wanted to say to my players. I just wasn't sure I'd be able to do it.

I hurried past the horde of newspeople already swarming Cowboys' headquarters. I gave my handwritten notes to Barbara and she barely finished typing them onto eight index cards for me before I walked out of my office and down the hall for my 9:00 scheduled squad meeting.

The players had already gathered in the large team meeting room at the corner of the sprawling locker room

area. I walked right to the lecturn in the front of the room—
the same room where Jerry Jones's press conference had
been held on Saturday night.

I took a deep breath and quickly scanned the assembled
group. Most of the team members had shown up for the first
morning of our winter mini-camp. A few Cowboys' employees stood in the back. The press had to wait outside.

This was the first official squad meeting in 1989. So I'd
been planning to lay out a challenge for the coming year.
Now, instead of a "first," it was a "last." And that's how I
started.

"Good morning," I said. "This will be the last time I'll
stand here . . . our last meeting together." I paused. *This was
going to be even harder than I thought*.

"We all have to go on with our lives. . . ." Then I
reminded them of something I'd told them many times.
"The way you react to adversity is the key to success. People
who succeed are the ones who respond the right way in
adverse circumstances. Right now . . . things are in turmoil
around here . . . how you react will be crucial . . . important
to what happens next season. I don't want you to concern
yourself with what has happened to me . . . you need . . . to
look forward . . . to playing football next September."

I tried to clear my throat but a huge lump remained. "I
want you guys to do everything you can to bring the
Cowboys back to the top of the NFL. I . . ."

I paused again. I told the players how proud I'd been of
their reactions over the past season. How much it meant to
me that "you never quit . . . that we never quit when . . ."

I could feel the tears rolling down my cheeks as I had to
take several deep breaths before I could go on. The room
seemed deathly quiet. A few of the players had their heads
down. Some had tears of their own.

I skipped to the end of my notes to say, "The thing I'm
going to miss most . . . is my relationships with the coaches
and you . . . you the players . . ." At that point I broke into
sobs.

Finally, after what seemed like forever I regained

composure and said as I looked aound the room, "I want you to know I'll always be with you in spirit. . . . God bless you and your families. . . . I love you guys."

The team gave me a standing ovation as I walked out of the room and hurried down the hall and into the restricted coaches' area to avoid the throng of reporters.

"How'd it go?" Barbara wanted to know.

I shrugged and tried to smile. "Okay, I guess. But I didn't make it through."

A few minutes later, after I'd regained my composure, I walked back through the training room and then out to the covered weights and workout area to say my good-byes to individual players. Once that was done I returned to my office where I posed as Barbara snapped pictures of me with various Cowboys' office personnel who came in to wish me well.

I talked for a while with my coaches, especially long-time assistants and friends Dick Nolan and Jerry Tubbs. Then I granted three separate interviews to the local network television stations.

Mike Ditka called from Chicago to check on me and we talked for a while. I telephoned my old friend Gene Stallings, head coach of the Phoenix Cardinals and a man I'd hired as an assistant after he was fired as head coach of Texas A&M. "Well, Gene," I laughed. "Here's another guy who had to get out of Dodge City."

I returned a few other phone calls, answered some correspondence, and finally it was time to go home. Barbara walked me to the front door and gave me a big good-bye hug. Outside, waiting to walk me to my car, stood Tom, Jr., who had dropped by in case I needed anything. He took one look at the small mob of television and newspaper photographers surrounding my car, shook his head, and said, "This is kind of morbid."

As I drove out of the parking lot for the last time, a few Cowboys' employees stood on the steps among the media people and watched me go.

*　　　*　　　*

When I arrived home, Alicia told me the phone had not stopped ringing all day. If it wasn't friends calling to say they were thinking about us and praying for us, it was some reporter from Oregon or Florida or South Dakota. By Monday afternoon people all over Dallas followed one DJ's suggestion that they tie a Cowboy-blue ribbon around a tree in their yard in protest of my firing.

Over the next few days it seemed some sportswriter on every paper in the country leaped to my defense with an article about me and/or my firing as coach of the Cowboys. I couldn't believe the emotional outcry. The Cowboys' sale and my firing became the topic of discussion on every talk show in Texas and the subject of a half-dozen songs that cropped up overnight on local radio stations.

And the phone continued to ring.

By Wednesday Alicia and I decided the only relief from all this attention was to get out of town for a while. We had planned to spend some time that month vacationing in Palm Springs, so we just took off early.

Since very few people knew where we were, our phone in Palm Springs was quiet. Until the White House called. The operator said the president wished to talk to me and if I'd be at this number between 8:00 and 8:30 EST the next morning, I could expect him to call. I suppose I could have reminded the operator of the time difference. But I didn't. I simply told her I'd be there. It wasn't as if I would have to cancel any plans for 5:00 the next morning.

I set my alarm. When it went off about four forty-five I got up and waited for the call. The phone rang a few minutes later and the White House operator told me to hold for the president. Then President Bush came on the line to ask how I was doing, express his personal sympathies at the news of my firing from the Cowboys, and say he wished me well in the future.

When the president learned I was in Palm Springs, he was most apologetic about calling at that hour; I told him to think nothing of it, I just appreciated the thoughtfulness and concern evidenced by his call. He again expressed his best wishes for me and Alicia in the next stage of our lives, I thanked him, and we said good-bye. Then, since it was still a little early to begin a round of golf, I went back to bed.

Another highlight of our time in California came when the NFL held its annual spring meetings in Palm Springs. We didn't go to any of the meetings, of course, but Mike and Diana Ditka, Dan and Pam Reeves, and Gene and Ruth Ann Stallings called and invited Alicia and me to join them for dinner at a local restaurant.

It felt like old-home week. Gene Stallings, an old Bear Bryant protégé out of the University of Alabama, worked with me for fourteen years before he left to become head coach of the Cardinals in 1986. Not only is he a fine football man and a dear friend, there's no one I respect more as a family man and a father than Gene.

Mike played and coached under me for thirteen years before he took over as coach of the Chicago Bears. Danny played and coached with me for sixteen. The two of them were as much like sons as assistants. In fact I sometimes had to give them a little stern fatherly advice.

I remember one day when they got so worked up at the officials that I sat them down after the game and said, "I think I'd rather lose a football game than ever have my assistants act that way on the sidelines again."

I don't know of anyone more fiercely competitive than Mike and Dan. And not just about football. I used to play a little tennis with them during training camps; for them tennis was a contact sport. They'd rather knock their partner down trying to get to a drop shot than lose an uncontested point.

Even across the net from Mike you weren't safe. You never knew what he'd do if he missed a particularly frustrating shot. I've seen him smash his racket on the court until it looked like an aluminum pretzel, then bend it back into its approximate original shape and go on with the match. One day when he blew a shot he angrily slung his racket at the net and missed—hitting me on the ankle and sending me hopping around the court on one foot.

They were just as competitive in whatever they did. Danny brought a dart board to Thousand Oaks one year and hung it on the wall of his dorm room. He and Mike went at it with such a vengeance they had to pay for a new wall when we broke training camp.

So we had a lot of memories to talk about and a lot of laughter to share in that Palm Springs restaurant. In fact, our evening together was such a poignant reminder of all that we'd enjoyed, all the associations that would never be again, that Alicia broke down and cried for the first time since my firing. For my sake, she'd been so strong for so long.

It was like everything finally hit her. A wonderful part of our life was really over. Sensing that completely, she finally let down and cried. But it was okay; we were among loving friends.

When Alicia and I returned to Dallas after three weeks we learned we had friends everywhere. More than we'd ever known.

So many thousands of letters of encouragement and support flooded the Cowboys' offices that I had to recruit my retired secretary, Marge Kelley, just to help sort it all. Cowboys' fans from all over the world wrote to say how much they would miss me. But a significant percentage of letters came from people who admitted they always rooted against the Cowboys—many Giants' and Redskins' fans— who wanted to let me know they were sorry and they cared.

And the expressions of support didn't stop with the mail.

While we'd been in Palm Springs the *Dallas Morning News* had published a 32-page Sunday supplement about my years with the Cowboys. And several billboards had gone up around Dallas saying, "Tom Landry—Thanks for 29 great years" or "We love you, Tom!" One even said, "Exchange the Fat Cat for the Hat. Landry for Governor."

I already felt overwhelmed when Roger Staubach called to tell me the city of Dallas was planning a big tribute to me, and the mayor had appointed him co-chairman of the festivities for a Tom Landry Day. He wanted to clear a date. I told Roger I was honored and would gladly be there. But Alicia and I figured all the postfiring furor would be long forgotten by the end of April; I couldn't imagine there would be very much public interest by then.

In fact, when the day arrived, as Alicia and I walked out of the house to head downtown for the celebration, she said, "Do you really think anybody will be there?"

Were we ever surprised. The Dallas police officially estimated more than a hundred thousand people lined the streets of downtown Dallas for the "Hats Off to Tom Landry Day Parade." For an hour and a half Alicia and I sat up on the back of a blue '54 Buick Skylark convertible, waving to the people who lined the entire parade route six or seven deep. The cheers, the applause, the waving banners and the constant calls of "Tom! Tom! We love you!" made me feel that never in my life had I been so affirmed, so loved.

And the parade merely started the day. Thousands then gathered in the Civic Center Plaza for ceremonies that went on and on. The mayor and the governor made presentations. The president and Billy Graham sent telegrams. Bob Hope called live to give his greetings and deliver a few one-liners.

Alicia and I were overwhelmed with special gifts. To name a few: Two airlines gave us lifetime passes; American Airlines gave me the keys for a ride in their 767 flight simulator and two round-trip tickets anywhere in the world; Braniff named one of its aircraft in my honor. The Mission Independent School District presented me with an old student desk.

Perhaps the most meaningful tribute was the presence of so many old Cowboys. Over ninety former players and coaches sat with me on the platform that afternoon. And when the ceremonies ended, Alicia and I were whisked away by helicopter to Texas Stadium for a special reception and a chance to coach some of those old players one last time in a Cowboys'-Redskins' Pro Legends Classic flag football game. After that a limo carried us to television station KSAS for a live, thirty-minute TV special.

By the time Alicia and I finally got to bed that night, we felt numb. The sense of love we experienced that day in Dallas meant more than any Super Bowl win.

I had heard so many kind words I felt a little like a man allowed to listen in at his own funeral. But if I was tempted to let all that praise go to my head, I had the perfect antidote.

KDFW-TV gave me several thousand letters written to me by Dallas area school children over the preceding weeks. And as I pulled those letters out to read a few at a time, I found they not only encouraged me, they helped keep all that had happened in perspective. Here are some samples complete with kids' creative spelling.

Dear Coach Landry,

I'm sorry you got fired and I hope you get rehired. I think you have a supercalifragilistic team. I said that because your great. It's not your fault you got fired its ther fault that's why I hope you get rehired. Your great and I swear your team is too.

Your biggest fan,
Randolph W.

P.S.   Will you pleas come to Mr. Wolff's reading class and bring Hurshle Walker with you.

Dear Coach Landry,

I am a real big fan of the Dallas Cowboys. If I could have two wishes it would be that the Cowboys won every football game. Also that you were always their coach. I wish you lots of luck.

Sincerely,
Codi D.

(She illustrated her letter with a drawing showing two football players and a most encouraging scoreboard reading "Redskins 14, Cowboys 21.")

Dear Coach Landry,

. . . I think that you were a good example because you always had a smile when you were winning but when you weren't winning you still had a straight face on!

> Your admirer,
> Suzanne H.

Dear Tom Landry,

. . . a good way to remember you is either naming the Dallas Stadium the Tom Landry Stadium or Irving, Texas Irving, Landry.

> Sincerely,
> Erin S.

Dear Tom Landry,

I think your the greatest couch in the world. I think you taught them a lot about football. I've watched every game since I was born. I think you have the greatest team. That's all I have to say.

> From Michael H.

I think the little girl who wrote the next letter has the makings of a journalist:

Dear Tom Landry,

How does it feel to not be the coach of the Dallas Cowboys? Why did you let Jerry Jones buy the Dallas Cowboys? How do the Dallas Cowboys feel about it? Do you like not to be the owner of the Dallas Cowboys or do you. Are you still going to watch the Dallas Cowboys play? Are you and Jerry Jones friends?

> From, Teresa

Dear Mr. Laundry,

. . . You were a very good coach. I am sorry you are leaving. One thing good about you leaving is you do not have to get up every morning and go to work until you get a new job. The Dallas Cowboys will never be the same without you. We will all miss you very much.

> Sincerely,
> Jessica J.

*   *   *

In the weeks and months after Tom Landry Day in Dallas I continued to receive many wonderful honors. Baylor University Medical Center announced it was going to name a new $16 million sports medicine and research center in my honor. My friends in the Fellowship of Christian Athletes paid me a wonderful tribute at a huge banquet.

An honor that took me by complete surprise was an invitation to enemy territory up in Washington, D.C., for my induction into the Washington Touchdown Club Hall of Fame. George Allen was even there for that one. I made it a point to remind him about that Clint Longley game, in case he'd forgotten. And I admitted to those at the special luncheon that I thought the Cowboy-Redskin rivalry had lost a lot of intensity during my last few years because Coach Joe Gibbs was such a nice guy.

I think my family and friends worried a bit about how I'd adjust to life without football. I wasn't sure myself how well I'd handle it. But after my first year off the sidelines I can say it's been easier than I ever dreamed.

I've enjoyed having more time to spend with Alicia, my kids, and my grandchildren. I've traveled more and played more golf than ever before.

Every day the mail brings a half dozen or more invitations to speak or attend some special event somewhere in the country. I could eat banquet dinners two or three times every week if I accepted all the opportunities.

I accept what I can. But President Bush appointed me to his National Drug Advisory Board and Dallas Mayor Annette Strauss asked me to become the founding chairman of a new International Sports Commission for the purpose of bringing more amateur sporting events to our city.

And then there's been the launching of my new career in country music. I had serious reservations when the folks from Quality Inn called and asked me to do a television commercial in which I'd pop out of a suitcase and sing a few bars of the classic country tune "Mamas, Don't Let Your

Babies Grow Up to Be Cowboys." I didn't want people to think I was knocking the Cowboys, so I turned the offer down.

Then a couple advertising agency executives flew to Dallas to propose a satisfactory adaptation of the song. And I agreed to do the commercial. I was still leery of the singing however. Remembering my old glee club strategy, I thought maybe I could just move my lips and they could dub in the voice of Glenn Campbell or even Don Meredith, who once recorded a little country music.

To reassure me, the Quality Inn people finally had musician Hugh McCracken call and ask me to try to duplicate the notes he would hum for me. When I did, he assured me I wasn't tone deaf. I'd be able to sing the commercial with him walking me through it by prerecording the music in a studio as he sang along with me over a headset.

So, with apologies to my Austin neighbor Willie Nelson, I sang "Mamas don't let your babies grow up to be Redskins" and had fun doing it.

On January 27, 1990, eleven months after I received the phone call from Tex Schramm saying he and Jerry Jones were flying out to meet with me, I was playing a round of golf out at Hidden Hills when another phone call came. This time it was good news. I'd just been elected to the Pro Football Hall of Fame in my first year of eligibility.

For me that election capped off what could have been the toughest year of my life. Instead, it may have been the best.

I do miss the interaction with players and coaches. I miss the challenge of creating a game plan. The anticipation and excitement of standing on the sideline in Texas Stadium on a crisp autumn afternoon.

It has saddened me to see the new management of the team deliberately dismantle so much of the tradition the Cowboys built up over the years. Within months after Bum Bright sold the Cowboys to Jerry Jones, my colleagues Tex

Schramm and Gil Brandt were gone. Good men I'd known and worked with for years, Tex's right hand man Joe Bailey and Cowboy PR Director Doug Todd soon followed. Numerous other Cowboys' employees with fifteen, twenty, twenty-five years of experience were fired or forced out of jobs ranging from team vice president to maintenance men to stadium announcer. All but two of my assistant coaches were let go before the '89 season. Longtime defensive great Randy White was encouraged to retire. So was veteran quarterback Danny White. The Cowboys traded Herschel Walker to Minnesota. Even Tommy Loy, whose trumpet solo of "The Star-Spangled Banner" preceded every Cowboys' home game for twenty-two years, was replaced by a trumpet quartet.

By the end of the '89 season I felt strangely detached from the Dallas Cowboys. Because the old Cowboys were gone forever.

As sad as that realization is, I know no one can take away the memories—memories shared with so many people who played and worked together to create a football team and a proud tradition that made Dallas, Texas, renowned throughout the world as the home of the Cowboys. For a time at least, America's Team.

As a boy growing up in Mission, Texas, I always dreamed of being a cowboy. For twenty-nine wonderful years I was one. And now, in my heart, I know I always will be.

part five
PERSPECTIVES

chapter twenty-two

ON COACHING
AND MOTIVATION

THE PRIMARY challenge of coaching in the National Football League can be boiled down to a one-sentence job description: To get people to do what they don't want to do in order to achieve what they want to achieve.

How do you do that?

A lot of my feelings and thoughts on coaching have been covered as I've recounted my coaching experiences in New York and Dallas. But I would like to clarify a few points on this subject.

THE CHANGES IN COACHING

My first NFL coach, Steve Owen, once defined football as "essentially a game played by two men down in the dirt. The fellow who hits first and harder will usually be the winner." He also said, "The best offense can be built around ten basic plays, the best defense on two. All the rest is razzle-dazzle, egomania, and box office."

In Steve's day, his summary of football was true. Football had begun as a very simple game and remained simple for decades.

On offense you had a quarterback who took the snap from center and either handed the ball to someone who would run with it or passed it to someone who would catch it. On defense everyone went for the man with the ball. And when a change of possession occurred, the same twenty-two players just exchanged roles. The game's basic strategy could be understood even by casual fans.

Coaching was probably never as simple as Steve Owen implied when he explained why he didn't need many assistant coaches: "A coach's job is to blow up the footballs and keep order, and that doesn't take much help." But the job of a coach definitely became more complex as the game changed.

We've already talked about how Paul Brown's Cleveland Browns led the transformation of football from a game of brute strength to a game of precision. Not only did the Cleveland style transform football strategy, it changed the requirements of coaching.

In the Knute Rockne era a coach's job was to teach fundamentals and motivate players. While those two challenges are still part of coaching, they have to be done differently today.

Before football became a precision sport, a coach like Rockne needed to rely on emotionalism and inspiration. With everyone following the same basic strategy, emotion and inspiration were the coaching tools that often spelled the difference between two teams.

Coaches in those early days didn't have film or video tape of every game their opponents played. They didn't have computers that spit out entire books containing information on every play run by every team they played. They couldn't study, analyze, and prepare the way coaches do today—even if they had wanted to.

But with the change to a precision style and the advent of technology, emotional motivation decreased in importance for a coach. Analysis became a more important skill. Even Lombardi, who maintained an emotional style, was very analytical in his approach to football. His back-to-basics football relied on precision in its execution.

THE ROLE OF EMOTION

In Lombardi's Green Bay system, the offense ran the same plays again and again, regardless of the defensive alignment. Success depended not on surprise or complexity but on execution. So Vince had to spur his players to an emotional pitch just to keep them performing their best against a defense that knew what was coming. Emotion wouldn't distract them because they knew in their sleep what to do; actually they had to stay very high emotionally in order to successfully execute their offense.

Over the years, especially when we always seemed to lose the big one in the playoffs, the Cowboys received a lot of criticism for not being an emotional team. But the Dallas system was different from the Packers'. In our multiple formation offense we had to take advantage of situations as they presented themselves. Everything we did from every formation didn't work against every defense. So we had to concentrate to be able to constantly adjust. Our defense too was complicated—depending on reading the offensive information and each player knowing exactly where to go.

Therefore the nature of response from the sideline had to be different for the Cowboys from a Green Bay-type team. The execution of our system required calm, clear, instantaneous decision-making on the sidelines as well as on the field. My players didn't want to see me rushing around and screaming; that would have been demoralizing, not motivating. They had to believe I was in control and knew what I was doing.

Now I'm not saying there isn't a place for emotion in football. I don't think you can play a contact sport like football very well without emotion. But it's a matter of how that emotion is fostered and whether the result is real or false emotion.

It's not difficult to work a team into a frenzy with a win-one-for-the-Gipper type pep talk before the kickoff. I remember doing it once when I felt the team wasn't ready for a game. They charged out of the dressing room and looked like a million bucks the first two minutes, scoring immediately. But then we lost by a score of 34–7. That sort of false emotion often dissolves with the first success, or the first setback.

Real emotion is built up over time and its foundation is preparation. Because it's almost impossible to keep a team emotionally high over an entire season—especially a season as long as the NFL's. When you get too high emotionally, the chances are you're going to slack off and be flat the next week. But careful preparation fosters confidence. That confidence becomes contagious and translates into a lasting kind of emotion that really pays off.

PACING FOR SUCCESS

I went into every season expecting my team to go through peaks and valleys. But I always wanted to get off to a good start so that when the inevitable valley came, we wouldn't sink right out of contention. Throughout our twenty-year winning streak, we almost always won our opener because we made it a high priority and spent the last few weeks of the preseason preparing specifically for that first game. Early season success helped set a pattern and an expectation for winning. Then, even though we would always hit a low point around midseason, we'd be in position to salvage a good season with a strong surge at the end of the year.

Perhaps the biggest factor in the Cowboys' reputation as strong finishers was our quality control program. When I first hired a coach for the sole purpose of studying our films and analyzing our own performance, we waited till the end of the year to evaluate which plays we ran well, which required fine-tuning, and what things needed to be thrown out or forgotten altogether. But I quickly concluded, "Why wait until after the season when it's too late to improve this year?'' That's when we began carefully evaluating the effectiveness of all areas of the team every four or five games.

As we entered the last few weeks of every season we would know, *These are the specific weaknesses we have to correct to make the playoffs.* Those would be the critical points we'd concentrate on in practice. When we corrected those specific problems, the team's play would move up another notch or two and we'd go into the playoffs with a winning surge.

Too many teams contentedly spend their practices working on the areas in which they're already good. Everyone likes to do that. It's easier and more immediately satisfying. But if you want a football team to improve, you need to identify the areas in which you aren't as good and practice those. Then you'll have a shot at the championship.

TEAMWORK

Football is more of a team game than perhaps any other sport.

Almost all the action in baseball revolves around individual performance. Each batter goes one on one with the pitcher. The success of every fielding play comes down to an individual performance: Does the man catch the ball or not. Even baseball's ultimate example of teamwork—the double play—boils down to a series of individual acts.

Basketball requires more teamwork. But you still have only five men playing at a time and much of the game is isolated into smaller segments of two-on-two or one-on-one maneuvering. An outstanding basketball player can often make his team a winner on the strength of his own individual performance.

The very best football players have to depend more on their teammates. All eleven men on a team have specific roles on every play. Unless each successfully does his part, the play won't work. It's a coordinated effort.

It's not enough for ten out of eleven defensive men to perform their assignments perfectly. Ninety percent performance can mean one hundred percent failure. Everyone has to do his job. If one blocker misses his block, the best runner in football can be tackled for no gain. If just one defensive player misses his assignment, you have a huge hole the offense can run through for a touchdown.

What this means is that in football no one individual can be more important than the team. Sometimes this is a hard lesson for the most talented athletes to learn; it's why some very gifted players bounce from team to team. It's also why in football the greatest superstars may not be the ones with the most physical talent; they're the ones who learn to adapt and fit their talents into the team concept. Prima donnas don't often make great football players and it's even more seldom that they make for a successful team.

RELATING TO PLAYERS

Over the years some observers, including a number of Cowboys, criticized me for not having a closer personal relationship with my players. Some of that can probably be attributed to personality shortcomings I've already talked about—my shyness, my demanding perfectionism, my emotionally undemonstrative nature, and that tendency toward tunnel vision that sometimes made me insensitive or oblivious to other people.

Without sounding too defensive, I'd like to have had a closer personal relationship with my players. But I never believed I could do that and still "get them to do what they didn't want to do in order to achieve what they wanted to achieve."

I felt if I got too close to my players they would be tempted to use that personal relationship as a crutch. And it would have made it harder to push them to achieve their best. I felt I could protect them from that temptation to slack off and take advantage of a relationship if I maintained a little distance.

Another major concern of mine was objectivity and fairness in my dealings with players. The toughest thing a coach has to do is make decisions he knows will affect the lives and careers of his players. The closer I felt to players the harder it was to make those decisions objectively.

I found it particularly painful to trade or cut players who had been with me for years and made valuable contributions to the team. I remember the decision to release defensive end John Dutton in 1987 after he'd been such a big part of the Cowboys for so long as one of the most difficult things I ever did as a coach. I almost broke down completely when I announced his release to the team.

Perhaps the toughest call for a coach is weighing what is best for an individual against what is best for the team. While I certainly believe the individual matters, I have to remember what's best for the team is also best for all those other individuals who make up the team. Keeping a player on the roster just because I liked him personally, or even because of his great contribution to the team in the past (like a Tony Dorsett at the end of his career), when I felt someone else could do more for the team would be a disservice to the team's goals.

The only way I could ever make those tough decisions was to try to remain as objective as possible. I never could do that without maintaining a measure of personal distance.

I had many players over the years I would have liked to be good friends with, individuals I greatly respected and admired not just as athletes but for the caliber of person they were—men like Bob Lilly, Roger Staubach, and Drew Pearson for example. Today they, like many former Cowboys, are good personal friends. But we didn't have that kind of relationship when they played because I felt it would have made their jobs and mine more difficult.

DISCIPLINE AND MORALE

I always believed if you're going to have good morale on a team, you have to have one set of rules, one standard for everyone. The biggest exception I made to this philosophy was with Duane Thomas in 1971. And I was willing to make that exception for two reasons: I thought it was the only hope for meeting his individual needs at the time, and I felt the team was mature enough to understand what was best for Duane was also best for the team. We were willing to make a major exception and live with the resulting morale problem in order to achieve the team goal of winning the Super Bowl. But once we reached that goal, I couldn't ask the team to go through the same thing another year. When Duane couldn't conform, we had to let him go for the sake of the team's morale.

Most successful players not only accept rules and limitations, I believe they need them. In fact, I believe players are free to perform at their best only when they know what the expectations are, where the limits stand.

I see this as a biblical principle that also applies to life, a principle our society as a whole has forgotten: You can't enjoy true freedom without limits.

We often resent rules because they limit what we can do. Yet without the rules that define a football game, you can't play the game, let alone enjoy it. The same thing is true in life. To live and enjoy the freedom we have in America, we have to live by the rules of society. To live life to its fullest and truly enjoy it, we need to understand and abide by the rules God spells out in the Bible. God isn't out to spoil our fun; he knows that life without limits results in anarchy and misery. It's only when we have absolute limits that we can be truly free to enjoy the best life has to offer.

CORRECTION

I think it's possible to be demanding without being critical. I didn't always succeed at that as a coach, but that was always my goal.

I could be pretty tough when it came to critiquing game films every Monday. But I tried to focus my comments more on what should have happened or what needs to happen next week than just to attack the mistakes or the people who made them.

Theoretically I always believed praise to be more effective than criticism. I was such a perfectionist I'm afraid I seldom doled out as much praise as I should have.

I did learn that having one set of standards for everyone didn't mean I shouldn't handle players differently. Some guys respond well when you correct them in front of their peers; they're that much more determined to do it right. Other players can be devastated when you get on them. So when they're not performing you need to take them aside, sit down with them, find out what's going on in their lives, and see if you can learn what the problem is.

As a general rule a coach needs to be the most demanding when his team is doing well, because there's a human tendency to ease up when you're winning. When things are going poorly, especially when the effort is there, that's when a team needs encouragement and affirmation more than it needs more pressure from the coach. That's the time to back off and let the team's own pride take effect—as we did after that devastating 38–0 loss to St. Louis in 1970. In a way, a coach's role is to provide balance and a realistic perspective. When the press and the fans think a team is the greatest, the coach needs to prod them to be better. But when everyone else is down on a team, the coach needs to take their side and show them he believes in them.

THE LIMITS OF COACHING

I believe coaching is far more than pumping up the balls and keeping order, as Steve Owen said. Yet I've always felt a coach gets too much credit when his team wins and too much blame when his team loses.

In professional sports especially, a team has to reach a certain level of talent before coaching kicks in and makes much difference at all. Often you'll see a new coach come into a program and there will be an initial surge that results in more victories. Then the team drops off to the same level of performance it had before.

Certainly some coaches are better than others. But no

coach can win without talented players. Coaching "genius" is overrated.

THE JOY OF COACHING

Every season was like starting over. As the players changed, so did the game. I loved that change. And I enjoyed the evolution of football. I once said, "If the whole emphasis is on repetition and execution and cutting out mistakes, the game comes down to one thing only—personnel. Well, I reject that as the idea of football. To me it's a great deal more than just trying to out-personnel the other team."

I loved the intellectual challenge of the game. I always found more of that coaching defense than I did coaching offense. You know what you're going to do on offense because you call the plays. But on defense you face the challenge of uncertainty, you have to outthink your opponent to anticipate what he's going to do before he does it. Which is one reason I kept coaching the Cowboys for twenty-nine years.

Oh, I enjoyed the winning. But the real appeal for me was the challenge of working with people and helping them achieve success. The Cowboys had many great players with incredible physical talent over the years—players like Bob Lilly, Mel Renfro, Chuck Howley, Tony Dorsett, Too Tall Jones, and Randy White. Those guys were certainly a joy to watch Sunday after Sunday. But I think the greatest satisfaction of all was seeing players with lesser talent— guys like Danny Reeves, Dave Edwards, Pettis Norman, Walt Garrison, Billy Joe Dupree, and Charlie Waters— become great football players because they reached their fullest potential.

To get men to do what they don't want to do in order to achieve what they want to achieve. That's what coaching is all about. That's the challenge I will miss.

chapter twenty-three

ON LEADERSHIP

THAT definition I used for coaching—getting people to do what they don't want to do in order to achieve what they want to achieve—is a pretty good description of any kind of leadership. Because the greatest challenge of every leader is getting the best out of people.

Thirty-five years of professional coaching didn't provide me with a simple formula for successful leadership, but I did discover a few basic requirements of leadership that apply not only to coaching but to other businesses as well.

KNOWLEDGE

The first requirement of leadership is knowledge. When I became player-coach of the New York Giants' defense in 1954, I was only twenty-nine years old. I couldn't establish my authority based on age or experience; I was younger and had less experience than several members of the defensive team I coached. And I wasn't the most talented defensive player on the team; others had more athletic talent and football skill. What I did have was knowledge.

With my limited athletic talent, knowledge had become my greatest personal survival tool as a defensive back. My only hope of covering faster receivers like Mac Speedie was to know what he was going to do, where he was going to run, before he did it. I had to learn to anticipate the action.

All the hours of study that required gave me an understanding of other teams' offenses, a knowledge that not only made me a more effective player, but in the process, prepared and qualified me to lead the Giants' defense. The ability to convey that knowledge to my teammates earned me the respect required to lead them effectively.

A leader doesn't have to be the smartest member of a group, but he does need to demonstrate a mastery of his field. Mastery means more than just knowing information and facts; it requires an understanding of the information and the ability to apply that information. When I could tell my Giants' teammates how I knew ahead of time what the opposing offense would do on a given play, that knowledge gave me the authority I needed to establish my leadership.

Knowledge is also foundational for the next key ingredient of leadership.

INNOVATION

If I had to pick my greatest strength as a professional football coach, I'd say it was innovation. But it started with preparation and knowledge. As a leader you have to understand the present system, situation, or problem you're faced with before you can react effectively—before you can be a successful innovator.

I had to understand the intentions of the Cleveland Browns' offense before I could design a coordinated 4–3 defense to counter it. Then when I went to the Cowboys, my entire offensive strategy rested on the understanding that the key to the 4–3 defense was the ability to recognize and anticipate what the offense intended to do. The result was our multiple-set offense, which shifted linemen, sent backs in motion, and often altered a formation two or three times before the snap of the ball—all in an attempt to stymie the defense by not giving it enough time to recognize a formation and anticipate the play in time to stop it.

A successful leader has to be innovative. If you're not one step ahead of the crowd, you'll soon be a step behind everyone else.

A BASIC PHILOSOPHY

One of the most innovative things I ever did with the Cowboys was to bring in an industrial psychologist to help teach us how to be better managers and develop a more successful football program. He was the one who convinced me how important it is for every leader and every organization to have a clearly understood philosophy.

Your philosophy is simply an abstract statement of what you believe. Out of that belief you develop your methodology and your goals. But everything goes back to the philosophy.

For example, our basic offensive philosophy on the Cowboys could be stated like this: "Offensively we must prevent the defensive team from recognizing our intentions and preparing effectively for our attack." The methodology we used to do that was our multiple-formation offense. And the execution of our methods required the establishment of specific goals that could be used to measure our effectiveness.

A basic philosophy that everyone agrees on can provide a powerful sense of unity within an organization. But it also means one of the responsibilities of a leader is to make sure everyone buys into the philosophy. This is easier to do when you build from within an organization as we did with the Cowboys for so many years. If you bring in someone from outside the organization, you have to be careful to hire people in tune with your philosophy or you have to be able to sell them on the philosophy. As I learned my last few seasons, trying to mix conflicting philosophies can create conflicts and disarray within an organization.

For many years the Cowboys' coaching staff annually reviewed our basic philosophy by asking, "Do we still believe in this?" If everyone can't buy into the philosophy it's time to adjust the philosophy, or to suggest those who can't accept it would be better off if they went somewhere else.

Not that there's only one way to do things. Vince Lombardi's system worked in Green Bay. Chuck Noll's certainly worked in Pittsburgh, as Bill Walsh's did in San Francisco. It's not a matter of one philosophy being better than another; it's a matter of unity and focus.

SHARED GOALS

Out of the philosophy we defined in 1965, we developed goals for our team. After five dismal losing seasons in a row, I sent a letter before that summer's training camp to all the returning players spelling out our team goals for the '65 season.

> All right—now that we have laid the foundation and our draft system is effective and our team is stocked with good men—how are we going to become a winner? You can read volumes of books on what makes people, teams, and organizations successful, and several important principles seem to re-occur. . . . Three important principles must be followed.
>
> First, you must have a clear-cut *objective*. As strange as it may seem, very few people really know what they want in life. They might not be satisfied with things as they are, but when you ask them what they want specifically, you will invariably get a vague answer. This should not be true in professional football because the objective is clear-cut—the World Championship. . . .
>
> Second, you must recognize every *resistance* that will prevent you from reaching your objective. We could immediately list fourteen resistances that stand between us and our

objective, because this represents the fourteen teams we must face this fall. We must be more specific and list the resistances that would prevent us from having the type of team that can defeat each one of our opponents.

Third, you must have *a plan of action* that will overcome the resistances. . . .

Now you have an idea what the coaching staff has been doing from December until July. We have analyzed every phase of our football team and have pinpointed each resistance that must be overcome. Our plan of action has been formulated.

The objective, the World's Championship, appears to be monumental. In the fifteen years I have been in the NFL, two teams have dominated the Eastern Division—New York and Cleveland—Philadelphia won it one year. Pittsburgh never has won the Eastern Crown. I submit to you the reason the other teams have not won it is because . . . they keep their attention on the objective without working through the other two steps. So it becomes more important to break down our *major objective*, the championship, into *minor objectives*—the resistances we must overcome. And each one of the *minor objectives* must be a *major objective* until it is attained. . . .

The minor objective we set for the team was to reach the first division—a .500 season in 1965. The thinking was once we reached that attainable goal, we could take the next step to a division title. And that's just what happened when we went 7–7 in 1965 and then won the Eastern Division Championship in 1966.

Under the team goals, in pyramid fashion, we set specific offensive, defensive, and special team goals. Things we had to do better to overcome those resistances to winning. For example, one of our specific minor objectives was to improve our pass protection. By emphasizing this in practice and developing some new techniques we did indeed reduce our quarterback sacks and yardage lost as well as cutting our quarterback fumbles from five lost in 1964 to one lost in 1965. That kind of emphasis in achieving secondary goals not only keeps a team focused on specific critical points but can provide encouraging signs of progress when a goal is achieved. The same sort of goal-setting works effectively within positions (for example, offensive line, defensive backs, pass receivers) and on down to individual players.

I don't believe you can effectively manage people without helping them understand where they fit into the goals of the organization. So individual goal-setting becomes an important means of communicating with a player and involving him in the team.

It's also an effective method of motivation—which is another key to leadership.

MOTIVATION

One way to motivate people is by using emotion. Vince Lombardi was a master of fear motivation. His players knew if they didn't perform they would pay the price of a tongue-lashing, extra work, or some other punitive indication of Vince's disfavor.

I believe fear motivation is always risky. It worked for Vince in Green Bay during the sixties because he had the talent to win. The negative sense of suffering Vince put the Packers through forced them to bond together as a group; when they won, the players forged a powerful sense of attachment to their teammates. What could easily have turned to hatred for Lombardi turned to love in the wake of victory—winning made it all worth it.

But if you don't win, fear motivation quickly backfires. There's no payoff to make players feel it's "worth it." And with all the emphasis on "individual rights" since the sixties, I don't think fear motivation can be very effective today.

I always believed knowledge could motivate a person. The better prepared you were, the better you felt and more confident you became in your ability to perform.

The goal-setting we've talked about became a means of motivating the team, as well as individuals. When we finally achieved success in reaching our goals and in winning football games, the Cowboys' winning tradition itself became one of our greatest motivators.

Another important factor in getting the best out of a player or an employee is making sure you have him in the right spot.

I guess I learned this lesson with Sam Huff who just didn't have the size to be a lineman, so I switched him to linebacker. Bob Lilly was another example. He had such tremendous skills but wasn't a tremendous defensive end. When we switched him to defensive tackle he dominated the game. Both Huff and Lilly became Hall of Fame football players because we tried to be flexible and find the perfect place for their talents.

Those two cases taught me a lesson I applied many times with many players over the years. When I saw someone who wasn't producing up to the level of their skills, someone who showed more talent than production, I automatically began looking for another spot to use him.

LIVING WITH THE DEMANDS

Coaching, like a lot of other professions, has seen its share of burnout victims in recent years—fine coaches like Dick Vermeil and John Madden. Even though I ended up tied with Curly Lambeau for the record of most consecutive years coaching the same professional football team—we both had twenty-nine—I understand the burnout phenomenon. Pressure is part of the price you pay for the privilege of leadership.

You can read any number of books on stress relief. But for me, two major factors explain my long survival.

The first is my faith. I've talked earlier about my life priorities as a Christian. Knowing your job isn't the most important thing in your life relieves a lot of the pressure. And because I felt I was doing God's will for my life I knew I didn't have to do it all in my own strength; God promises the necessary strength to those who follow him (1 Cor. 12:9 and 2 Peter 1:3).

Finally, doing my job for the Lord gave me extra incentive to keep going, and God's Holy Spirit gave me extra support and encouragement to get back up when I was down. Like I was after those Cleveland losses in '68 and '69.

The second factor was the ownership style of Clint Murchison. Most owners in professional sports put pressure on coaches to win or else. Clint was unique in that he constantly attempted to reduce the pressure for me—by his encouragement, patience, and confidence. And by giving me the security of that ten-year contract. Without Clint, and Tex's hands-off style under Clint, I would probably have burned out before I coached ten years.

HANDLING ADVERSITY AND CRITICISM

As a leader you have to understand you will face adversity. In fact, it's so much a part of leadership that in the final evaluation, your reaction to adversity will determine your success or failure as a leader.

A big part of the battle is a matter of attitude. As the philosopher and psychologist William James said, "The greatest discovery of my generation is that human beings can alter their lives by altering their attitude of mind."

You need to approach difficulties and adversities as a challenge to overcome rather than a problem to worry about. While you want to learn from past mistakes, you can't afford to look back. You have to be planning ahead. A leader can't afford to get too emotionally upset about the last mistake or the last play; you have to focus on what you will do differently next time.

A leader always has others watching to see how he reacts when things are going bad. If he wants to maintain control of his followers he has to stay in control of himself. That requires confidence in the basic philosophy. If I hadn't believed in what I was doing during those dark early days, I would never have lasted long enough to see the Cowboys become winners.

A leader also needs to think clearly under pressure. For

me that required total concentration. The better prepared I was, the easier it was to maintain my concentration, shut out negative thoughts and attitudes, convey a sense of confidence to my players, and stay focused on our goals and objectives.

Another crucial test for any leader is how he handles criticism. Everyone makes mistakes. But when a leader makes one, people almost always notice and criticize him for it. As a football coach, the crowd boos when the play you called fails; the commentators in the broadcast booth question your thinking. There's no place to hide on that sideline when you know you made a mistake.

It's even harder to accept criticism for a right decision. Such as when people don't understand a personnel move and you don't want to explain because you don't want to hurt the person any more than you have by cutting him or trading him.

Sometimes a good leader has to be able to listen to criticism and change his plan accordingly. Other times he's better off just ignoring the critics. The trick is in deciding which to do when. That often means considering the source. Some of my critics I paid attention to because I knew them to be thoughtful, knowledgeable people who took the time to try to understand my position before they criticized it. Others I found easy to ignore because they had no idea what they were talking about.

Perhaps the most important step in dealing with criticism is realizing it's part of the job.

COMMITMENT TO EXCELLENCE

Vince Lombardi's most famous quote was one he borrowed from an old John Wayne movie in which the Duke played a football coach who said: "Winning isn't everything, it's the only thing." While I'm sure that statement worked well in a rousing pep talk, I don't think it's true. And while I don't doubt Vince used it to make a good point with his players, I don't think he believed it either.

If winning is the only thing that matters, then you'd do anything to win. You'd cheat. You'd sacrifice your marriage or your family to win. Relationships wouldn't matter. People wouldn't matter. Winning would be worth any price you had to pay. I don't believe that; after working with Vince Lombardi day after day for six years, I know he didn't believe it either.

As a competitor, Vince Lombardi had few equals. He hated to lose as much as he loved to win. But a more accurate reflection of his feelings would require a revision of that famous quote. Something like: "Winning isn't everything; it's the effort to win that matters."

We had our own quote on a sign in our Cowboys' locker room that said, "The quality of a man's life is in direct proportion to his commitment to excellence." What that means is that you have to get up each morning with a clear goal in mind saying to yourself, "Today I'm going to do my best in every area. I'm not going to take the easy way; I'm going to give 100 percent."

Having that kind of commitment doesn't guarantee we'll reach our goals. Some of the time we'll fall short. Occasionally we'll hit an insurmountable obstacle and be bounced back like Deacon Dan Towler off the goalpost. But the determination to strive to do our best will inevitably improve the quality of our lives.

The apostle Paul is one of my favorite biblical characters because he was such a competitor. He was stoned, shipwrecked, imprisoned, and still he wouldn't quit. He explained some of his motivation in a letter to the Corinthian church saying:

"In a race, everyone runs but only one person gets first prize. So run your race to win. To win the contest you must deny yourselves many things that would keep you from doing your best. An athlete goes to all this trouble just to win a blue ribbon or a silver cup, but we do it for a heavenly reward that never disappears. So I run straight to the goal with purpose in every step. I fight to win. I'm not just shadow-boxing or playing around. Like an athlete I punish my body, treating it roughly, training it to do what it should, not what it wants to. Otherwise I fear that after enlisting others for the race, I myself might be declared unfit and ordered to stand aside" (1 Cor. 9:24–27, *The Living Bible*).

Paul understood what it took to be a champion and a successful leader. He realized the quality of a man's life is in direct proportion to his commitment to excellence.

When I think of people I've seen in my career who embody this truth, I think of Roger Staubach. Twenty-three times he brought the Cowboys from behind to win—fourteen times in the last two minutes or overtime.

Roger's commitment to excellence improved the quality of his own life and the lives of everyone around him. During his career the Cowboys went to five Super Bowls. He started at quarterback in four of them, winning two championships. And in the two Super Bowls we lost, Roger was throwing the football into the end zone, giving us a chance to win, as time ran out.

That kind of commitment to excellence—the kind of will to win Paul wrote about—is absolutely essential to successful leadership.

chapter twenty-four
ON CHARACTER

WHEN things went so badly during the '88 season, a good friend of mine, former Cleveland Browns' coach Sam Rutigliano, sent me an encouraging note that included this quote from Harry Truman's book *Plain Speaking*: "The way in which you endure that which you must endure is more important than the crisis itself."

What he was really talking about was the need for character.

Horace Greeley once said, "Fame is a vapor; popularity an accident. Riches take wing; those who cheer today will curse tomorrow; only one thing endures—character."

I believe that because I've seen the difference character makes. It was strength of character that enabled the 1970 Cowboys to rally after everyone in the country wrote us off and come back to win seven straight games and go all the way to the Super Bowl. It was great maturity of character that enabled the 1971 team to ignore the controversies and distractions and press on to the goal of becoming Super Bowl champions. I believe it was character that enabled the 1985 Cowboys to play beyond their abilities and win the Eastern Division over two more talented football teams. And it was also character in my final team, the 1988 Cowboys, that enabled them to survive disappointing loss after disappointing loss without ever quitting.

I've seen the difference character makes in individual football players, too. Give me a choice between an outstanding athlete with poor character and a lesser athlete of good character, and I'll choose the latter every time. The athlete with good character will often perform to his fullest potential and be a successful football player while the outstanding athlete with poor character will usually fail to play up to his potential and often won't even achieve average performance. Of course when you can find an outstanding athlete with outstanding character you have the sort of rare player you can build a team around—people like a Bob Lilly, a Roger Staubach, or a Herschel Walker.

In my opinion, character is the most important determinant of a person's success, achievement, and ability to handle adversity.

How do we develop character?

I believe most of a person's character is developed as a child. It's the result of values learned from family and other significant people early in life—which is what makes our role as parents and the role of those who coach kids so important.

We also develop character by going through adversity. Coaches sometimes talk about a losing year being a "character-building season." There's truth to that as I've seen from experience. That strength of character so crucial to the 1970 Cowboys who rallied from almost certain failure to go on to the Super Bowl was forged through those difficult years when we couldn't win the big one.

They were perfect illustrations of what the apostle Paul was saying in those verses I referred to in an earlier chapter, "We know that suffering produces perseverance, perseverance, character, and character, hope."

Yet the truth remains, most of our character is established early in life. Adversity can help build it. Coaches can help mold it. But in our adult years, the only thing I've seen that can radically change a person's basic character is a relationship with Jesus Christ.

Just what does that mean?

I think there's a lot of confusion in the world today about what it means to be a Christian. Unfortunately, a lot of well-meaning Christian athletes contribute to that confusion.

Since the time I committed my own life to God, I've tried to be very open about that fact. I've talked about it here in this book because it's the most important thing in my life. And I think it's important for Christians to speak out and explain what they believe.

But I have to admit that I'm troubled a little and have very mixed reactions when I see a football player kneel down in the end zone and thank God after a touchdown. I have the same feelings of misgiving when I hear from winning locker rooms the excited testimonies of happy players who say, "I just want to thank the Lord because without him this victory wouldn't have been possible!"

Don't get me wrong. I think an athlete should feel gratitude for his God-given abilities. I think we all ought to regularly give thanks to our Creator for our blessings, our opportunities, for life itself. But I'm afraid these little "God helped me score a touchdown" and "God helps me be a winner" testimonials mislead people and belittle God.

I don't believe God plays favorites like that. Neither do I believe God cares who wins a football game. Despite the old joke in Dallas that the reason Texas Stadium was designed with a hole in the roof was so God could watch his favorite team play every Sunday afternoon.

While I don't believe God helps Christian athletes run faster, jump higher, or hit harder, I do believe a personal faith in Christ can be a very real advantage in life—as a football player, a surgeon, a business executive, a teacher, a student, or even a parent. Because a personal faith in God can change and improve anyone's character.

A Christian, a person who is trying to put the teachings of Jesus Christ into practice in his life every day, should begin to take on some of the character—the integrity, the patience, the truthfulness, and so on—of Christ. That's what being a Christian is all about. But I think a Christian's faith does much more than provide him with a character model.

Faith frees a person to do his best, to achieve his potential. How?

Think for a moment about the factors that most often prevent anyone from reaching his or her greatest potential—in whatever the field. In my experience as a football coach, I've seen two common barriers that most often prevent people from performing to their fullest potential. The first is a pattern of past failure and past mistakes. The second thing holding people back is a fear of failure.

The basic tenets of Christianity address both those problems and remove both barriers. As a Christian I believe my past is forgiven; I can start over with a clean slate. The mistakes of the past need not hold me back. Neither does my fear of failure—because as a Christian I believe God is in ultimate control of my life. While that doesn't mean I'll always win the championship or never get fired, it means I can believe the promise of Romans 8:28, which says God can bring good out of every experience for those who trust in him. So I don't need to worry about failing.

Without the burden of past mistakes or anxiety about failing in the future, I'm free to concentrate on doing my very best in the present. And I believe that's how a real, personal Christian faith can make it easier for anyone to reach his or her highest potential.

Having said that, I realize a lot of people think the idea of a "personal relationship" with God sounds disturbingly exclusive, somehow presumptive, and more than a little pious. I thought the same thing before I read what the Bible said and decided to become a Christian.

According to the Bible, this idea of having a personal relationship with God isn't at all presumptive. It was God's idea. And it's not at all exclusive. It's available to anyone who accepts God's offer.

As far as sounding pious, or giving the idea that a personal relationship with God makes a person better than everyone else—just the opposite is true. Because the first step in establishing that relationship is admitting you're as much a sinner as the worst human being and you need forgiveness.

In fact, the most important lesson I've learned in my life is that God is so gracious that he accepts me, my failures, my personality quirks, my shortcomings and all.

It's hard for a perfectionist like me, but I have to admit I can never be good enough. No matter how sound my strategy, how much I study, how hard I work—I'll always be a failure when it comes to being perfect. Yet God loves me anyway. And believing that gives me the greatest sense of peace, calm, and security in the world.

It's that belief, that faith, more than anything else, that enabled me to last twenty-nine years on the sidelines of the Dallas Cowboys. It's that faith that has allowed me to keep my perspective and not feel devastated or bitter about being fired. And it's that faith that gives me hope for whatever the future holds for me outside of professional football.

Index